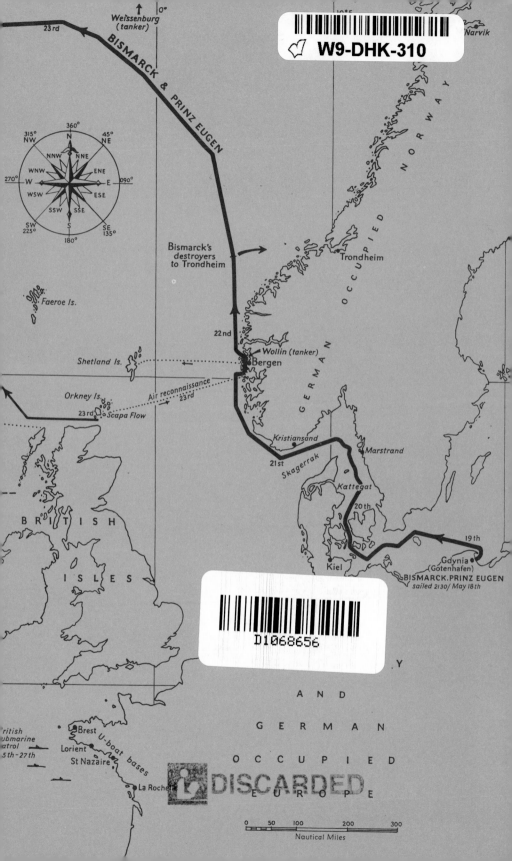

PURSUIT
The Chase and Sinking
of the Bismarck

T.

PURSUIT :

The Chase and Sinking of the Bismarck

LUDOVIC KENNEDY

COLLINS

St James's Place, London

1974

William Collins Sons & Co Ltd
London · Glasgow · Sydney · Auckland
Toronto · Johannesburg

First published 1974
© Ludovic Kennedy 1974
ISBN 0 00 211739 8
Set in Monotype Bembo
Made and Printed in Great Britain by
William Collins Sons & Co Ltd Glasgow

For my friend and former tutor
DAVID CECIL
This tale of unquiet lives.
With gratitude and affection

My subject is war, and the pity of war.

Wilfred Owen

Contents

Illustrations

Acknowledgements

I am very grateful to the many people who have helped me in the preparation and writing of this book; firstly to Captain Stephen Roskill, not only for so generously putting his papers at my disposal but for advice and encouragement at every stage, often given when he was busy with other things; also to Vice-Admiral Friedrich Ruge for allowing me to draw so freely on his great knowledge of the German Navy. To Rear-Admiral Peter Buckley and his staff at the Naval Historical Section and Naval Library at the Ministry of Defence I owe a great debt, especially to Captain Donald Macintyre, Mr J. Lawson and Mr David Brown; similarly to Mr D. P. Mayne and his staff at the Photographic Department of the Imperial War Museum, especially Mr R. E. Squires. I am grateful to Commander Wolfgang Brost, Assistant Naval Attaché at the German Embassy in London for help in tracking down photographs in Germany, to Dr Sidney Hamilton for permission to reproduce the photograph on the dust-jacket and plate 27, 'The Pursuit'. and to Lieutenant-Commander Peter Wright and the officers of H.M.S. *Rapid* for information and hospitality in the last of the Navy's steam-driven destroyers.

I wish also to thank Vice-Admiral Edwin Hooper, Curator of the U.S. Naval Archives, for making available wartime documents; Lieutenant-Commander Peter Kemp for much sound advice and helping unravel the complex events of May 25th 1941; Rear-Admiral Gerhard Wagner and Commander Paul Schmalenbach for their comments on the German aspect of the operation; Lieutenant Commander M. R. Healy, Christine Smith, Prince Weikersheim, and Mr David Woodward for translations from the German —Mr Woodward too for putting me right on many tiny historical details; Mr Robert Kee for arbitrating on a disputed point between my publishers and myself; the British Broadcasting Corporation for permitting extracts from radio talks given by participants after the operation and from contributions to my own television documentary *Battleship Bismarck*, first shown in 1971; Joyce Turnbull and Nancy Winch for unflagging secretarial help and Hazel Plenderleith for her typing; my wife for many wise comments on points as they arose during a year's writing; and lastly all those kind people who gave so generously of their time in talking or writing to me about the operation, and whose names will be found in the list of acknowledgements at the end.

There have been many books about the *Bismarck*, some good, some bad, but nearly all partisan. This book, written more than thirty years after the event, aims not to be partisan. If it is pro anything, it is pro humanity.

Edinburgh 1973   LUDOVIC KENNEDY

Author's Note

To a person in a ship facing forward, the right-hand side is starboard (Green), and the left-hand side port (Red).

An object seen from a ship to be lying in an area between right ahead and 90° on either side (abeam) is said to be on the bow, and lying between right astern and 90° on either side to be on the quarter.

Courses and bearings are determined by compass markings of 360°, North being 000° (or 360°), East 090°, South 180°, West 270°, etc.

A knot is speed through the water measured in sea miles per hour. A sea mile is 2,000 yards, so a knot is fractionally faster than its equivalent in land miles (1760 yards) per hour.

Part 1

VICTORY

Now entertain conjecture of a time
Shakespeare: Henry V

CHAPTER

1

•

It was a May evening of 1941, a time when most of Europe had
yielded to Hitler, and across the narrow moat that had made and
saved her, a truculent Britain faced Germany alone. To the west,
across the steep Atlantic, and to the east, beyond the Vistula, the two
giants marked time: their turn would come, but now they were
spectators, uneasily neutral, also alone.

Nature, indifferent to wars, was neutral too. Farmers in Wessex
and Württemberg, Hanover and Hampshire listened to the song of
blackbird and cuckoo, took long scythes to cut the newborn grasses,
shook the rich blossom on the pear-tree's boughs. On hills in Scotland and Bavaria men weary from work or war stood in streams
swollen with the melting snows and tossed in little flies to bring
trout to the surface and benison to their souls. Nightly the bombs
fell, on suburbs of Germany and England, but in gardens of the
Midlands and the Ruhr daffodils died too, and brave young tulips
reached for the sun. If April is the cruellest month, May is for gesta-
tion, breeder of schemes in mice and men, a time of promise for
buttercup and battleship, affidavit for a harvest at journey's end.

In the daytime, in the country, you hardly knew a war was on.
Dusk was for remembrance, in cities especially, Coventry, Hamm,
Hamburg, Devonport, Genoa, Brest: then the blackout curtains
were drawn and the street lights doused, and the streets became like
long tunnels and men and women rabbits, diving in and out of
bright warrens, shutting away until morning the perils and per-

adventures of the night. It was like that always, even when the bombers didn't come, and when they did come, it was another story.

In a few places in Europe the lights still shone. In Stockholm, for instance, considered by some to be a dull, clean city servicing dull, progressive people, but then, like its partners in neutrality at the other end of Europe, Madrid and Lisbon, a buzzing beehive of espionage and intrigue. Here the Germans and the British had embassies and other front organisations, spied on each other, bribed Swedes and others to spy for them, touted for hot tips like how much iron ore was coming down from Narvik, and the wavebands of British radar, coded dark secrets for London and Berlin, and sent them by radio or aeroplane, in the trouser-legs of sea-cooks and the incredible memories of agents.

An unlikely man to find mixed up in all this was Captain Henry Denham, Royal Navy, who liked nothing better than sailing and racing small boats. He'd been naval attaché in Copenhagen in 1940 when the Germans overran Denmark, and getting out, had been asked to go to Sweden to do the same. Why, he never knew: he understood no Swedish, it was the only European country where he hadn't been.

He reached Stockholm in June 1940 via Narvik and the North Cape, crossing the frontier to Finland with the Wehrmacht half a day behind. At first, lacking the language and contacts, it had been uphill work. But he had persevered, called on the right people, been congenial at parties, and now, a year later, had several useful informants, in the Swedish armed forces and without. He lived in a comfortable, small flat in the Riddargatan, but he met informants elsewhere, at the embassy or in the woods. He knew his flat was watched from the building opposite, and that his telephone was tapped, and he suspected bugging too.

On this evening in May Captain Denham was in his flat when the telephone rang. It was the British embassy in the Strandvägen. Colonel Roscher Lund had arrived to see him. It was urgent.

Colonel Roscher Lund was the military attaché of the exiled Norwegian government in London, a friend and colleague of Denham and the most reliable of his informants: he knew many Swedish officers, having done liaison work with their interception and cryptography service before the war. One man he knew well was Major Törnberg, himself half-Norwegian and Chief of Staff to Colonel Petersën, head of the Swedish secret service. Törnberg hated the Germans for what they had done to Norway, felt no disloyalty to his own country in passing on to Roscher Lund information that might be useful to Britain in the prosecution of the war. Twice a week, in the evenings, Roscher Lund brought papers to Denham at the embassy: Denham made abstracts of what he thought important and Roscher Lund returned the papers to Törnberg's office before it opened in the morning. Denham and Roscher Lund referred to Petersën as 'P' to preserve his security.

Denham got out his bicycle and set off for the embassy, five minutes away on the waterfront. Never before had Roscher Lund asked for a special meeting, so he guessed something unusual was up.

At the embassy they went to Denham's office. Roscher Lund's message was brief and undramatic. It was a report from 'P''s office that two big German warships with sea and air escort had been sighted that afternoon off the south coast of Sweden. There was no indication of the source, which was in fact the Swedish cruiser *Gotland*: so delicate was the matter that not even Roscher Lund knew of it. As a result Denham doubted its reliability, and it wasn't until long afterwards that he realised that someone in 'P''s office, Törnberg probably, knowing this intelligence to be vital to Britain, had taken special, cautious steps to see that he was informed.

Roscher Lund left, and Denham drafted a telegram to the Admiralty, classified Most Immediate, graded B.3.[1] Within an hour it had been put into cipher and was zinging its way from the Gothenburg radio masts across the North Sea to London.

'Kattegat today 20th May. At 1500 two large warships, escorted by three destroyers, five escort vessels, ten or twelve aircraft, passed Marstrand course north-west. 2058/20.'

The secret was out. *Bismarck* and *Prinz Eugen* were on their way. Operation *Rheinübung* had begun.

The head of Hitler's Navy was Erich Raeder, Grand Admiral in the

German Fleet, a handsome square-faced man of 65, highly intelligent and approachable, son of a teacher of languages near Hamburg, like his parents deeply religious. He joined the Navy in 1894, was navigator of the Kaiser's famous yacht *Hohenzollern* in 1911, then for five years was Chief Staff Officer to Admiral Hipper, commanding the scouting forces. With Hipper he'd seen action on that other May day in 1916, off the coast of Jutland, when Jellicoe's Grand Fleet and Scheer's High Seas Fleet had their only rendezvous of the war and by next day twenty-four ships were at the bottom and over 6,000 British and 2,500 German sailors had died.

It was Churchill who said of Jellicoe that he was the only man on either side who could lose the war in an afternoon, and Scheer and Hipper and Raeder knew it. For Britain's sustenance depended and depends on the ocean trade-routes, and the Grand Fleet was all that prevented the High Seas Fleet starving her into defeat. As it was, Scheer's battleships were boxed in, collectively by Jellicoe's battleships, individually by limitations of fuel. The U-boats had nearly pulled it off by their massive sinkings in the Atlantic in 1917, but in the end the convoy system had thwarted them. After Germany's defeat, the sending of the High Seas Fleet to Beatty for disposal, and the scuttling of it by von Reuter at Scapa Flow, Raeder remembered these things. He remembered also the accusations of inactivity, even timidity, that had been levelled at the High Seas Fleet.

Raeder became head of the Navy in 1928, so that when Hitler came to power five years later, there was already the nucleus of a new German fleet. First came the U-boat arm, forbidden by the Versailles Treaty, started with secret constructions in dockyards in Finland and Spain; then the far-ranging armoured cruisers or pocket-battleships, *Deutschland, Admiral Graf Spee, Admiral Scheer;* later cruisers and destroyers, the fast battleships or battle-cruisers *Scharnhorst* and *Gneisenau*, the huge *Bismarck* and her sister *Tirpitz*. (These ships were all designed to look alike, an idea which later and quite unintentionally, paid rich dividends). For years Hitler assured Raeder he need never fear a war with Britain; even in 1938 when the nightmare looked like reality he promised him another seven years grace. So Raeder prepared his 'Z' plan, 250 U-boats, six more battleships even vaster than *Bismarck* and *Tirpitz*, and swift, light cruisers to scout for them, all to prowl about the Atlantic like hungry tigers and drive British shipping from the seas. And then a year later came war, and an unprepared Raeder found what foreigners had found before him, that his master's promises were dust.

'On land I am a hero,' Hitler once said, 'but at sea I am a coward'. He was fascinated by battleships, talked knowingly about their technicalities, but of sea-power and its influence he knew nothing. So he left things to Raeder, and of all the arms and institutions of the Third Reich the Navy was the least affected by Nazi ideas and practices. Raeder was able to impress on the Navy his own high standards of morality. He retained the old naval salute for all routine occasions: he forbade officers to become involved in party politics and dismissed the few who did, including a naval aide to Hitler: he retained, despite opposition, the Chaplain Corps of the Navy, expanded it as the fleet expanded, encouraged corporate worship. He refused to retire Jewish officers like Backenköhler, Grassmann, Rogge, and when in 1938 the infamous 'Crystal-night' took place, the burning and looting of the synagogues, and outraged senior officers like Lütjens and Dönitz protested, he conveyed their protests, and his, to Hitler. Navies by their nature exist at the periphery not the centre of their country's events: Raeder's rules about no politics ensured that the German Navy was insulated from the régime's grosser excesses, that its sailors mostly were straightforward, uncorrupted men.

With the coming of war in 1939 Raeder lost no time in putting his aggressive policy into action. *Graf Spee, Deutschland* and several U-boats were already on the trade-routes, and in November *Scharnhorst* and *Gneisenau* put to sea. Off Iceland they sighted and sank the British armed merchant-cruiser *Rawalpindi*,[2] an action which caused some alarm in the British and French Admiralties, for no home-based German battleship in wartime had ever been this far north before. In the spring of 1940 Raeder committed most of the Navy to the invasion of Norway: the losses were heavy (at Narvik about half the entire German destroyer force) but considering the success achieved, tolerable. *Scharnhorst* and *Gneisenau* under Admiral Lütjens covered the Narvik landings from seaward and briefly engaged the battle-cruiser *Renown: Gneisenau* was hit three times and several of her crew killed and wounded. Two months later when the British were evacuating the port (and Captain Denham struggling to cross into Sweden), the two ships returned to the same waters under Admiral Marschall and sank the aircraft-carrier *Glorious* and two destroyers.

That summer the conquest of France gave the German Navy a foothold on the very edge of the Atlantic battlefield: U-boat bases were set up at Lorient, Brest, La Rochelle, St Nazaire. German merchant raiders operating on the world's trade-routes had orders to send prizes to French ports, so did *Admiral Scheer* when she left Germany in October for a five months' cruise in the Atlantic and Indian Oceans. In December the heavy cruiser *Admiral Hipper* broke out, like *Scheer*, through the Denmark Straits between Greenland and Iceland, and after a brush with an allied troop convoy, put into Brest, the first German heavy warship to do so. Finally in January 1941 Admiral Lütjens again took *Scharnhorst* and *Gneisenau* north, this time to operate in the Atlantic. On passage through the Faeroes-Iceland gap, they were spotted by the British cruiser *Naiad*, retired at speed to the Arctic, refuelled from a waiting tanker and a week later passed through the mists and darkness of the Denmark Straits unseen. 'For the first time in our history,' Admiral Lütjens signalled to his two ships on reaching the Atlantic, 'German battleships have today succeeded in breaking through the British blockade. We shall now go forward to success.'

In a two-month cruise, supported by supply ships and tankers, the battle-cruisers sank 116,000 tons of allied shipping before turning for France: they would have sunk more if some convoys sighted had not had battleship escorts like *Rodney* and *Malaya*, which Lütjens's orders forbade him to attack. The Atlantic Battle was now mounting to a climax as successes against shipping by U-boats, warships, raiders and aircraft mounted. In March 1941 Atlantic losses were the severest so far, over 350,000 tons, in April in all theatres a record of nearly 700,000 tons. To Admiral Raeder it was clear that the tide was running in his favour: such losses could not be sustained indefinitely. Now was the time to go *banco* with all he had; and he signalled to Lütjens not to delay unduly his arrival in Brest, as *Bismarck* was almost ready for service and preparations were under way for *Scharnhorst, Gneisenau,* and the new heavy cruiser *Prinz Eugen* to join with her on a fresh operation in the Atlantic under his command.

She was built by Blohm and Voss of Hamburg and went down the slipway there on St Valentine's day, 1939, the anniversary of Nelson's great coup at the battle of Cape St Vincent. The German government declared the ceremony a state occasion. Hitler, Raeder, Keitel, Göring, Goebbels, Hess, Ribbentrop, Himmler, Bormann, von Schirach were all present on the podium, and Hitler in a speech hoped her future crew would be imbued with Bismarck's iron spirit. The bands played, the Nazi flags curled in the air, Hitler and Raeder beamed happily and a vast crowd cheered to see Bismarck's granddaughter, Dorothea von Loewenfeld, christen their greatest ship with the name of their greatest Chancellor. She was a sixth of a mile long, 120 feet wide, designed to carry eight fifteen-inch guns and six aircraft, with thirteen-inch armour made of specially hardened Wotan steel on her turrets and sides. Listed as 35,000 tons to comply with the London Treaty, she would in fact be 42,000 tons standard displacement and over 50,000 tons fully laden. There had never been a warship like her: she symbolised not only a resurgent Navy but the whole resurgent German nation.

During the next eighteen months, in peace and war, she lay alongside the quay fitting out, an iron antheap swarming with dock-yard workmen. There were welders and fitters to fashion her super-structure plate by plate, men with cranes to step her masts, lower her twelve boilers, swing on board her four gun turrets each of a thousand tons, Anton and Bruno forward, Caesar and Dora aft,* electricians to make light and power circuits, fire-control and tele-phone systems, fix radio panels, suction fans, compasses, radar; shipwrights to stow anchors and cables; plumbers to install wash-basins and wastepipes; carpenters to fit cabins, messes, operations room, charthouse. That summer, while the Wehrmacht sketched in

* The Germans called their turrets A & B forward and C & D aft, the British A & B forward, X & Y aft.

the boundaries of a new German Empire from the Pyrenees to the North Cape, the Atlantic to the Oder, the ship took shape. Key officers joined, like Adalbert Schneider, gunnery commander, Gerhard Junack, engineer officer in charge of damage control. Later came others, Walter Lehmann, chief engineer, Wolf Neuendorff, navigating officer, Hans Oels, executive officer. Third gunnery officer was Burkard, Baron von Müllenheim-Rechberg, of an old Alsatian family, father killed in the army in the first world war, brother Wendelin killed in the Luftwaffe at the beginning of this one. Before the war he'd been assistant naval attaché under Ribbentrop at the embassy in London, had a flat off Grosvenor Square and many English friends, had already seen action twice, in *Scharnhorst* when she sank the *Rawalpindi*, later as second in command of the destroyer *Erich Giese* when she sailed to Narvik.

Last came the captain, Ernst Lindemann from the Rhineland, aged forty-five, clever and cool, top of his term as a cadet, specialist in gunnery, chain-smoker and coffee-drinker, blond hair sleeked back. Junack admired him, respected his knowledge of engineering, called him the right man in the right job. With him came his steward, ex-waiter of his favourite Hamburg restaurant, a man nervous about military service but happy to be taken to sea in something so large and safe. By August 24th the ship was ready to be handed over: the band played on the quarter-deck, the Nazi naval ensign was run up, *Bismarck* was commissioned into the German Navy.

During the next month *Bismarck* continued fitting-out and completing her complement: signalmen, store-keepers, sick-berth attendants; cooks, coders, clerks; seamen, stokers, stewards. Like the rest of the German Navy they were all volunteers and regulars, had to pass a strict examination to be accepted, most of those who applied failed. They signed for four years initially with an option at the end of a further twelve. Their average age was twenty-one: few had seen action of any kind, and for most this was their first ship: they worked on board in the daytime, lived in accommodation ships like the *Oceania* and *General Artigas* at night. Later, as the ship prepared for sea, they moved into messes, like the British Navy had hammocks to sleep in, lockers for clothes: each mess peeled its own

24

potatoes but the cooked food was fetched in containers from central galleys: unlike the British Navy beer was available instead of rum, and there was a weekly free issue of cigarettes. As the sailing date neared, the ship filled with stores: flags, flour, duffel coats, typewriters; bandages, carcasses, signal pads, paint; sausages, crockery, charts, binoculars; soap, blankets, cipher books, cigarettes; hammocks, potatoes, light bulbs, lavatory paper; everything to meet the wants of this floating town and the 2,000 men who were to make their home in her.

On September 15th 1940 *Bismarck* was weaned, left the crèche of Hamburg, slipped the cords that tied her to the shore, glided down the lazy Elbe towards salt water and the open sea. And those who saw her pass on the long journey from Hamburg to the river's mouth and through the Kaiser Wilhelm Canal to Germany's other side, housewives in Altona, sailors and dockers in Brunsbüttel, farmers and soldiers on guard in Schleswig-Holstein, marvelled at what they saw. Warships combine uniquely grace and power, and *Bismarck*, massive and elegant, with the high flare of her bows and majestic sweep of her lines, the symmetry of her turrets, the rakish cowling of her funnel, her ease and arrogance in the water, was then the most graceful, most powerful warship yet built. No German saw her without pride, no neutral or enemy without admiration.

In the enclosed waters of Kiel Bay she underwent acceptance trials, adjusted compasses, tested degaussing gear, ran machinery and speed trials over the measured mile, worked up to 30 knots. Some trials didn't go as smoothly as expected and in the first week of December she was back in Hamburg for extensive adjustments. Here she was joined by another child of Blohm and Voss, the newly built U-boat *U.556*, which came and fitted out alongside her, ferret at the tail of a tiger. The Captain of *U.556* was Herbert Wohlfarth, known as 'Parsifal' in the U-boat Service because of his fastidiousness on a pre-war cruise, cartoonist and a bit of a joker, experienced though and brave, Dönitz called him brilliant, this was his third command.

Wohlfarth and his men often heard *Bismarck*'s band practising on the quay above them, and as the day of their commissioning approached in February 1941, they thought, how nice if we could get the band to play at our commissioning ceremony. But how to ask for it without inviting rebuff?

It happened that 'godparenthoods', adoptions by towns of ships and regiments, were all the rage in Germany then (and in Britain too): *U.556* had herself just been adopted by the district of Bergisch-land. So Wohlfarth and his officers prepared a grave document, charred at the edges to show its age, the 'adoption' by *U.556* of the mighty *Bismarck*, a promise to protect *Bismarck* from all dangers that might beset her in the oceans, seas, lakes, ponds, puddles of the world for ever and ever amen; and there were two drawings, of the knight Parsifal deflecting torpedoes from *Bismarck* with his sword, and of *U.556* towing her. Wohlfarth sealed the document with his thumb-print and took it over to Lindemann, and Lindemann laughed and had it framed and hung in the wardroom next to pictures of Hitler and Bismarck, and for *U.556*'s commissioning sent along the *Bismarck*'s band.

By March *Bismarck* was ready to take to sea again, and returned to Kiel for further trials, this time successful. Then she filled her bunkers with oil, and magazines with ammunition, and sailed east to the Bay of Danzig, to Gdynia or Gotenhafen as the Germans had renamed it, there to carry out a long programme of exercises and training, away from the attention of British bombers. The great guns spoke and deafened the novices with their blast. The Arado aircraft were catapulted from their launching rails, spotted fall of shot, flew on search patrols, alighted and were recovered. Land-based aircraft with drogues passed down the ship's sides as targets for the flak crews. There were exercises in towing and being towed, in oiling from tankers while under way, in electrical failures, fire-fighting, damage control. Soon *Bismarck* was joined by the new heavy cruiser *Prinz Eugen*, 14,000 tons, named after the Prince of Savoy, the liberator of Vienna, recently completed at the Germania works at Kiel, with lines so like *Bismarck*'s that from afar you could barely tell them apart. She had eight eight-inch guns, and a speed of 32 knots: her captain was a class-mate of Lindemann's, Helmuth Brink-mann from Lübeck.

One day in *Bismarck* they practised flooding of the steering gear compartment, down aft by the rudders. Ordinary Seaman Herbert Blum on damage control duty there jokingly asked his lieutenant permission not to obey orders, as if the compartment had really been knocked out, he and his mates would be dead. 'Quite right,' said the lieutenant laughing, 'so you'd better play dead, put your caps on back to front, lie down on the deck and everyone will know you are bodies.' After the exercise the lieutenant said, 'The chances of getting a hit there are a hundred thousand against'. At the time Blum didn't pay much attention to this remark, weeks later he was to remember it.

Another day *Bismarck* was preparing for a sub-calibre shoot, when who should turn up but *U.556* and Wohlfarth? Seeing the towed target Wohlfarth asked if he might loose off a few rounds first. Permission was granted, *U.556* opened up and to Wohlfarth's and Lindemann's astonishment the target was immediately hit. 'I hope you will be as successful in the Atlantic,' signalled Lindemann, 'and earn the Knight's Cross as well,' and the noble Parsifal replied, 'I hope we may *both* earn the Knight's Cross in joint action together. Later, passing *Bismarck* en route for *U.556*'s first patrol, Wohlfarth, remembering his protective role, signalled, 'Don't worry when your turn comes to follow. I'll see you suffer no harm.' It was a prophecy that was to come within an ace of fulfilment.

On April 2nd, 1941, just two weeks after the arrival of *Scharnhorst* and *Gneisenau* in Brest, the German naval staff issued preparatory orders. In the next new moon period at the end of the month *Bismarck*, *Prinz Eugen* and *Gneisenau* were to rendezvous in the Atlantic for a combined attack on allied shipping: *Scharnhorst* would be unable to join them because of repairs to her boilers. Unlike Lütjens's order on the previous operation which forbade him to attack a battleship escort, this time *Bismarck* had discretion to draw enemy fire, while *Gneisenau* and *Prinz Eugen* attacked the ships of the convoy. Otherwise action with enemy warships was to be avoided, the object of the operation being the destruction of merchant shipping.

Had this squadron, even without *Scharnhorst*, put to sea, it might have been disastrous for Britain, indeed could have altered the whole course of the war. But luck was not with the Germans. Two days later there was a British bombing raid on Brest and a bomb fell without exploding into the water of No. 8 dock where *Gneisenau* was lying. The ship was moved to a mooring in the harbour, and here at 9 a.m. on 6th April she was attacked by a torpedo-carrying plane of British Coastal Command. Her pilot, Flying Officer Kenneth Campbell, a Canadian, went in low over the harbour mole, brave beyond the call of duty, shells and bullets screaming at him from every side. He and his crew crashed almost at once, but before hitting the water they released a torpedo which struck *Gneisenau* near the stern, smashed a propeller shaft, flooded two engine rooms and put the ship out of service for six months.[3]

So what had once been a formidable force of one battleship, two battlecruisers and a heavy cruiser was reduced now to the still powerful *Bismarck* and *Prinz Eugen*. Should Raeder postpone the operation until *Tirpitz*, which had recently arrived at Gotenhafen for her own working-up exercises, was ready to join them? On balance there was little to be said for it. The longer the operation was put off, the shorter the northern nights, the less chance of breaking out unseen. America might soon be in the war against them, and the range and quality of aircraft patrolling the Atlantic were increasing monthly. Finally, on the very day that *Gneisenau* was torpedoed, the German army began pouring into Greece on its drive south towards Crete and the Eastern Mediterranean, and any diversion to prevent reinforcements from reaching Admiral Cunningham's hard-pressed Mediterranean Fleet was to be welcomed. Raeder must have reached his decision quickly, for two days later, on 8th April, Admiral Lütjens flew to Paris to confer with his old friend Karl Dönitz, Admiral commanding U-boats, about co-operation between *Bismarck* and submarines.

But on 24th April a further setback took place. A magnetic mine exploded a hundred feet from *Prinz Eugen*, damaging a coupling. Repairs would take two weeks, so the earliest the squadron could now sail was the new moon period towards the end of May. Should postponement be considered again? Raeder thought not but felt he should put his views to the Fleet Commander; and Lütjens flew to Berlin.

Günther Lütjens was then 51, a long, lean, lamp-post of a man, with cropped hair like most German officers, and a dour, tight expression which some said concealed a dry sense of humour. He was born in Wiesbaden, son of a merchant, entered the naval college at Kiel in 1908, passed out 20th from a class of 160, had a reputation for mastering whatever he studied. He'd fought in torpedo-boats in the first war, off Flanders and in the Channel, in the thirties commanded the cruiser *Karlsrühe* on a trip to the Americas while Dönitz was commanding the *Emden* on a voyage to the Far East. On return the cruisers rendezvoused in Vigo, Spain, steamed back to Germany together. Later Lütjens became Chief of Personnel and Admiral commanding torpedo-boats. In the Norwegian Campaign of 1940 he'd deputised for Admiral Marschall in *Gneisenau* as Fleet Commander, been awarded the Knight's Cross.

Lütjens was a man wholly dedicated to the service, courageous, single-minded, stoical, austere, taciturn as a Cistercian monk. He was not a Nazi, gave Hitler the naval not the party salute, always wore an admiral's dirk of the old Imperial Navy, not one with a swastika. His friend Admiral Conrad Patzig who succeeded him as Chief of Personnel called him 'one of the ablest officers in the Navy, very logical and shrewd, incorruptible in his opinions and an engaging personality when you got to know him'. Few did. To those who admired him, he was shy and withdrawn, to others aloof and remote. He believed that young officers should wed themselves to the Navy, and when Chief of Personnel was inflexible about the rule that no officer should marry until earning a certain level of pay. He practised what he preached, didn't marry until forty and then very happily, two children now and a third on the way. His sister had married his friend Captain Backenköhler, Marschall's former Chief of Staff.

Raeder asked Lütjens what he thought about postponement, and Lütjens said he was in favour of it at least until *Scharnhorst* or *Tirpitz* was ready. But Raeder's mind was already made up and he trotted out all the reasons for not postponing. Lütjens, was in Raeder's words 'perhaps not entirely convinced by my views' yet agreed to accede to them. As he told Patzig later, what else could he do? Patzig also wondered what need there was for the Fleet Commander and his valuable staff to embark for what had now become a single operation. 'We can't afford to lose any more Fleet Commanders,' said Patzig jokingly, referring to Boehm and Marschall, both of whom Raeder had recently sacked. Lütjens agreed but said any such suggestion must come from the Admiralty planning staff, and made Patzig promise not to propose it himself. Already a sense of fatalism, that was increasingly to show itself, was beginning to colour his thinking. 'I realise,' he said to Patzig, 'that in this unequal struggle between the British Navy and ourselves I shall sooner or later have to lose my life. But I have settled my private affairs, and I shall do my best to carry out my orders with honour.'

At the beginning of May Lütjens flew to Gotenhafen and embarked with the officers of his staff. They were his Chief of Staff, Captain Harald Netzbandt, former captain of *Gneisenau*, a tubby, little man whom Lütjens had grown to know and like during the Norwegian campaign; Commander Paul Ascher, fleet operations officer, former gunnery officer of the *Graf Spee* in her actions in the South Atlantic, interned in the Argentine after her scuttling and escaped back to Germany; Captain Emil Melms, fleet gunnery and personnel officer; Commander Nitzschke, fleet signals officer, fond of art and literature; Commander Thannemann, fleet engineer, in the *Blücher* when sunk in 1940 trying to force the Oslo narrows, Dr Riege, fleet medical officer, Dr Langer, deputy judge advocate of the fleet. There also embarked Dr Externbrink, the navy's senior meteorological officer and his staff, a U-boat liaison officer from Admiral Dönitz's staff and a Luftwaffe liaison officer, Major Grohé.

The operation was given its code-name, Rheinübung (Rhine Exercise), and a starting date of 18th May. On 5th May Hitler and his staff travelled to Gotenhafen by special train to inspect *Bismarck* and *Tirpitz*. Raeder did not accompany him, the first time in eight years on such a visit he had not done so. He gives no reason in his memoirs, as though it were something to be hushed up, but elsewhere he speaks of Hitler's malign influence and the ease of succumbing to his wishes. Aware of Hitler's lack of enthusiasm for surface ship operations, fears of sinkings and loss of prestige, he had not given him the squadron's exact sailing date: he may have felt that Hitler would have wormed it out of him, panicked at realising there was less than two weeks to go, ordered its cancellation. All Lütjens had to do if asked was say he didn't know.

Instead of Raeder, there went with Hitler General Keitel, Chief of the General Staff, later to be hanged at Nüremberg. Captain von Puttkamer, Hitler's naval aide, was also present and Walther Hewel, Ribbentrop's liaison officer at the Führer's headquarters.

At Gotenhafen ('the very hideous Gotenhafen' Hewel called it) the party embarked in the yacht *Hela* in the inner harbour, and steamed out to where *Bismarck*, massive and graceful, was lying at anchor in the roads: perhaps even Hitler caught his breath at the sight of her. The crew were lined up on deck with Admiral Lütjens, Captain Lindemann, Commander Oels and the officers of the watch waiting at the gangway to receive him. Hitler was piped over the side, the officers presented to him. He then inspected the crew and the ship. In the fore gunnery transmitting station he stayed nearly half an hour listening to Sub-Lieutenant Cardinal explaining how speed, course, wind-direction, temperature were fed into the machine, how the machine came up with the right angles of deflection and elevation for the guns. It was this sort of technical talk that Hitler liked, much better than old Raeder gassing about sea-power. Keitel, a gunner himself, found it absorbing too.

Then Lütjens took Hitler to his cabin, with von Puttkamer but without Keitel. Lütjens gave an account of his earlier cruise with *Scharnhorst* and *Gneisenau*, then told Hitler that this time because of *Bismarck*'s superiority, he would be able to take on any convoy escort while *Prinz Eugen* attacked the merchant ships. Was there then nothing to worry about, asked the cautious Hitler, what about torpedo-carrying aircraft? Yes, agreed Lütjens, that was a worry, his biggest worry, though he thought the ship's tremendous fire-power could cope with it – on another occasion he told a friend that with *Bismarck*'s armour, torpedo hits would be felt as bee stings that hurt but didn't damage. He might have added what all senior officers felt, that had the intriguing Göring not denied the Navy its air arm, had the aircraft carrier *Graf Zeppelin*, lying even now in the yards at Gotenhafen, half-completed and abandoned, been accompanying him, his worries would have been considerably less. Hitler, said von Puttkamer, was pleased to find that the experienced Lütjens shared his concerns. He then went ashore in the *Hela* and inspected the *Tirpitz* in the harbour. Captain Topp begged him to allow his ship to accompany *Bismarck* on her first operation. Hitler listened but said nothing. The party then returned to the train. 'Visit unbelievably impressive,' Hewel wrote in his diary that night. 'Concentration of force and the highest technical development.'

On 16th May Lütjens reported the squadron ready to proceed from midnight on the 18th–19th, and during the next two days support ships sailed from French Atlantic and Norwegian ports to take up waiting positions: the tankers *Weissenburg* and *Heide* to the Arctic Ocean, the tankers *Belchen* and *Lothringen* and reconnaissance ships *Gonzenheim* and *Kota Penang* to an area south of Greenland, the tankers *Esso Hamburg*, *Friedrich Breme* and supply ship *Egerland* between the Azores and Antilles. These ships would keep *Bismarck* and *Prinz Eugen* supplied with oil, ammunition, food and water for at least three months. In addition four weather ships were sailed and the tanker *Wollin* was ordered to stand by in Bergen harbour.

On the morning of Sunday 18th May Admiral Lütjens held a final conference in his cabin, attended by his staff officers and Captains Lindemann and Brinkmann. His operational brief from Admiral Carls of Naval Group Command North in Wilhelmshaven (his shore authority until he crossed the line Southern Greenland/ Northern Hebrides when it became Group Command West in Paris) recommended sailing direct to Korsfjord* near Bergen, there anchor for the day while *Prinz Eugen*, whose radius of action was very limited, topped up with fuel, then sail direct for the Atlantic through the Iceland/Faeroes gap. Now Lütjens said he had decided on a change of plan. The squadron would not call at Korsfjord but proceed directly to the Arctic Ocean, oil from the tanker *Weissenburg* near Jan Mayen Island, then go at high speed into the Atlantic through the

* Now called Krossfjord.

32

1. 'People in Britain saw her too, in spring and summer . . . ' H.M.S. **Hood**
entering Portsmouth, April 28th, 1937

2. 'massive and elegant . . . the most graceful, the most powerful warship yet
built.' **Bismarck** exercising in the Baltic. Taken from **Prinz Eugen**

3. Left 'He knew his flat was watched . . . that his telephone was tapped, and he suspected bugging too.' Captain Henry Denham, British Naval Attaché, Stockholm, 1941

4. Right 'would now never see the Harlequin Duck or Arctic Tern or Icelandic Falcon' Lieutenant Esmond Knight, R.N.V.R.

5. Left 'And so Lieutenant Jean Philippon of the French Navy . . . became a spy for France.' Philippon as First Lieutenant of the submarine **Ouessant,** 1940

6. Right 'He sent coded messages via the local bus driver . . . Viggo Axelssen of the Norwegian Resistance

Denmark Straits. Typically Lütjens gave no reason for the change. Group North had recommended the Iceland/Faeroes passage as the shortest route, saving time and fuel, but it was here that Lütjens had run into the cruiser *Naiad* in January and been obliged to turn back. The Denmark Straits route had been used successfully by *Scheer*, *Hipper*, and other raiders, and as he had subsequently negotiated it himself with *Scharnhorst* and *Gneisenau*, he had cause to think it the safest.

After the conference Lütjens went in his barge to the harbour to inspect *Prinz Eugen* and her crew, but neither to them nor her officers did he say a word about the impending operation. During the rest of the day the two ships topped up with oil fuel. Earlier in *Bismarck* while cleaning the oil tanks several Polish labourers had been killed by fumes, and this may have resulted in the decision not to oil to full capacity: the ship is believed to have sailed 200 tons short. Whatever the reason it was an omission that Captain Lindemann was later profoundly to regret.

Various last-minute supernumeraries joined the two ships, a hundred officers and men from the merchant service as prize crews for all the merchant vessels they hoped to capture, a batch of midshipmen from *Tirpitz* for war training, reporters and cameramen from Dr Goebbels's Propaganda Ministry, hungry for pictures of sinking British ships. Dr Menke, of the Navy's legal department, came on board to discuss with Dr Langer and Commander Oels disposal of men under arrest. Two of these were a Sickbay Petty Officer who had been caught stealing from his messmates, and a cadet charged with drunkenness. The Sickbay Petty Officer was sent ashore for disrating and punishment, and so missed the ship's sailing. The cadet asked and was given permission to have his punishment ashore postponed until after the operation, and so remained on board.

In the afternoon *Prinz Eugen* left the harbour and proceeded into the bay for degaussing trials against magnetic mines, and then *Bismarck* weighed. As the anchor came up from the Baltic seabed and the crew on the fo'c'sle hosed down the cables, the band on the quarter-deck a sixth of a mile away played '*Muss 'i denn?*' ('Must I leave?'), a ballad of grief and parting. It was the first time they had played it and later it was to be criticised as a possible breach of security. People on shore watched the two ships exercising until evening when they disappeared into the dusk.

They proceeded independently through the night and at 11 the next morning rendezvoused off Arkona, the northernmost cape of Prussia, with a flotilla of minesweepers and the destroyers *Friedrich Eckholdt* and *Z.23* under the command of Captain Schulze-Hinrichs. At noon Captain Lindemann addressed *Bismarck*'s crew on the loudspeaker system and told them officially what they had already guessed, that they were going on a three months cruise in the Atlantic to destroy British shipping. He finished: 'I give you the hunter's toast, good hunting and a good bag!' The news was welcomed, for it dispelled mystery, cleared the air, challenged the spirit: *Bismarck* was the most powerful warship in the world, Führer, admiral, captain had said so, they could see it too, there was nothing in the world she and they could not do. One or two perhaps, those who had read of the British Navy's strength and traditions, looked over the side at the grey Baltic slipping astern, wondered uneasily what the future might bring.

All that day and night the squadron sailed in formation westwards and northwards, the escorts leading, then *Bismarck* with the admiral's flag, white with a black cross fluttering at the fore, then *Prinz Eugen*. They passed through the Fehmarn Belt, skirted the eastern edge of Kiel Bay where they were joined by the destroyer *Hans Lody*, sailed through the Great Belt which divides two parts of Denmark, and on through the waters that Nelson had taken on his way to victory at Copenhagen 140 years before. At 4 a.m. a signal was received saying air reconnaissance of the British fleet at Scapa Flow had not been possible the day before because of cloud. Dawn broke to reveal a calm and empty sea, for as a security measure Group North had frozen all shipping movements in the Kattegat and Skaggerak during the squadron's passage. They had not reckoned with the *Gotland*, though, which showed up soon after, grey in the sunlight against the green of the Swedish coast, steaming on a parallel course. She kept company with the German ships for several hours: then off Marstrand they swung away to port, shaping a north-westerly course across the Skaggerak for a landfall at Kristiansand in southern Norway. *Gotland* sent a routine signal to Stockholm, and Lütjens wirelessed to Group North that he believed his presence had been betrayed.

In Kristiansand's Vesterveien a party of people were walking by the shore. They were Viggo Axelssen, a well-to-do young ship's chandler, his friends Arne Usterud, solicitor, a photographer called Wintersborg and half a dozen others. They had just been to see the launching of Axelssen's new boat, built to replace one commandeered by the authorities, and were now on the way to the local club for a celebratory dinner.

Viggo Axelssen, a bachelor, worked in the Norwegian resistance movement for the Oslo-Stavanger circuit. His job as ship's chandler gave him easy access to the port and harbour master's office where he noted things like the positions of minefields and arrival and departure of convoys. He sent coded messages via the local bus driver Arne Moen, who hid them in a pocket in the casing of his engine, to a radio operator called Gunvald Tomstad who lived at Helle near Flekkefjord sixty miles away. The Germans knew there was a transmitting-post at Flekkefjord but so far had been unable to find it. In Kristiansand only the two Arnes, Usterud and Moen, knew of Axelssen's activities.

The group stopped at the place called Runningen to admire the view. It was a still, calm evening and they could see far out to sea, beyond Oksøy lighthouse eight miles away. As they looked they saw a group of ships steaming west at high speed, the white foam curling at their bows. Wintersborg had with him an old-fashioned spy-glass, and Axelssen borrowed it to look at the group closer. He saw two big, camouflaged warships which he knew must be German, with aircraft circling above and escort craft ahead, steaming urgently in the direction of the Norwegian fjords. Quietly he returned the spy-glass to Wintersborg and said it was time to get along to the club.

On the way he told the others he had to call in at his office to fetch something. They took this to be a bottle of schnapps and laughed, all except Arne Usterud, who realised something was up. In his office Axelssen coded a message of twelve words, then took it along to Arne Moen before the bus left for Flekkefjord.

Late that evening the message was at Helle in Tomstad's hands. He and another agent, Odd Starheim, noted its urgency, decided there would be no time, as usually there was, to take the transmitter from beneath the hay in the barn and set it up at some remote spot. So they put it in Tomstad's 'dark-room', erected the aerial and began transmitting at once. And soon a second message about Rheinübung was going out across the ether to confirm the earlier truth of what Captain Denham had said.

And on that same night, far out in the long reaches of the Atlantic to which *Bismarck* and *Prinz Eugen* were bound, Herbert Wohlfarth in *U.556* along with other U-boats got in among the homeward-bound convoy H.X. 126 and sank five ships.

CHAPTER

2

At Scapa Flow in the Orkney Islands, ten miles from the north coast of Scotland across the racing waters of the Pentland Firth, lay the British Home Fleet. Scapa was ideal for guarding the approaches from the North Sea to the Atlantic, a sweep of water ten miles by eight ringed almost entirely by islands, a natural refuge for war-weary ships. Once on a time the Vikings had come here to plunder and settle, gave to the islands their old Norse names, Pomona on the north, Hoy to the west, Flotta and Hoxa to the south, Burray and South Ronaldsay in the east. Here a generation earlier Admiral Jellicoe had commanded the Grand Fleet, steamed out that May evening of 1916 with his squadrons of battleships to meet the High Seas Fleet. Here at war's end the High Seas Fleet were brought in like lambs, lay rotting at anchor for months while the politicians argued their disposal, until on Midsummer's Day 1919 at a signal from their admiral, the crews opened their sea·cocks and they all guggle-guggled to the bottom: some were raised and broken up, others still littered the sandy floor between Bring Deeps and Cava. And here one October night at the beginning of this war the bold Günther Prien had cocked a snook at British sea-power, taken his U-boat into the Flow through a narrow, unguarded eastern channel, torpedoed and sank the battleship *Royal Oak* with huge loss of life, crept out on the ebb as unobtrusively as he had come, returned to a hero's welcome in Germany.

Admiral Beatty called Scapa the most damnable place on earth, most of the lads agreed. The islands were heather and grass, seabirds and sheep, and across the bare face of the Flow tempests blew, often for days on end. There were no shops, restaurants, girls, just a couple of canteens to dispense warm beer, a hall for film-shows and the occasional concert-party, football fields that too often fathered the signal, 'All grounds unfit for play'. And yet now in the summertime when the Flow sparkled blue in the morning sun and the hills of Hoy were touched with purple and green, at night-time too when the Northern Lights wove pale patterns over the sleeping ships, the place had a rare beauty.

It was here, while Admiral Lütjens was steaming up the Norwegian coast in his new flagship *Bismarck*, that the British Admiral, Tovey, lay moored off Flotta in his new flagship *King George V*. Tovey was 56 now, a small, blue-eyed, twinkly man, last of a family of eleven. He entered the Navy at fifteen, won his spurs at Jutland commanding the destroyer *Onslow*, helped sink the German light cruiser *Wiesbaden*, at one moment in the battle was quite close to Raeder. Like Raeder he was deeply religious, prayed night and morning, once asked publicly why people were so shy of talking about faith, not realising others were different from himself. He was a natural leader, radiated confidence, could be quite fierce sometimes but it soon passed. A jokey admiral wrote of him when captain of the *Rodney*, 'Captain Tovey shares one characteristic with me. In myself I would call it tenacity of purpose. In Tovey I can only call it sheer bloody obstinacy.' Churchill found the same, called him stubborn, tried to get rid of him. Tovey did what he thought right, refused to kow-tow to titular superiors, hated 'Yes-men' in others. He was a civilised man, dressed well, liked good food and wine and company, had a golf handicap of 4, played for the Navy. Like many naval officers he would address foreigners loudly and slowly, was often astonished to find they spoke English too. He liked Poles and Americans especially, and he adored King George the Sixth.

On board the flagship was a green telephone which, when the fleet was in Scapa, was connected to a special shore line to the Admiralty in London. It was the same line on which Jellicoe had spoken to Churchill when he was First Lord of the Admiralty twenty-six years earlier. On this telephone, in the early morning of 21st May, Tovey's secretary, Captain Paffard, and his Chief of Staff, Commodore Brind, learnt from the Admiralty of Denham's signal, received during the night. To them, as to Tovey, it came as no surprise. It was known from intelligence that both *Bismarck* and *Prinz Eugen* had completed training, and one agent's report that new charts were being delivered to *Bismarck* and another's from France that battleship moorings were being prepared at Brest, made it clear her time in the Baltic was coming to an end. Further, during the past ten days there had been an unusual increase in German air activity, daily reconnaissance flights over the Flow, additional flights over the Denmark Straits and between Greenland and Jan Mayen, so that on 18th May, at the moment Lütjens was leaving Gotenhafen, Tovey ordered the cruiser *Suffolk* on patrol in the Denmark Straits to keep a sharp look-out, especially near the ice-edge, and her sister ship *Norfolk* to sail from Iceland to relieve her, that in case of emergency both ships might have full tanks.

There were two things to be done immediately; make an aerial search of the Norwegian fjords, which the Admiralty had already arranged, and to bring the fleet to short notice for steam. A signal went out from the flagship's bridge, and from across the Flow the ships in company answered: the old battlecruiser *Hood*, 42,000 tons, for twenty-one years the pride of Britain's Navy, the biggest warship in the world; the new battleship *Prince of Wales*, sister ship of *King George V*, fresh from the builder's yard, with two turrets not yet free of teething troubles and dockyard workmen still aboard her; the brand new aircraft-carrier *Victorious*, with 48 crated Hurricane fighters on board for beleaguered Malta, and due in two days' time to join the battle-cruiser *Repulse* off the Clyde and escort the valuable Middle East troop convoy WS8B to the southwards; and a score of cruisers and destroyers. Men in these ships wondered what the crisis might be, some went below and flashed up second and third boilers.

During the morning Tovey spoke several times to the Admiralty on the green telephone, conferred with his staff officers in his comfortable cabin, but until he had further news there was little more he could do. He had made his dispositions, *Norfolk* and *Suffolk* in the

39

Denmark Straits, the cruisers *Manchester*, *Birmingham* and five trawlers in the Iceland-Faeroes passage, and a request for air patrols from Greenland to Orkney: the main fleet would be divided into two groups of two ships each, *Hood* flying the flag of Vice-Admiral Holland, and *Prince of Wales;* and *King George V* and the battle-cruiser *Repulse* which the Admiralty had signalled they were sending from the Clyde.

The morning wore on. Drifters puttered about the Flow, bringing stores and mail, motor-boats chugged inshore, taking men to the pay office and dentist. Above the grey ships the white gulls hovered like mobiles, waiting for titbits from the emptied trashcans. It was a warm, summer day, a day for golf perhaps or fishing or walking the hills of Hoy. At around noon Admiral Tovey heard that two Spitfires of the Photographic Reconnaissance Unit of Coastal Command had just taken off from Wick, across the Pentland Firth, heading for the Norwegian coast. One went east towards Oslo and the Skaggerak, the other, piloted by Flying Officer Suckling, made for the Bergen fjords.

Through the night the German squadron steamed northwards up the Norwegian coast, steering a zigzag course to avoid British submarines. To those newly-joined the weather was kind: a calm sea with a gentle wind from the north-east. A signal from Group North reported photographic reconnaissance of Scapa Flow the day before as showing (correctly) three heavy ships (*King George V, Prince of Wales, Hood*), a carrier (*Victorious*) and several cruisers and destroyers. A further signal reported the decoding of a British message to all coastal aircraft to look out for the German squadron, reported on a northerly course, but a note in the *Prinz Eugen*'s log reveals that this didn't come to Captain Brinkmann's attention until evening. At breakfast on the messdecks there was cheering news on the wireless: the day before German paratroops had made a massive descent on Crete.

Now Admiral Lütjens did the very thing he said he wouldn't do at his conference at Gotenhafen three days before, signalled the squadron to enter the Norwegian fjords. Just before 9 a.m. off the island of Marstein the two ships turned to starboard and entered the quiet waters of Korsfjord, the tongue of water that leads to Bergen. Pilots came aboard, took *Bismarck* to Grimstad fjord, just south of Bergen, *Prinz Eugen* to Kalvanes Bay, north-west of it, the three destroyers to Bergen. *Bismarck* anchored close inshore, a stone's throw from the grey rocks and trim red and yellow wooden houses and sheep grazing on the young grasses. Farmers and fishermen stared with astonishment at what they saw, the sailors stared back, conquerors and conquered, neither comprehending, so near together, worlds apart. Four merchant ships were ordered alongside each of the big ships, one on each beam and quarter, as anti-torpedo protection for the engine-rooms, propellers and rudders. Admiral Lütjens signalled *Prinz Eugen* to oil from the tanker *Wollin* and to be ready to sail in the evening.

What reasons caused Lütjens to reverse his decision not to enter Korsfjord we shall never know, for typically he left none. Possibly he felt that by topping up *Prinz Eugen*'s tanks he could defer the decision whether to break out by the Denmark Straits or the Iceland-Faeroes passage or even the Faeroes-Orkney passage until the last moment. Whatever the reason it was as foolish a decision as that of allowing the ships to leave home waters by the Baltic rather than the North Sea. Had they gone through the Kiel Canal, left Brunsbüttel in the afternoon, oiled at Trondheim or Narvik or even steamed straight to the *Weissenburg* in the Arctic, they would have stood a good chance of getting out unobserved. To send them by daylight through the narrow waters of the Kattegat and Skaggerak was to invite the attention of neutrals and agents, which was exactly what happened. Further, Raeder knew it; for a signal sent that very morning from Admiral Canaris, head of the *Abwehr* or Counter Intelligence Service, stated that he had proof positive of British agents' reports of the squadron's outward movements. For the squadron, in the light of this knowledge, to be permitted to enter Bergen, the nearest Norwegian harbour to British air bases, was asking for trouble, like a burglar loitering outside his local police station.

And trouble came. At about 1.15 p.m. Flying Officer Suckling in his Spitfire, almost at the end of his search, spotted two warships 25,000 feet below. They looked like cruisers: he turned, made a run over the fjords, opened the shutter. At the time no one in *Bismarck* or *Prinz Eugen* saw him: it wasn't until fifteen minutes later that the alarm bells sounded, by which time Suckling and his happy snaps were quarter-way back to Wick.

At Wick the Station Intelligence Officer looked at the wet prints, assessed the ships as one battleship and one cruiser, informed Tovey's staff. The Air Ministry agreed to an Admiralty request to mount a bombing attack that night, but the Chief of Coastal Command, Air Marshal Sir Frederick Bowhill, once a seaman himself, wanted his own staff to evaluate the photographs further. The only pilot and plane available to take them the 650 miles to London was Suckling and his Spitfire, so he climbed in again, set off south. At nightfall he found himself short of petrol and near Nottingham where he lived. He landed, roused a garage-proprietor friend who had a car and petrol, drove through the black-out at 50 miles an hour, handed over the prints in the early morning: and later Admiralty and Air Ministry experts confirmed the appreciation of Wick.

At Scapa Admiral Tovey had assumed the same: and when the *Victorious* came into the Flow in the late afternoon after exercises, there was a signal at the flagship's yardarm for her captain, Henry Bovell, to come on board. Tovey asked Bovell whether his Swordfish aircrews, who had flown on board from nearby Hatston only a day or two before, were capable of mounting a torpedo attack on the ships in the fjord. Bovell said he doubted it; few had any operational experience, some had just landed on a carrier for the very first time. Were the ship and her aircrews, asked Tovey, sufficiently trained to sail with the fleet at all? Bovell said he thought so, but he wanted the advice of his flight operations officer, Commander Ranald, and the brave Eugene Esmonde, his senior squadron commander. They arrived presently and all three agreed the ship should go; but Tovey was left under no illusions as to the rawness and lack of sea experience of most of the carrier's aircrews.

Nor was he much happier about *Prince of Wales*. Two days before her captain, John Leach, sensing that something was afoot and not wanting to miss it, had reported to Tovey that *Prince of Wales* had completed her working-up, was now ready to join the fleet as a fighting unit. In fact, as Tovey knew, her guns were far from satisfactory and civilian technicians from Vickers-Armstrong were still working on them. Now, this evening, having heard of the report from Bergen, Leach had his ship's company mustered on the quarter-deck, mounted the roof of Y turret, told them what he'd told Tovey, thanked them for their hard work during exercises, and hoped they'd acquit themselves well if and when battle came. They, knowing nothing of the enemy's movements, speculated where they might be sent. Some thought an Atlantic patrol, or escorting a convoy down to the Cape, others, more prophetic, recalled the Saturday night concert-party and their own version of a famous naval ditty:

'We'll all get promotion
This side of the ocean
When we've sunk the old *Bismarck* and all'.

Lieutenant Esmond Knight, RNVR, actor, artist and ornithologist, discussed with another bird-fancier the possibilities of Iceland; a chance to see the Great Skua, Arctic Tern, Harlequin Duck.

In *King George V* Tovey waited anxiously for further news. But now came a change in the weather, a mist settled over the sea, it began to rain. The hours went by and a creeping fear started to gnaw at Tovey's heart, that the German ships had sailed, were even now heading towards the Atlantic where no less than eleven allied convoys were at sea. If so, there were no heavy ships to stop them. It was nine in the evening and growing dark when he made up his mind. To Vice-Admiral Holland in the *Hood* he made a signal to take the *Prince of Wales* under his orders together with the destroyers *Electra*, *Anthony*, *Echo*, *Icarus*, *Achates*, *Antelope*, proceed to Iceland to refuel and then take up a position south-west of the island so as to cover both the Iceland-Greenland and Iceland-Faeroes gaps.

Just before midnight the destroyers slipped their moorings in Gutter Sound, formed line ahead to pass through the Switha gate. Outside the Flow, at the edge of the Pentland Firth, they waited for *Hood* and *Prince of Wales*. On the quarter-deck of the *King George V* which, for exercise he paced so often, Admiral Tovey watched the old battlecruiser and the new battleship weigh, swing round on their engines, glide southwards through the mist and darkness towards the Hoxa gate. *Hood* led the way, proud and elegant, Admiral Holland's flag fluttering at the fore. The crew of the gate-vessel drew aside the huge underwater anti-submarine netting, the two ships passed through, the destroyers took station ahead. Twenty-one years before *Hood* had sailed this way to Scandinavia, on the first mission of her long and wonderful career. She had been here many times since. Now she was leaving for the last time. No landsman would ever see her again.

At Kalvanes during the afternoon *Prinz Eugen* oiled from the *Wollin*, the destroyers from a tanker in Bergen harbour. *Bismarck*, incredibly, didn't oil at all, despite having sailed short and burned over a thousand tons since leaving Gotenhafen. It was an astonishing omission, in sharp contrast to the British Navy's wartime rules that on reaching harbour oiling took priority over everything else. Admittedly the tanker *Weissenburg* in the Arctic was only a day's steaming away, and there was little likelihood of meeting the enemy *en route*. Yet the decision allowed no margin for error or change, it showed an amateurishness in planning, a lack of experience of ocean warfare for which in the end Lütjens would have to pay.

Also in the afternoon crews of both ships painted out camouflage markings, substituted battleship grey to confuse them with British ships; and Lütjens and his staff closely examined the previous days' aerial photographs of Scapa sent down by special car from Bergen. Fighter planes circled the two ships continuously, 'buzzing' Norwegian boats that got too near: patrol craft moved to and fro across the entrance to the fjords, Norwegians ashore noticed their crews peering over the sides. Later, when painting over the camouflage was finished, the men of both ships were allowed to laze about, sleep, read, play games on deck. Many wrote last letters home, taking care not to say where they were: Lindemann gave his to a Luftwaffe officer who went ashore just before the squadron sailed.

At about 7.30 *Bismarck* weighed, turned north, went to anti-aircraft action stations. Off Bergen Schulze-Hinrichs's destroyers were waiting, took station ahead, off Kalvanes *Prinz Eugen* was waiting, took station astern. In single line the five ships steamed at 20 knots up Hjeltefjord and the Fedjeosen. A few officers not on duty stood about on the quarter-deck, smoking and chatting in the evening air, watching the wooded islands slip by. Commander Nitzsche passed with a signal for the admiral, told Müllenheim-Rechberg it was the intercept message from British Coastal Command telling all aircraft to look out for the squadron. At the end of the Fedjeosen they dropped the Norwegian pilot, then swung to port past the Skerries to enter the open sea.

Here the destroyers took up screening positions ahead, the ships started zigzagging. The wind was astern from the south-east, ahead there were low, dark clouds. At a little before midnight, at about the time that *Hood* and *Prince of Wales* were leaving Scapa, the ships turned due north, heading for the Arctic Ocean. Presently look-outs reported, far away to the south, enemy aircraft dropping flares and bombs over Korsfjord – good news for Lütjens, for it showed the British had no idea he had sailed. At five in the morning he dismissed Schulze-Hinrichs and the destroyers to Trondheim. Schulze-Hinrichs signalled good luck, hung about a little expecting Lütjens to take advantage of this opportunity not to break wireless silence by giving him a visual message for Trondheim on his latest intentions. But from the admiral's bridge on the foretop no further message came. Perhaps Lütjens was asleep; perhaps at this moment he didn't clearly know his intentions; perhaps as he'd already said at Gotenhafen he would go via the *Weissenburg* and the Denmark Straits, he felt no need to say it again. Disappointed, Schulze-Hinrichs turned his destroyers to the east, watched the two great ships disappear northwards into the morning mists.

At Scapa Tovey was woken with gloomy news: because of the weather only two of the eighteen bombers that had set out from Wick during the night to bomb the German ships had found the target area, neither had seen anything, both had bombed blind. And the latest weather reports showed a blanket of rain and mist spreading over the whole of the northern part of the North Sea. Reconnaissance aircraft that had left for the fjords before dawn had all had to turn back. From his cabin Tovey couldn't see more than half-way across the Flow.

Were *Bismarck* and *Prinz Eugen* still at Bergen or had they sailed? And what was he to do? These were the questions that tugged at Tovey's mind. If the German ships had sailed the night before, were already four to five hundred miles on their way to the Atlantic, then he too should be at sea chasing them. But say they had not sailed, were still sitting snug in the fjords near Bergen. That would mean that he, Tovey, would be charging aimlessly about the ocean using precious fuel, every drop of which he might need when the moment came, while the Germans, choosing their own moment, could sail with full tanks. Yet if they had left or were leaving by either of the exits between Greenland and the Faeroes, there were cruisers and aircraft watching for them and *Hood* and *Prince of Wales* well placed to intercept; while if they were planning to go through the Faeroes-Orkney gap, Scapa was the best place to wait news of them. The temptation to sail must have been overwhelming, but Tovey resisted it, decided to stay until he had something further to go on.

The day wore on, the weather over Norway remained thick as ever, the ships at Scapa stayed motionless, mute. In mid-morning Coastal Command reported all reconnaissance flights to the Norwegian coast cancelled until further notice. To Tovey, leaning over the charts with his staff officers, 'Daddy' Brind, 'Baron' Bingley, Frankie Lloyd the Master of the Fleet, and others, pencilling in for the umpteenth time *Bismarck*'s 'farthest on' position, it must have seemed his God had deserted him. He looked out of the scuttle at the mists that blotted out Hoy, clung to the hilltop on Flotta. Was there *nothing* that could be done?

There was, thanks to Captain Henry St John Fancourt, Royal Navy, commanding officer of the naval air station at Hatston, on the other side of the Flow. Hatston was used mostly as a training base, for flying off new aircraft to carriers (it was from Hatston that the *Victorious*'s aircrews had flown on board) providing towed targets for the fleet. But it had also an operational squadron of Albacore torpedo planes, and when Captain Fancourt heard the German ships were in Bergen, he was given permission by Coastal Command to move these to Shetland, a hundred miles nearer Bergen, with a view to launching an attack.

For his Albacores then, as much as for Tovey and Coastal Command, Captain Fancourt wanted news of the enemy. His second in command at Hatston was one Geoffrey Rotherham, a pen-pusher now, but a trained observer and aerial navigator of long experience, learnt his trade in the old string and glue days, a man to whom the shape of a wave and the look of wind on water said much, who in the filthiest weather had a knack of 'feeling' his way from one place to another. Captain Fancourt asked Commander Rotherham whether in existing conditions he felt like making a trip to Bergen in one of the old twin-engine American Marylands they used for target-towing, the only suitable plane since the Albacores had left. Commander Rotherham, who reckoned his operational flying days were over, said he'd like it very much, when could they start? Noel Goddard, leader of the target-towing squadron, insisted on being pilot and a volunteer telegraphist/air-gunner was soon found.

At 2 p.m. Fancourt telephoned his idea to the staffs of Tovey at Scapa and Bowhill in London and got the blessings of both. The afternoon was spent planning the flight in detail, for there was a real danger that the Maryland would run slap into the side of Norway without ever seeing it. Rotherham decided to make a landfall on Marstein Island, as Neuendorff had done in *Bismarck* the morning before, run up Korsfjord from there. Coastal Command advised the best approach would be at 200 feet and that the enemy's fighters were in strength.

They took off at 4.30 p.m., it was ducks and drakes most of the way. Rotherham wanted to skim the sea but Goddard felt there was a danger of diving into it and after a bit insisted on going up to the clouds. Presently Rotherham wanted to see the sea again. Twice they came down to under a hundred feet without seeing it. Third time lucky, Rotherham noted a change in the wind, gave an alteration of course, then it was back to the clouds. Within minutes of their estimated landfall Rotherham signalled Goddard to go down again. The clouds parted momentarily, there right ahead lay Marstein Island and its light. They flew up Korsfjord, looked into Grimstad and Kalvanes fjords, found them empty. They took a look at Bergen harbour just to be sure, raced over the housetops and docks while every gun in the place opened up at them, were hit but not badly, ran up Hjeltefjord for a further check, then, satisfied the birds had flown, headed seawards and home.

Fearful of being shot down before Tovey heard the news, Rotherham scribbled an urgent message for the radio operator. The operator couldn't raise Coastal Command, so called Hatston on the target-towing wave. Target-towing exercises were in leisurely progress, when the Hatston operator was startled to find himself taking in an urgent operational signal. He passed it to *King George V* and when the Maryland touched down in Shetland at 7.45, Rotherham found a message to ring Commodore Brind. To him he confirmed that there were no enemy warships of any size in the fjords of the Bergen area.

For Tovey it was negative news but at least he was no longer completely in the dark. He signalled *Victorious*, the cruisers *Galatea*, *Hermione*, *Kenya*, *Aurora* and the destroyers *Inglefield*, *Intrepid*, *Active*, *Punjabi*, *Windsor* and *Lance* to be ready to proceed with him at 10.15 p.m. He signalled *Suffolk* to join *Norfolk* immediately in the Denmark Straits, *Arethusa* to join *Birmingham* and *Manchester* in the Iceland-Faeroes passage, and the battle-cruiser *Repulse* in the Clyde to join his flag north of the Hebrides in the morning. Then, like other great commanders before him, he sat down with his staff to dinner.

Rotherham's news reached London too, and on no one did it make more of an impression than the Prime Minister, Winston Churchill. With his experience of naval affairs in two wars he knew of the fearful havoc the German squadron could cause among the Atlantic convoys, and of the effect on the war. In December 1940 when it became known that *Tirpitz*'s completion was not far behind that of *Bismarck*, he had written to his friend Franklin Roosevelt: 'We have

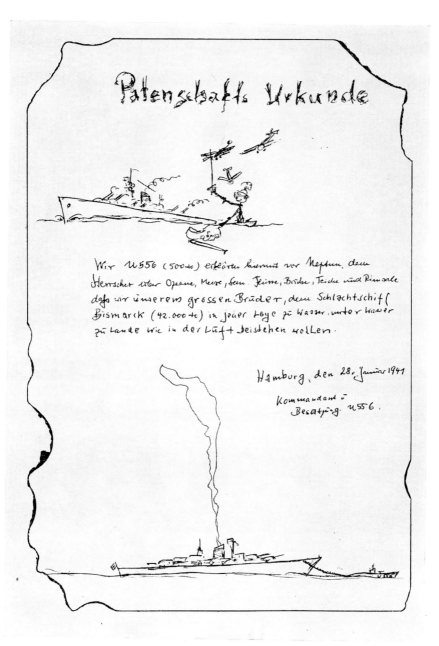

7. '. . . a grave document, charred at the edges to show its age . . . drawings of the knight Parsifal deflecting torpedoes from **Bismarck** with his sword, and of **U 556** towing her.' A facsimile, made by Herbert Wohlfarth in 1973, of the drawings he gave to Captain Lindemann in return for **U 556** borrowing **Bismarck's** band

8. 'a class-mate of Lindemann's, Helmuth Brinkmann from Lubeck.' The captain of the **Prinz Eugen** on her commissioning day

9. 'gave Hitler the naval, not the party salute.' Admiral Lutjens welcomes the Führer on board **Tirpitz** at Gotenhafen

. . . to consider for the first time in this war a fleet action in which the enemy will have two ships at least as good as our two best and only modern ones' (i.e. *King George V* and *Prince of Wales*). Now he sent the American President a direct appeal for help. 'Should we fail to catch them going out, your Navy should surely be able to mark them down for us . . . Give us the news and we will finish the job.'

Yet if the British Prime Minister and his admirals knew a fraction more than they did of the German squadron's movements, the German Chancellor knew nothing at all – not of the sailing from Gotenhafen nor of the voyage through the Kattegat and Skaggerak nor of the arrival at and departure from Bergen. Raeder had long discovered that timing was the essence of his dealings with Hitler, and it wasn't until the first part of the break-out was successfully completed that he felt able to go to the Berghof, the Führer's retreat at Berchtesgaden, and in the presence of Keitel, Ribbentrop and von Puttkamer, tell Hitler the news. At first, as he feared, Hitler expressed profound misgivings and wanted the ships recalled: he was worried about American reactions, about complications connected with the coming attack on Russia, about the risk of torpedo damage from British carriers. Raeder stressed the most difficult part of the journey was now over and the naval operations staff had the highest hopes for its success; and after further discussion Hitler allowed it to proceed.

After Schulze-Hinrichs's departure on the morning of the 22nd, the squadron continued northwards at 24 knots. Lütjens was still uncertain whether to go north or south of Iceland. There was some discussion on the matter among his staff, and a signal from Group North to Admiral Dönitz warned U-boats to be prepared for either. What may have finally decided Lütjens to stick to the original plan was the continuing poor visibility which Dr Externbrink and his fellow meteorologists, conspicuous about the ship in flimsy white coats, predicted would last to southern Greenland. At noon Lütjens signalled *Prinz Eugen* his intentions to go direct for the Denmark Straits but not to oil from *Weissenburg* unless the weather lifted.

49

The decision to forgo *Weissenburg* was bold in view of *Prinz Eugen*'s limited endurance and the depletion of *Bismarck*'s own stocks, but Lütjens believed it correct. His information from Group North was that British air reconnaissance was active only around the lower half of the Norwegian coast, and that while Luftwaffe reconnaissance of Scapa had not been possible the day before because of weather, monitoring of British wireless traffic gave no indication that any British ships had sailed in pursuit or that the enemy had any idea where the squadron was.

This was faulty intelligence, but all that Lütjens had to go on. If he spent precious hours diverting to *Weissenburg*, he might not only lose the foggy weather but would be giving the British more time to track him down. At present the only possible barriers to a dash through the Denmark Straits to his tankers south of Greenland were patrolling British cruisers. These might not be there; if they were they might not see him; if they did there was every hope in fog patches and snow showers of giving them the slip. And if the oil situation became really acute he could always double back to *Weissenburg*, which would take much longer from the Faeroes-Iceland route. Dr Externbrink mentioned to Müllenheim-Rechberg that he had urged Lütjens to go faster to keep up with the weather but Lütjens had refused: it could be that with the *Weissenburg* oiling now cancelled, a more economical speed was thought essential.

At midday the squadron altered from due north to north-west. To Lütjens and Netzbandt these were familiar waters from their days in *Gneisenau* – during the Norwegian campaign the year before and more recently in the January break-out with *Scharnhorst*. As no German aircraft were likely to be met from now on, men in both ships painted out the aircraft recognition markings on the gun turrets, the big Nazi swastikas on quarter-deck and fo'c'sle. All afternoon and evening the foggy weather continued, at times so thick that *Bismarck* was blotted out and had to shine a searchlight astern for *Prinz Eugen* to follow in her wake. An entry in the *Prinz Eugen*'s log reads: 'The weather seems as though made for a break-through.'

If Lütjens wanted confirmation of the wisdom of going direct to the Denmark Straits, he got it that night in a signal from Group

North that although no photographic reconnaissance of Scapa Flow had been possible that day because of weather, visual reconnaissance had reported three heavy units, a carrier and several cruisers and destroyers – an exact repetition of the photographic report of the 20th, giving the impression no heavy units had sailed and the situation was unchanged. This was an example of the sometimes sloppy work of the Luftwaffe when detached on naval assignments, work which they (unlike the R.A.F.'s Coastal Command) often resented. For of the three heavy units the observer had seen on a quick swoop from the clouds, two were wood and canvas dummies (the other was *King George V*) and so it escaped Group North's attention entirely that *Hood* and *Prince of Wales* had sailed. Had Lütjens got to know of this, he would certainly have recast his plans, might even have turned the squadron back.[1]

Further encouragement to push on came from a second piece of faulty intelligence – a signal from Group North that the ships of the formidable British Force H (the battle-cruiser *Renown*, the carrier *Ark Royal*, the cruiser *Sheffield* and destroyers) based at Gibraltar and obviously a danger to Lütjens, were now at sea, probably en route to Crete. In fact they were all at Gibraltar.

At eleven that night when *Bismarck* and *Prinz Eugen* were some two hundred miles north-east of Iceland, and Tovey and the main British fleet clearing Scapa Flow, Lütjens turned south-west for the first leg of his run through the Denmark Straits. In this latitude it was light all night but still foggy. It was also very cold. At four in the morning, perhaps in answer to Dr Externbrink's pleas, the squadron went on to 27 knots. At ten they started entering the mush ice and reduced to 24: in *Prinz Eugen* an ex-trawler skipper from Bremerhaven with much experience of sailing through ice (one of the spare crew for prizes) was called to the bridge to help Captain Brinkmann and Commander Beck with the navigating. In mid-morning both ships exercised action stations. The weather still held foggy and misty, the sea calm with patches of sea-smoke on the surface where the cold Polar winds brushed the warmer water: in *Bismarck* there was a continuous tinkling sound as the ship's great bow scythed a passage through the frozen crystals.

Now the squadron was approaching the most dangerous part of the break-out, the narrow passage, at this time of year not more than thirty to forty miles wide, separating the edge of the Greenland ice-pack from the limits of the British declared minefield that stretched northwards from the Icelandic peninsula of Vestfirdir. Presently the pack-ice came into sight to starboard, the ships turned to steer parallel to it, went on again to 27 knots. Soon they were among the big, flat ice floes that had broken off from the pack-ice and were drifting southwards. There were frequent alarms as look-outs mistook floes for ships and at times swift avoiding action had to be taken; but Lütjens maintained the speed of the fleet, knowing the next few hours were critical.

It was late afternoon when Dr Externbrink's worst fears were realised: the weather began to clear. The fog melted away, the pack-ice, broad, dense, blue-white and green, unravelled itself ahead and to starboard: beyond and far away against an azure sky rose the tops of Greenland's icy mountains, sharp and clear in the gunnery range-finder lenses. Ahead, for the first time in nearly thirty-six hours, there was a clear path of water between three and ten miles wide. Only to port in the direction of Iceland did a thick wall of fog still lie, yellow-grey in colour, mottled with shifting patterns of white, what sailors call the ice-blink, the fierce reflection of the glare from the pack-ice.

Word of the change soon spread, and young Germans who until a week or two before had never been outside home waters, peered through the slits of turrets and round the corners of doors, silent with wonder at what they saw. This was the edge of the world, the land beyond the rainbow, out there in those empty wastes were to be found Polar bears like in the Berlin zoo, real, live Eskimos and the road to the North Pole. How strange to be here, the young ones thought, if only the family could see me now.

On the bridge of the *Prinz Eugen* too the officers, cold in their leather trousers and winter woollies, gazed through binoculars at the transformation of this twilight world: Captain Brinkmann, tall and heavy, leaning on the port side of the bridge, naval cap perched on top of balaclava, gloved hand holding a smouldering cigar: Commander Beck, the navigator, Lieutenant Reckhoff, officer of the watch and like Ascher in *Bismarck* a fugitive from the Argentine after the death of the *Graf Spee*, Commander Busch, a popular naval writer, married to an English wife and sent on board by Berlin to describe the operation. Captain Brinkmann trained his binoculars on the thick wall of fog to port and said: 'If they're anywhere in these parts, they're in there'.

He was right, they were; and a little later, while Commander Busch and other officers were finishing a quick meal in the dimly-lit wardroom aft, the ship's alarm bells rang.

For the men of the *Norfolk* and *Suffolk*, the three-funnelled eight-inch-gun cruisers that were part of the First Cruiser Squadron, patrolling the Denmark Straits was not a popular job. They had been doing it for days, weeks, though it seemed like months, years. To and fro, up and down they went, nothing but the division of watches to mark the passing time. Today the weather was tolerable, mostly it was vile. Seas the size of houses would come from every side, so that on duty or off one could rarely rest, was always bracing the body, bending body and knees like some frozen skier to meet the motion of the ship. The bows dug deep into the dark sides of the travelling water-hills, flung the spray upwards where the Polar wind caught it, hurled it over the ship, on deck and superstructure and the faces of crouching men, froze it on steel and skin. One saw nothing but an agony of water, grey-green or blue-black, spume tossed, marble-streaked, heard nothing but the thunder of the seas against the sides, the yell of the wind above. Off duty men ate and slept like automatons, browsed in magazines or comics. The wireless was popular, it required no effort: Tommy Handley with his 'Itma' show and the spy Funf, Vera Lynn, the Forces Sweetheart, the singer with the catch in her voice, these made you forget where you were, made you think of London or home. Churchill too was good value, talking of *Herr* Hitler and the *Narzies*, Churchill was good for morale.

The captain of the *Suffolk*, Robert Ellis, was very tired. When on 18th May he got Admiral Tovey's order to oil, his ship had already been ten days on patrol in the vilest weather. He made a fast night passage to Hvalfjord on the west of Iceland, remaining on the bridge most of the time, snatched a few hours' sleep while oiling was in progress, returned to the bridge for another night passage back. It wasn't too bad a trip, for during the ship's last refit the bridge had been 'arcticised', that is closed in and steam-heated: this was luxury compared to the open bridge of the *Norfolk*, though it made for a tendency to sleep.

While Captain Ellis was on his way back to the Straits, his admiral Frederick Wake-Walker in the *Norfolk*, was steaming to Isafjordur, a deep cleft on Iceland's north-west peninsula of Vestfirdir, to look at a new radar station: *Suffolk* was to join him there to receive final instructions. Wake-Walker was a torpedo specialist who in 1940 had superbly organised the evacuation of the British Army from the beaches of Dunkirk, a tall impressive-looking man, very technically minded, not much humour or imagination, a friend of Tovey. His hobbies were shooting, sketching and looking for wild flowers. He took the shooting on a farm at Scapa, and in Iceland, said David Kelburn,[2] his flag-lieutenant, 'he'd go thundering off in search of saxifrage and that sort of thing'.

At ten on the foggy morning of 23rd May the *Suffolk* edged in to the entrance to Isafjordur, the bleak cliffs of Vestfirdir towering above, and soon a signal lamp was winking from *Norfolk*'s bridge. *Suffolk* was to proceed within radar distance of the pack-ice opposite Vestfirdir, there patrol parallel to it in a south-west/north-east direction, each leg of the patrol to last for three hours. *Norfolk* would station herself some fifteen miles to the south of her, in case the Germans risked skirting the edge of the minefield. If nothing had been sighted by the following morning the two ships would rendezvous to check positions.

Ellis swung his ship round and made off through the fog towards the pack-ice. He was in a buoyant mood, for it looked as though he might be using a new toy in which he had taken a great interest, a radar set of an improved kind which had been fitted on the last refit. Radar then was in its infancy: this set had a range of thirteen miles and covered all sectors except either side of the stern.

On reaching his patrol area Ellis found, as Lütjens was soon to find, clear water along the ice-edge, good visibility over Greenland, but on the Icelandic side the fog stretching a long way in either direction. When, therefore, he was on his north-easterly run, i.e. facing the direction in which the enemy might come, he kept in the open water near the ice-edge, knowing his radar would pick them up a long way ahead. But on the south-westerly leg when the bridge superstructure and funnel smoke obscured the view astern and the radar was blind, he steered down the edge of the wall of fog, ready to slip into it if an emergency arose. It was not his business to fight the *Bismarck*, but keep in touch with her until bigger ships arrived.

The afternoon passed without incident. Look-outs and radar operators in the *Suffolk* and *Norfolk* – and farther south too, in the cruisers *Manchester*, *Birmingham*, *Arethusa*, in trawlers like *Northern Sky* and *Northern Isles*, in the *Hood* and *Prince of Wales*, *King George V* and *Repulse* now steaming with their cruisers and destroyers to positions south of Iceland, pilots and observers of Coastal Command seeking gaps in the overcast between Iceland and Orkney – all these were sweeping the seas with instruments and binoculars in search of the German ships. There hadn't been a whisper of them since Suckling had seen them in the Bergen fjords two days before: in that time they could have steamed over a thousand miles: they could be just over the horizon, already at the edge of the Atlantic, on their way back to Germany, at anchor in a Norwegian fjord. Everyone had his own theory, no one had a clue to work on.

It was Able Seaman Newell in the *Suffolk* who brought suspense to an end. The ship was on her south-westerly leg when at 6 p.m. he took over the position on the bridge of starboard after look-out. An hour and a quarter later, when sweeping his sector between the beam and the stern for perhaps the fiftieth time, he saw something which for the rest of his life he would never forget – the *Bismarck*, black and massive, emerging from a patch of mist on the starboard quarter, not more than seven miles away. 'Ship bearing Green One Four Oh,' he shouted, as though his life depended on it, which it did, and then as the *Prinz Eugen* swam into his lenses, ' *Two* ships bearing Green One Four Oh.'

The *Suffolk* sprang to life. Captain Ellis ordered hard a-port and full speed ahead to get into the fog. Another officer pressed the alarm bells, all over the ship men leapt from mess-bench or hammock, slid into sea-boots, snatched coats and scarves, lifebelts and tin hats, raced down passageways and up and down ladders to reach their action stations: others, luckier, went thinly dressed to the warmth of engine-room or wireless office. Swiftly the ship answered the helm, leaned heavily to starboard: in the wardroom where dinner had started, crockery and cutlery went crashing to the deck. On the quarter-deck Ludovic Porter, the ship's commander, took off for the bridge, 'as though airborne'. A midshipman, surfacing from a deep sleep, caught a glimpse of the German ships as he tottered to his action station, thought they were *Hood* and *Prince of Wales*.

It was going to take a couple of minutes for *Suffolk* to reach the fog, and everyone on the bridge watched *Bismarck* coming on at them, noted the high V of her bow-wave, waited fearfully for the crash of her first salvoes. Miraculously they never came, *Suffolk* breached the fog wall unharmed. Safe inside she waited, sending out a string of enemy reports, watching the two blips on the radar scan that represented the German ships pass from right to left. When the enemy was some thirteen miles ahead – at the limit of *Suffolk*'s radar range but well within scope of *Bismarck*'s guns, she ran out of the fog and took up position in *Prinz Eugen*'s wake.

Norfolk, meanwhile, fifteen miles away inside the fog, had picked up the first of *Suffolk*'s signals: her captain Alfred Phillips was in his sea-cabin eating cheese on toast when the Yeoman of Signals burst in with the news. Phillips at once increased speed and steered for the open water, but in his eagerness not to lose touch, he misjudged the direction, emerged from the fog to find *Bismarck* only six miles ahead, coming straight at him. This time there was no doubting her readiness. As *Norfolk* swung to starboard to get back to the safety of the fog, *Bismarck*'s guns roared in anger for the first time. On the *Norfolk*'s bridge they saw the ripple of the orange flashes and brown puffs of cordite smoke, heard the scream of the shells – a sound which some have likened to the tearing of linen and others to the approach of an express train. Admiral Wake-Walker saw the sea to starboard pocked with shell splinters, observed one complete burnished shell bounce off the water fifty yards away, ricochet over the bridge. Great columns of milk-white water rose in the air, two hundred feet high. Five salvoes in all *Bismarck* fired before *Norfolk* regained the mist: some straddled, and splinters came on board; but there were no casualties or hits.

Now *Norfolk* waited for *Bismarck* and *Prinz Eugen* to pass, as *Suffolk* had done, and when they were decently ahead, took station on the enemy's port quarter in case he suddenly altered course to port. *Suffolk* remained more or less astern of the enemy, knowing that he couldn't make an alteration to starboard because of the ice. Sometimes the German ships could be seen far ahead. When they disappeared in mists and snow flurries, Wake-Walker relied entirely on *Suffolk*'s radar, for *Norfolk*'s set, with its fixed aerials, was to all intents and purposes useless.

Ever since *Suffolk*'s contact with *Bismarck*, she had been sending out a stream of wireless reports of the enemy's position, course and speed. But none had reached base because of icing to her aerials and it was *Norfolk*'s sighting report that was first picked up by ships and shore establishments of the Atlantic command; by Admiral Tovey in *King George V*, then 600 miles to the south-east, as relieved as Churchill and the Admiralty in London, that his dispositions had been correct; by the battleship *Rodney* which with four destroyers and the troopship *Britannic* had left the Clyde the day before for a refit in Boston, and was now 800 miles to the south; by the ships of the troop convoy WS8B which had also left the Clyde the day before, bound for Suez via the Cape and now feeling somewhat naked without *Victorious* and *Repulse;* by Vice-Admiral Sir James Somerville of Force H in Gibraltar harbour, to whom the news was then only of academic interest; and by the special cryptographic teams in *Bismarck* and *Prinz Eugen* who were decoding the signals within minutes of transmission (and mistaking the call sign of *Norfolk* for that of *King George V*). But the man to whom the news was of greatest moment was Vice-Admiral Holland in the *Hood*, which with *Prince of Wales* and their destroyers were now only 300 miles away and steering on a converging course.

CHAPTER

3

If any one ship could be said to have been the embodiment of British sea-power and the British Empire between the wars, it was 'the mighty *Hood*', as Britain and the Navy called her, and for later generations it is hard to convey the blend of affection, admiration and awe in which she was held, not only at home but by hundreds of thousands throughout the world.

She was an old lady now, one of the oldest in the Navy, laid down in 1916 in the Clydebank yards of John Brown, who later built the great Queens, named after a family who had given the Navy four famous admirals, Lord Hood who helped Rodney defeat the French in the West Indies in the eighteenth century, his brother Lord Bridport who was with Howe at the Glorious First of June, Sam Hood who helped Nelson win the battle of the Nile, Horace Hood killed at Jutland when his flagship *Invincible* blew up. She was launched by his widow, Lady Hood, in August 1918, just three months before the Armistice, the biggest warship ever built, longer even than *Bismarck* (860 feet as compared to 828) though narrower in the beam, with – like *Bismarck* – eight fifteen-inch mounted in pairs in four turrets. Her maximum speed of 32 knots made her the fastest warship of her size in the world, going flat out it took a ton of oil to drive her half a mile. She was a beautiful ship, elegant and symmetrical like *Bismarck*, yet dignified and restrained, without the aggressive sweep of *Bismarck*'s lines or the massiveness that spoke of held-back power. But she had one great defect, a lack of armour on her upper decks. *Hood* had been laid down before Jutland where three British battle-cruisers were destroyed by German shells which, fired at long range, had plunged vertically through the lightly protected decks, exploded inside. All big ships built after Jutland had strengthened armour. *Hood*'s armour was strengthened on her sides but not on her decks: they were to be her Achilles' heel.

Between the wars, when a quarter of the globe was still coloured red for Britain, the *Hood* showed the flag, as they used to say, to the Empire and the world. She went on cruises to Scandinavia and South America, to the Mediterranean and the Pacific, to the old world and the new. Her *1923–24* world tour, in company with *Repulse* and five cruisers, was described as 'the most successful cruise by a squadron of warships in the history of sea-power'. They visited South Africa, Zanzibar, Ceylon, Singapore, Australia, New Zealand, the Pacific Islands, San Francisco, the Panama Canal, Jamaica, Canada, Newfoundland. Their arrival anywhere caused huge crowds to gather, filled the pages of the local press. A girl in Melbourne noted: 'Every road and pathway was thick, and many families were making a day of it, taking out all the children and hampers of food and bottles of beer. The Bay was dotted with sailing boats'. The mist lifted to reveal *Hood* and her consorts coming in. 'It was a wonderful sight – something I shall never forget, everyone cheering and the kids running up and down and the sirens of all the ships in the harbour going off.' In *Hood*'s eleven-month voyage millions of people saw her, hundreds of thousands came aboard. She was a unique blend of strength and beauty, the outward and visible manifestation of sea-power: looking at her one understood what 'Rule Britannia' meant. Her visitors fingered the brasswork and fondled the guns, walked the long decks and climbed the superstructure, took snapshots galore, stunned by the scale and wonder of it all. Her public relations too were immaculate. Finding in Honolulu that a Boy Scout chosen to represent Hawaii at an assembly in Copenhagen had missed the steamer to the United States, *Hood*'s admiral gave him free passage on the boys' mess-deck, won a garland from the American press. When she arrived in San Francisco, the mayor, bowled over by her size and beauty, said: 'We surrender our city unto you. We capitulate'.

The days were filled with parades, receptions, sport, the nights when the squadron lay shining and still in the harbour like golden scarabs, with more receptions, dinners, dances, so that it was a relief to get to sea, catch up with letters and paperwork, slip back into the comfortable, familiar routine, time parcelled out in watches. Then there would be nights of leisurely steaming between tropical islands, phosphorescence in the wake and a skyful of stars above, young men on fo'c'sle and quarter-deck remembering hospitality received and given, girls kissed or laid, wondering how it might be next time. They left goodwill where they went, for the British sailor, insular but gregarious, had a knack of being congenial to those he met, Imperial cousins or foreigners with funny ways. When they got home, says *Hood*'s biographer, 'they had strengthened friendships and revived alliances. They had become a fireside story, and one ship – her photograph in thousands of homes – had become a legend.'

. People in Britain saw her too, in spring and summer when she visted the Forth and Clyde and Invergordon, Plymouth and Portsmouth and Liverpool; on open days the locals swarmed aboard, the children were given rides on the capstan, sent whizzing down special chutes, fed sticky buns and ginger pop and ship's ice-cream. One moment the ship would be there, at the town's edge riding gracefully at anchor, the next she would be gone and people would hear the rumble of her guns far out at sea, like summer thunder echoing in the hills, and be comforted, for that was her real business, and yet be concerned, for her business was war.

In the thirties war and talk of war was increasingly in the air. This was when *Hood* was supposed to go into dock for a long refit, have her main deck armoured as it always should have been, but by now Hitler and Mussolini were in power, crisis followed crisis, and to have allowed *Hood* to go out of commission for the months needed for the alterations was unthinkable.[1] She had a brief refit just before the war, mainly to put anti-aircraft guns on her upper deck: these and other additions increased her deep load by 3000 tons, made her aft an even wetter ship than usual, so that in heavy seas her quarter-deck often went under, she lay down and wallowed like a dog.

In August 1939 she put away the deck awnings and light bulbs that had been such a feature of her life for nearly twenty years, painted herself overall a dull grey, rigged black-out curtains in every passageway, took on reserve officers and men, embarked tin hats and duffel coats and morphine, went out on patrol in the grey North Sea. She was at Plymouth when the *Rawalpindi* was sunk, sailed to join a French squadron from Brest led by the battle-cruiser *Dunkerque* whose admiral, Gensoul, being senior to *Hood's* admiral, took command of the force; and *Hood's* watch-keeping officers had the novel experience of having to adjust course and speed to that of another ship when usually others adjusted to them.

In amity and alliance the combined squadron swept up the west coast of Ireland in a fruitless search for an enemy that was already going home. But six months later, after France's defeat and when Gensoul was commanding the French fleet at Oran, Admiral Somerville showed up in the *Hood* with the carrier *Ark Royal* and the battleships *Valiant* and *Resolution*. His orders from London where the Cabinet was fearful of the French ships falling into German hands, were to persuade Gensoul to join the British fleet, or to take his ships to a British or French colonial port, or to scuttle them. Gensoul refused. Somerville regretfully hoisted the signal to open fire and *Hood's* guns, with those of the other ships, spat out at the man whose flag she had recently obeyed, savaged his fleet, killed fifteen hundred of his men.

And now on this May evening of 1941 *Hood* was on her way to do what she had been designed to do twenty-six years before, engage on the high seas her country's enemies in battle. The wind, from the north, was rising, and she pushed her long nose into the oncoming swell, threw great gouts of water aside, rose and fell, wet but marvellously steady. Astern and a little on the quarter was *Prince of Wales*, ahead the screening destroyers. Two had gone to Iceland to refuel, four were left: the gunner of the *Electra*, Mr Cain, looking at the flagship across the darkling sea, thought her never so impressive. 'With *Hood* to support us we felt we could tackle anything . . . there was no beating her . . . it was inconceivable to think that anything could happen to her.'

On *Hood*'s bridge stood Vice-Admiral Lancelot Holland who had come on board only ten days before. Holland was 54, a gunnery specialist, a short slim man with almost white hair. He was shy at first but companionable when you got to know him, had a wry sense of humour, was well read, very able, intensely ambitious: one evening in his cuddy he thumbed through the Navy List with his flag-lieutenant, said it was either him or Bruce Fraser for First Sea Lord. In 1936, his only child, a gifted youth of eighteen who wrote poems and painted, died of polio, he and his wife had never got over it. As an admiral he'd already seen action in the Mediterranean in November when on Somerville's orders he'd taken five cruisers to attack the Italian battlefleet off Cape Spartivento, a bold, brave thrust that might have paid dividends if the Italians had not turned and run.

From the wing of *Hood*'s bridge Holland looked astern at where *Prince of Wales*'s great bulk lifted and fell, felt reassured, despite her deficiencies, to have her with him. Since leaving Scapa he had exercised the two ships in range and inclination practice and signalled tactical intentions: if *Hood* and *Prince of Wales* were together when the enemy was met, fire would be concentrated; if apart, they would fire independently and report each other's fall of shot: radar was not to be used unless action was imminent for fear the enemy might pick up its transmissions and alter course away. Preparations had been made and now there was nothing more to do but leave things, as Nelson once said, to the Great Disposer of Events. For the first few hours of the voyage tension in the squadron had been high, for it seemed as though battle was imminent: Esmond Knight reflected it when he wrote of a feeling of unrest and excitement, 'I lay on my bunk and tried to read but the lines refused to register. I sat at the desk and tried to draw a funny picture for the ship's magazine, but the idea just would not come.' But now nearly two days had gone by without further news: tension had eased and it began to seem as though this trip, like so many others in the past, was just one more false alarm.

The bubble was pricked at four minutes past eight on the evening of the 23rd when *Hood* picked up the first of *Suffolk*'s reports. With his staff officers Admiral Holland studied the chart closely, plotted *Bismarck*'s position and course relative to his. Then he signalled the squadron to increase speed to 27 knots on a course of 295°, and for the destroyers to follow at best speed if they could not keep up. Over the loudspeakers the ship's companies were told that action was expected within a matter of hours.

The blast from *Bismarck*'s guns when firing at *Norfolk* had put her forward radar out of action, and she was now blind ahead. A desire to have eyes in front of him and also perhaps a fear that *Suffolk*, *Norfolk* (and/or *King George V*) might creep up on *Prinz Eugen* in bad visibility, caused Lütjens to signal to *Prinz Eugen* to take station ahead. *Bismarck* dropped a few knots and the big cruiser started inching up on her starboard side. Lütjens, watching her bow creaming the water, her officers on the bridge, her long, sleek lines, was moved to unexpected loquacity. 'From Admiral to Captain,' he signalled to Brinkmann, 'you have a wonderful ship'. A moment later he nearly had no ship at all, for as *Prinz Eugen* came abeam, *Bismarck*'s wheel (it was an electric, push-button wheel, not the old, spoked variety) suddenly jammed, and she began heeling to starboard. Brinkmann sensed what was happening at once, ordered his own helmsman to go hard-a-starboard, and with forty degrees of wheel on and keeling over, *Prinz Eugen* swung away. Lindemann, who according to Müllenheim-Rechberg, was aft at this moment attending to something, also gave a quick, correcting order to the bridge by telephone, and so disaster was avoided.

Now *Prinz Eugen* was in the lead, *Bismarck* astern of her, *Norfolk* and *Suffolk* ten to fourteen miles astern of *Bismarck*, all going at nearly thirty knots, for the weather was calm, all creaking and groaning at the strains being put upon them. Four bows churned white furrows out of the leaden sea, the water slapped against the sides with quick, sharp blows like a wet towel, then fell back, hissing and frothing like detergent on the troubled swiftly-passing surface, white on peppermint green. Aft, beneath each stern, a great plume of water was thrown up like a burst water-main by the thrashing screws, collapsed and disappeared in the bubbling champagne wake.

In all the ships was heard the sucking, hollow drone of the ventilation fans drawing the air into the interior, the insistent, high-pitched whine of the turbines turning at maximum speed. The vibration was terrific, especially aft in the tiller-flats and engine-rooms where the plates shuddered and juddered and cried out, and things left unsecured in cabins and messes went tumbling to the deck, despite an even keel. Even in *Suffolk*'s charthouse, high up near the bridge, the plotting officer David Paton found his hand shaking as if with Parkinson's disease, could barely keep pencil and ruler steady.

As the chase settled down, some of the German crews were puzzled why the world's greatest battleship should be running away from two British cruisers; so Lindemann and Brinkmann broadcast that their orders were to avoid action with enemy warships in order to reach the Atlantic undamaged and destroy merchant shipping. These same orders had given Lütjens discretion to turn back on meeting *Norfolk* and *Suffolk*, but thinking the British fleet was still at Scapa, he saw no reason to: when darkness came, he and his staff hoped, they would give the cruisers the slip. This optimism was shared by those in *Prinz Eugen*. In the vacant staff medical officer's cabin that had been allocated to him, Commander Busch sat up late with Commander Jasper, the gunnery officer and Lieutenant Albrecht, a first world war U-boat officer but now a civilian from Siemens, an expert on naval guns, drinking out of toothglasses beer they'd got from *Wollin*. They were cheerful and confident. 'The feeling of absolute security,' wrote Busch (echoing what Cain in *Electra* was feeling as he looked across at *Hood*) 'was shared by every man in the ship's company. In our beautiful ship and in *Bismarck* too, the men felt safe,' adding that if things got bad, they could always rely on superior speed to get away.

But in this quiet sea they had no superior speed and could not get away. Often *Norfolk* and *Suffolk* were blotted from sight in snow flurries and fog patches, but when the visibility cleared, there they still were; and their situation reports to the Admiralty when decoded by the German cryptographic teams showed them aware of Lütjens's every alteration of course or speed. At first the Germans believed the British must have some sensitive, underwater, hydrophonic detection

64

gear similar to their own; then, that they were picking up German radar transmissions. It was some time before they realised that at least one enemy ship was equipped with a radar set far superior to theirs. The question of British naval radar had not been discussed in the operation orders because the German naval staff believed they had none. The discovery of it at this time and place was for Lütjens and his staff a shock.

The hours passed, the four ships continued thundering south. In *Prinz Eugen* they went to second degree of readiness, four hours on watch, four hours off, but in *Bismarck*, *Norfolk* and *Suffolk*, they remained at action stations, allowing men to doze off, go and relieve themselves, fetch chocolate or cigarettes, in ones and twos at a time. Night came on, a bosky half-light in which sky and sea merged. Black-out curtains were drawn across passageways, smoking forbidden on exposed positions on deck. On the bridges of the four ships, where the only light came from the upward glow of the compass rose, shadowy figures moved about: the two admirals, Lütjens and Wake-Walker, the four captains, Lindemann and Brinkmann, Philips and Ellis, officers of the watch, navigating and torpedo officers, signalmen, communications ratings, bridge messengers, look-outs, officers from other positions snatching a few minutes to get the latest news. German or British, these men were doing the same sort of thing, wearing the same kind of uniforms, using the same sort of instruments, giving the same commands, differing only in the causes they were fighting for, the countries where they came from, the patterns of their speech. On *Suffolk*'s bridge cold stomachs were warmed by bully-beef and cocoa, in *Prinz Eugen* by soup and coffee. Once the chase had settled down, there was little to disturb its monotony save, in the British ships, the fear of losing contact, in the German ones, the hope of getting away. Near *Suffolk* a snow goose detached itself from a passing flock, kept the ship company, flying above the fo'c'sle. Some officers wanted to shoot it down, have wardroom goose for next day's dinner, but Captain Ellis, remembering the Ancient Mariner, said no.

As the long day came to an end, the visibility worsened, less because of light than an increase of snow-flurries, rain showers, mist.

Soon after 10 p.m. the officers on *Suffolk*'s bridge saw *Bismarck* disappear into a rain-storm, a few moments later were horrified to see her emerging from the storm and coming straight at them, the thing they had always feared, before rain again blotted her out. *Suffolk*'s wheel was put hard over to an about turn, but as the minutes passed and no *Bismarck* appeared, they realised they had been tricked by a mirage. Luckily *Suffolk* had a few knots in hand, and after some hard steaming she made contact again.

The distance between Holland and Lütjens continued steadily to close; and far away to the south-east Tovey debated whether to signal Holland to station *Prince of Wales* ahead of *Hood* so that the better protected ship might draw the enemy's fire. In the end he decided against it ('I did not feel such interference with so senior an officer justified'). Yet before many more hours had passed, he was to wish profoundly he had.

At about this time another event occurred which, small in itself, was later to affect the outcome of the whole operation. The Admiralty in London, increasingly concerned by *Bismarck*'s southward progress and the vulnerability of the troop convoy WS8B, now two days out from the Clyde, sent a signal to Admiral Somerville in Gibraltar for Force H to raise steam for full speed. And so, two thousand miles away from Greenland's icy coasts, naval patrols went ashore in the warm Gibraltar night to comb Main Street and its bars, visit the Rock Hotel, have messages flashed on cinema screens to tell the officers and men of the aircraft-carrier *Ark Royal*, the old battle-cruiser *Renown*, the 6-inch-gun cruiser *Sheffield* and their destroyers to return to their ships at once. They came in twos and threes, some grumbling, some singing, some resigned, embarked at Ragged Staff Steps in the waiting liberty-boats, were ferried out to the darkened silent ships. And in the dead watches of the night, while the Gibraltar garrison and the barmen of Main Street and the whores in La Linea slept, Force H, under Admiral Somerville, crept to sea. Usually their orders took them east into sunshine and blue water, on operations against the Italian fleet or for the relief of Malta, but this time they turned west, past Tangier and the edge of Africa, then north-west towards the grey Atlantic, past the two capes of Trafalgar and St Vincent where Nelson and Jervis had won immortality so many years before. They steered so as to meet Convoy WS8B in two days' time west of Brest and south-west of Ireland. It was a rendezvous they never kept: more dramatic things were waiting for them than that.

The men of *Hood, Prince of Wales* and their destroyers, told that action was expected before the night was out, felt the chill of fear in their bowels, a heightening of sensation, a quickening of the blood. They were about to undergo a novel experience, do what the ship had been built for and they had been trained for: fight. For most, so far, war had been what for most participants it always is, boredom and discomfort, long patrols in winter weather, seeing nothing, meeting nobody, dog days in harbour when you had to listen to the radio to know a war was on. And now the moment which had lived only as an embryo in the wombs of their minds, had gestated, was at the point of birth, there was absolutely no avoiding it. And everywhere men wondered – all but the very unimaginative, the very brave – how it might go for them; whether they would be mutilated, lose a hand or eye or testicles; whether they would die, in agony, or without knowing a thing about it; how they would acquit themselves, whether discover untapped reserves of courage and calm, or, seeing men killed beside them, blood and splintered bone and the spilling out of friends' insides, they would break down, vomit, scream they couldn't go on, be paralysed with terror. And they looked at one another, each alone in his cell, hoping, doubting that others felt the same. But none spoke, for all were ashamed of their fears.

By 9 p.m. the squadron had worked up to 27 knots, which in the rising sea was as much as they would manage. It was rougher here than where the *Bismarck* was, and the destroyers were finding it increasingly uncomfortable. Their bows lunged at each oncoming wave like a steeplechaser at Beecher's, breasted the crest, rose on and up until they were pointing at the sky and it seemed the ship must become airborne, hung there a moment, then as the wave passed astern, fell like a roller coaster towards the trough, hit the water with a crack like a cannon so that keel plates shuddered and it felt as if the ship must come apart with the shock.

To Cain in the *Electra* the water parted on either side in green-white walls, and the spray cascaded over the ship like sheets of heavy rain. Sometimes from *Hood* and *Prince of Wales* the destroyers were lost to sight in spray, ghost ships sailing in a cocoon of ectoplasm. The big ships were taking it green too: Cain, watching them rise and fall from the juddering bridge of the *Electra*, the water streaming from the nostrils of the hawse-holes in their bows, saw them as two angry dragons.

At ten the squadron began preparations for battle. In the ward-room of the *Prince of Wales*, before it was turned into an emergency casualty station, Esmond Knight attended a briefing by the ship's gunnery officer. Then he went to the cinema flat, where only a few days before he had been watching Bing Crosby, to join a queue waiting for anti-flash gear, white gloves and strange white hoods like those of the Ku Klux Klan, to protect hands and faces from burns. In all the ships, officers and men went to cabins and messes and put on clean underwear and socks, a ritual the British Navy has always observed before battle to prevent wounds from infection. While there, they sat down, many of them, wrote farewell notes to parents, wives, sweethearts, for no one doubted the gravity of what lay ahead.

In his cabin Esmond Knight wrote two letters, then took down pictures, photographs and other breakables and wrapped them in the bedclothes, for the blast from *Prince of Wales*'s own guns would soon smash them, let alone anything *Bismarck* could do. He dressed carefully, tucked trouser-legs into seaboots, put on several sweaters and a warm scarf – for his action station was in the exposed Air Defence Position above the bridge – tied a lifebelt round his chest, saw that tin hat and binoculars – a German Zeiss pair he had bought in Austria before the war – were handy, then sat down in a chair to try and compose himself. He thought of the birds he loved to watch, remembered with pleasure the sight of two fulmar petrels which had kept company with the ship all day, skimming the water one on

68

either side, travelling at over 25 knots, yet hardly ever seeming to move their slender wings. He recalled too the mountain caps of Iceland which he had seen away on the starboard beam just before coming down, and how strangely pink they looked.

But try as he would he could not keep his mind off the coming battle. 'All the time there was a persistent little voice crying out from every nook and cranny in the ship that we were to be in action before many hours, and that nothing could avoid it.' The unaccustomed creaking and groaning and vibration as the ship raced through the water seemed somehow doom-laden. He thought of Hamlet, as any actor would. 'To die – to sleep no more'. Was this how it would end? A fellow officer looked in, said he found it impossible to sit still, was going forward to see what was happening. Esmond dozed, saw as others did in their troubled minds weird shapes and fancies dance before his eyes.

Presently the squadron went to action stations, and everywhere men closed up, in the wind and spray of the upper deck, in the fug of the engine-room, in the cool and claustrophobia of shell-room and magazine. Water-tight doors were closed, ammunition hoists tested, communications checked, guns elevated and trained: in each of *Prince of Wales*'s turrets the civilian technicians from Vickers-Armstrong, never dreaming they would be required to fight a sea-battle and wishing they were snug at home in bed, stood by to keep the guns in action. Down below, men looked more carefully than usual at temperature and pressure gauges, listened more acutely to orders from the bridge, to wireless messages coming in from the ether. Cooks damped down the fires of galleys, and in sickbay and wardroom doctors and sickberth attendants sterilised instruments, prepared anaesthetics and morphine. On his way to the bridge superstructure Esmond Knight passed his ornithologist friend who shouted at him and pointed excitedly to starboard. Esmond turned, expecting to see *Bismarck* on the horizon at least, saw instead what he and his friend had longed to see for years: bobbing contentedly on the water not a hundred yards from the ship, a Great Northern Diver.

The signals from *Norfolk* and *Suffolk* continued streaming in, and at midnight the enemy was estimated to be just over a hundred miles away. If Admiral Holland continued on his present course and speed, and the enemy on theirs, he would cross some sixty miles ahead of their track by about 2.30 a.m. thus effectually barring their passage to the Atlantic. But it would also mean going into action at high speed in the darkest period of the night, with all the uncertainty and confusion that this would involve. If on the other hand he turned north towards *Bismarck* now, he could with advantage bring action on. The two squadrons would close at a mean rate of 50 knots and should meet at around 2 a.m.: sunset in this latitude was at 1.51 a.m., so while *Bismarck* and *Prinz Eugen* would be silhouetted against its afterglow, the British ships would be in darkness, could approach rapidly and unseen from a range where *Bismarck*'s shells could do the maximum damage to *Hood*, to one where *Hood* would be on terms of greater equality. The Germans would not be expecting an attack from this quarter, and so he would have all the advantage of surprise.[2]

Accordingly at twelve minutes past midnight Holland signalled his squadron to turn 45° to starboard, i.e. from a course of a little north of west to a little west of north, and reduce to 25 knots. Five minutes later, probably on decoding Captain Ellis's signal timed 00.09 of 24th May that *Bismarck* was hidden in a snowstorm, and that *Suffolk* had come round from south-south-west to south, Holland turned another 15° to due north to allow for the possibility of *Bismarck* also having turned south; this meant the two squadrons were now closing on almost reciprocal courses. Holland further signalled for the squadron to hoist battle ensigns – the outsize white ensigns the Navy traditionally wears when going into battle – and to prepare to make contact with the enemy any time after 1.40 a.m. *Hood* and *Prince of Wales* would engage *Bismarck* while *Norfolk* and *Suffolk* took on *Prinz Eugen* (which Holland assumed was still in the rear); but he didn't radio these intentions to Wake-Walker for fear of disclosing his whereabouts, and for the same reason he maintained radar silence.

It was a bold plan, and might well have succeeded had not *Suffolk* temporarily lost contact. Her first signal to suggest this (it contained no enemy report) was sent at 12.28 a.m. and about the same time Holland signalled that if they had not sighted the enemy by 2.10 a.m., he would turn south until the cruisers regained contact: this was so that if the *Bismarck* had maintained her southerly course, he would still be ahead of her. An hour and a half passed without sight of the enemy or any further news from *Norfolk* and *Suffolk* so reluctantly Holland swung his ships round and steadied on 200° or south-south-west, the course that *Bismarck* was steering when the cruisers lost contact. But he told the destroyers to continue searching to the north. In the event he missed Lütjens by a hairsbreadth. The British ships were steering an almost perfect intercepting course and were only twenty miles away when at 1.41 a.m. the German ships altered a little to the west to follow the line of the Greenland ice-pack. They passed only ten miles to the north-west of Admiral Holland's destroyers, and had the visibility then not been down to between three and five miles, would almost certainly have been spotted.

The men of *Hood* and *Prince of Wales* had now been at action stations for more than four hours, and those not actually on duty were told they could doze at their posts. Some cradled their heads in their arms, others lolled forward on lifebelt or counter, but most were still too keyed up to lose consciousness. Not wanting battle in the first place, they had yet steeled themselves to it, and now it had been denied them, they felt let down, oddly disappointed, annoyed at having to make another psychological adjustment. And mixed with this was a feeling of relief, instant joy that this night at any rate they might not have to spill their blood, die their deaths after all. Those who had not liked to admit their fears, could afford a few quips now that danger had receded. 'Pity, there goes my V.C!' and 'Those bastards in *Bismarck* don't *know* how lucky they've been,' they said, helping to take themselves and others out of their private cells, re-establish comradeship, ease the tension.

It was just before 3 a.m. that *Suffolk*, steaming south at 30 knots, signalled that she was in touch with the enemy again, and on *Hood*'s plot this showed *Bismarck* to be 35 miles to the north-west, with the British just a fraction ahead. During the past hour the two squadrons had been steaming on slightly divergent courses, Lütjens on 220°, Holland on 200°, which accounted for the now increased distance between them.

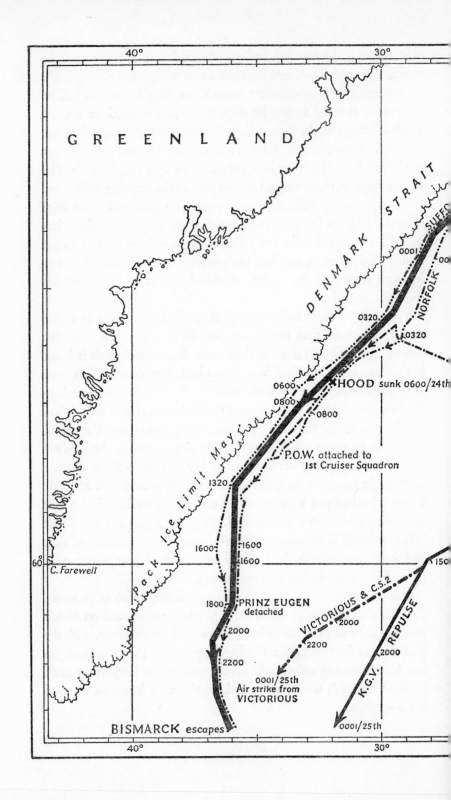

GREENLAND

DENMARK STRAIT

SUFFO

0001

NORFOLK

0320

0320

00

0600

✕HOOD sunk 0600/24th

0800

0800

P.O.W. attached to
1st Cruiser Squadron

Pack Ice Limit May

1320

1600

1600

1600

60°

C. Farewell

150

1800

PRINZ EUGEN
detached

VICTORIOUS & C.S.2

REPULSE

2000

2000

2000

2200

2200

K.G.V.

2200

0001/25th
Air strike from
VICTORIOUS

0001/25th

BISMARCK escapes

40°

30°

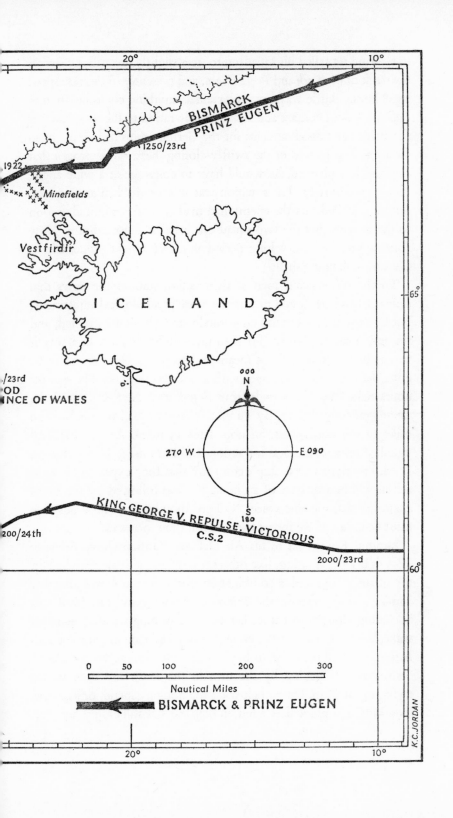

20°   10°

BISMARCK
PRINZ EUGEN

1250/23rd

1922

xxxx Minefields

Vestfirdir

I C E L A N D

/23rd
OD
NCE OF WALES

000
N

270 W ———————— E 090

S
180

KING GEORGE V. REPULSE. VICTORIOUS
C.S.2

200/24th

2000/23rd

65°

60°

0   50   100   200   300

Nautical Miles

BISMARCK & PRINZ EUGEN

K.C.JORDAN

20°   10°

Holland signalled his squadron to steer slightly inwards, i.e. across the track of *Bismarck* and *Prinz Eugen*, and presently to increase speed to 28 knots. Battle was now as certain as anything could be, though *Suffolk*'s loss of contact and *Bismarck*'s alteration to the west had put the British at a disadvantage: for the German ships had now got so far ahead that instead of the swiftly-closing 'head on' approach that Holland had planned, he would have to converge at a wide angle, much more slowly. The situation was worsened when at 3.20 a.m. *Suffolk* signalled that the enemy had made a further slight alteration to the west so that the two squadrons became almost abeam. Now there would be a very long period when *Hood* was vulnerable to *Bismarck*'s plunging shells.

To the officers and men at their action stations the news that *Bismarck* had been found meant one more psychological adjustment; but by now they were too emotionally and physically drained, and the action too imminent, for it to make much impact. In a way it was to be welcomed, for it meant an end to doubt; if it had to be done, let it be done and over with as soon as possible. The quarter hours ticked by, the signals from *Suffolk* and *Norfolk* showed the range gradually closing. By 4 a.m. the enemy squadron was only 20 miles to the north-west, an hour later 15 miles. At 5.10 Holland signalled instant readiness for action, and in *Prince of Wales* Captain Leach broadcast to the ship's company that they expected to be in action within a quarter of an hour. He was followed by the ship's chaplain's flat, metallic voice: 'O Lord thou knowest how busy we must be today. If we forget thee, do not thou forget us.'

Esmond Knight sat in his Air Defence Position above *Prince of Wales*'s bridge, wearing, like others round him, a tin hat perched on top of anti-flash hood, a combination that seemed to him somewhat comic. Ahead, fine on the *Prince of Wales*'s bow, the *Hood* was bucketing along into battle, her screws churning up a tremendous wake, her huge white battle ensign curling and flapping in the wind. Astern, and still out of sight beyond the funnel haze, were the four destroyers, left behind by the turn to the south and now vainly trying to catch up. Down below on the bridge, captain, officers and look-outs kept binoculars fixed on the clear but still empty horizon.

Captain Leach gave an order, and a lad of eighteen, Knocker White by name, was given a pair of glasses and a spare coat, told to go aloft at once, up the swaying mast to the crow's nest, keep his eyes glued to the starboard beam, sing out loud and clear when the enemy's topmasts came into sight. The minutes passed, agonisingly slowly: any moment now, thought Esmond Knight, they would see the great ship which until this moment had been to all of them only a name. No one on the bridge said anything, every eye, every pair of binoculars was trained to starboard: there was no sound but the bows slicing the water and the wind tearing and snatching at the halyards. Then, from above, came the voice, a thin, reedy cry, but no doubting its urgency: 'Enemy in sight!' Everyone looked up and there was Knocker White, leaning out of the crow's nest and pointing excitedly to starboard. 'Enemy in sight!' he cried again, so there should be no mistake. On the bridge they trained binoculars in the direction of the boy's arm, the 14-inch guns in their huge turrets and the director tower and rangefinder began swinging round too. For a few moments there was nothing to see, the bridge being so much lower than the crow's nest; then from below the rim of the horizon the tops of two masts appeared, the superstructures, the ships themselves. Black they seemed to Esmond Knight in the dawn light, black and sinister and powerful. This was the enemy, come out of its lair, and to those in the British ships who had never seen a German warship before, there was something evil in the silent, purposeful, way they raced southwards, hell-bent on their mission of destruction, as if the Atlantic was suddenly theirs.

The range on sighting was 17 miles,* too far to open fire accurately. How quickly would Holland close it? While most of those on *Prince of Wales*'s bridge gazed, as if hypnotised, at the enemy ships, one man had his telescope trained firmly on the flagship's yardarm. He was the Chief Yeoman of Signals, and as he watched the little coloured flags run up the halyards, it was his turn to speak. 'From *Hood*, sir,' he shouted against the wind, 'Blue four. Alter course forty degrees to starboard.'

* Approximately the distance between Piccadilly Circus and Hampton Court Palace or a little more than that between Central Park South and La Guardia.

It was a big alteration and the new course meant approaching the enemy at so fine an angle that *Hood* and *Prince of Wales*'s after turrets would not be able to bear – what the First Sea Lord later called 'going into battle with one hand when you have two'. On the other hand it meant exposing *Hood*'s vulnerable upper deck to the enemy's long-range fire for the minimum time. Captain Leach gave the orders to the helmsman, the bows of *Hood* and *Prince of Wales* swung round, pointed more acutely across the paths of *Bismarck* and *Prinz Eugen*. The range began closing rapidly: in minutes now the battle would begin.

A rather less hectic night had been passed by the crews of *Bismarck* and *Prinz Eugen*, quite unaware of the movements of *Hood* and *Prince of Wales*. A signal from Group North made late on the evening of the 23rd that there was still no enemy operational activity discernible must have given Lütjens pause for thought when two enemy ships had been trailing him for hours and one of them was reported by his cryptographers as having the call sign of *King George V*. On the other hand these could be part of the routine patrol the British kept in these waters, and if so, and Group North's report was correct, there should be nothing further ahead of him. It was true that all attempts to shake off the shadowers, lay smoke screens and violent alterations of course, had so far failed, but once in the Atlantic, with rougher weather and longer nights, they should be able to get clear.

In the staff medical officer's cabin in the *Prinz Eugen*, after Jasper and Albrecht had finished their beer and left, Commander Busch lay down for a couple of hours, fully dressed, on the cold leather bunk. He was up again a little before midnight to prepare for the middle watch. He put on bridge coat, scarf and binoculars, crossed the ante-room leading to the captain's day cabin, now unoccupied, passed the pay office with the guard mounted outside the door, skilfully avoiding the hammocks in the passageway of those sleeping near their action stations, reached the heavy, steel door that led to the upper deck, unbolted the clips. A flurry of snow met him, thick, white flakes that blotted out all visibility. It was in this storm, a few minutes later, that *Bismarck* and *Prinz Eugen* went on to 30 knots, and *Norfolk* and *Suffolk* lost them. Busch put his head down, groped his way along the upper deck, climbed the steel ladder to the bridge.

Jasper was already there, and Paul Schmalenbach, the second gunnery officer, was handing over the watch. There was little to report. *Bismarck* was in the same position, a mile astern, and some way astern of her were *Norfolk* and *Suffolk*, whose signals to the Admiralty were being decoded and sent up to the bridge within minutes; from here they were being passed by lamp to *Bismarck*, whose own wireless office was having difficulties with reception. The radar screen ahead was clear, but there were a few small ice floes about, which meant occasional alterations of course. The captain was on his chair at the back of the bridge.

Schmalenbach and the rest of the port watch went off for four hours' sleep. Busch looked over the edge of the curved bridge-rail. The snow had stopped but the wind had freshened, and the seas were breaking over the forward gun turret and shipping the spray up and over the bridge. Relief communication ratings, earphones on heads, had taken up their positions on the wooden gratings at the feet of the gunnery commander and officer of the watch, 'like hens', said Busch, 'on the roost'. From the earphones thin cables trailed away to a switchboard panel at the side of the bridge. Inside the armoured control position the helmsman rested his hands lightly on the press buttons of the electrical steering gear, kept his eyes fixed on the dimly-lit rudder indicator and compass.

Friebe, the bridge orderly, brought round soup and coffee to ease the bitter cold. Captain Brinkmann, at the back of the bridge, sipped his, spluttered and swore. 'God dammit! Someone's been throwing cigarette ends into the tureen, and I've got one. Friebe, you will be shot at dawn.' The captain was always coming out with things like this and everyone liked him for it. The watch dragged on, and throughout the ship – and in *Bismarck* and in the British ships too – men's thoughts turned to what they most desired. A few days before it might have been steak and eggs, an evening on the beer, the body of a beautiful girl, but for most now it was nothing more demanding than eight hours' sleep in a warm, still bed. Captain Brinkmann thought of the Kaiserhof in Berlin and the many good meals he had had there, Busch's mind turned to his home in Steuben Square, Charlottenburg, the big block of flats and the pretty women who lived in them, the provision store near the underground station run by the ex-sailor who always dressed in white.

These home thoughts from sea were interrupted by the voice of Petty Officer Hertel, repeating a message from the foretop. 'Aircraft to port!' followed by another voice shouting 'Aircraft alarm from *Bismarck*.' The aircraft alarm bell was sounded – short, short, long, short (Frederiiicke) – and those in the port watch who had turned in only an hour before ran to their battle stations. It was a Catalina flying boat, L of 269 squadron, one of several Coastal Command machines that had been sent out from Iceland to search for the German ships. Oddly enough, although those in *Bismarck* and *Prinz Eugen* saw the plane clearly against the sky, the ships themselves merged with the leaden sea and in the half-light the pilot and observer missed them. The plane flew down the port side and disappeared, the port watch returned to hammocks and sleep.

At 3 a.m. the *Prinz Eugen*'s wireless room picked up the first enemy report from *Suffolk* for nearly three hours, and passed it to *Bismarck*. Lütjens and his staff had noted that none of *Suffolk*'s or *Norfolk*'s signals since midnight had mentioned enemy bearings, only their own course and speed, but as the signals were coming in strongly, it was reasonable to assume the British were still in touch. Had Lütjens realised he had shaken the cruisers off, he would probably have altered course drastically to make certain of it.

At 4 a.m. a refreshed Schmalenbach reappeared to take over from Jasper and the starboard watch. There wasn't much news. It was getting lighter all the time, the sea was moderate: *Suffolk* and *Norfolk* were sending out regular reports, the radar screen was clear, the captain was sleeping in his cabin. Schmalenbach settled down to the prospect of another four hours of high speed steaming. He was joined on the bridge by Lieutenant Hane of the Luftwaffe, the senior of the ship's three aircraft pilots, who had come to sniff out the chances of his taking off that morning on reconnaissance. 'Good, I would think,' said Schmalenbach, 'we know what's behind us, but as to what's ahead, who can tell?' Hane said he hoped they would get off, he was sick of having his leg pulled in the wardroom about the airmen's extra ration of fried eggs for breakfast.

It was about an hour later that the listening post reported the sound of screws of two fast-moving ships approaching on the port bow. The bridge checked with the radar in the foretop, but they had nothing; it was not surprising, for *Hood* and *Prince of Wales* were still more than twenty miles away, over the horizon.[3] It was the third gunnery officer who, high up in the foretop position, saw in his rangefinder smoke far away to the south-east. Once again the alarm bells were pressed – this time the succession of long trills that warned of surface action – once again men leapt from hammocks and bunks and passageways, raced to their action stations. Captain Brinkmann was on the bridge in a flash, sending an enemy report to *Bismarck*. Schmalenbach, the expert on warship silhouettes, grabbed Weyer's *Handbook of Foreign Navies* and made for the gunnery control in the foretop. Jasper hurried there too, from his cabin below the bridge, and Graf von Matuschka, the young rangefinding officer, later to do well in U-boats. In the engine-room the chief engineer, Commander Graser, switched the engines and power supply to action duty, checked the emergency lighting. From all over the ship officers and men reported to the bridge or foretop that their positions were ready for action.

In the gunnery control position they watched through the range-finders the smoke become masts, the masts become ships, the ships take shape.

'Any idea what they are?' said Jasper.

Schmalenbach took his time in answering.

'The one on the right is more squat than the one on the left, and has a tremendous bow-wave. The one on the left is obviously a more modern vessel.' He paused. 'I think the one on the right is the *Hood*.'

In the control position they heard this with astonishment. The *Hood*? Impossible. Jasper laughed out loud. 'Nonsense!' he said, 'it's either a cruiser or destroyer.'

'I'll bet you a bottle of champagne,' said Schmalenbach, 'that it's *Hood*.'

79

'Taken', said Jasper, thinking he was on to a good thing. 'Load with high explosive shell and impact fuses.'

These shells were ideal for bursting on the exposed decks of lightly armoured cruisers or destroyers and causing casualties among the crew. Had Jasper believed Schmalenbach, he would have loaded with armour-piercing shell with delayed fuses, designed to penetrate *Hood*'s deck and explode inside. Indeed had Brinkmann known earlier and for certain that the ships were *Hood* and *Prince of Wales*, he would have dropped out of the line, for German Fleet orders expressly forbade cruisers to engage capital ships. Lütjens did not order him to do so because in *Bismarck* they were also confused as to the identity of the British ships: the gunnery officer Commander Schneider thought them both cruisers.

And in the British ranks there was confusion too, caused by the similarity of *Bismarck*'s and *Prinz Eugen*'s silhouettes. Assuming that *Bismarck* must be leading the enemy line, Holland signalled to *Prince of Wales*, 'Stand by to open fire. Target left-hand ship.'

CHAPTER

4

And so the two admirals, Lütjens and Holland, riding on their great chargers, came at each other like knights of old, with guns for lances and armoured bridges for visors and pennants streaming in the wind. And beneath their feet, on the airy decks and in the warm bellies of their mounts, were their six thousand young seconds, half on either side, who felt no personal ill will towards each other at all, who in different circumstances might have played and laughed and sung together, kissed each other's sisters, visited each other's homes, but now, because of this time and place, were at each other's throats, concentrating as never before to ensure that they killed first, that their knights' lances toppled the other in the tourney.

In the gun turrets of the four ships, the first shells and cartridges and silken bags of cordite had been sent up from shell rooms and magazines far below, were even now rammed home in the barrels of each gun, the breeches had been closed and locked, the gun ready lamps were burning: the guns of *Hood* and *Bismarck* were over twenty yards long, weighed 100 tons apiece. The rangefinding ratings leaned heads forward on rubber eye-cushions: the German rangefinders were stereoscopic, which meant centring the little yellow *Wandermark* on the base of the enemy's superstructure: British rangefinders were co-incidental, presented an enemy vessel in two images which required merging into one. The British Navy had considered stereoscopic equipment after the first war, for it was deadly accurate, especially at initial ranges; but it required special aptitudes and a cool head which might be lost in the heat of the battle, so in the end they rejected it. The ranges both visual and radar were fed by electrical circuits to computers in transmitting stations deep below each bridge, along with own course and speed, enemy's course and speed, wind velocity, air density, rate of range-change, and, thus programmed, the computers fed to the gun-turrets an ever changing stream of directions for the training and elevation of the guns. In four gunnery control positions above each bridge, the four gunnery control officers – Schneider, McMullen, Moultrie and Jasper, saw the gun ready lamps burn in front of them, stood by to open fire.

For a few moments then, as the two squadrons raced towards each other in that cold, pale dawn, with the eastern sky pink and violet on the low cirrus and a hazy blue above, there was in all the ships a silence made more striking by the knowledge of the thunder that was to come. Men's voices and hands had done all they could by way of preparation: the only sounds now were sea sounds, bows slicing the water, whistling wind and spray.

On *Hood*'s bridge a man with headphones on his ears began singing out softly the closing ranges as given from the gunnery control position, like the conductor of a Dutch auction. And at about the same time as Admiral Holland's Chief Yeoman of Signals was hoisting the preparatory signal to open fire to *Prince of Wales*, Admiral Lütjens was ordering his Chief Yeoman to hoist JD, the signal to open fire to *Prinz Eugen*. When the range was down to 13 miles,* Admiral Holland said, 'Execute.' The Chief Yeoman shouted to the flag deck, 'Down Flag 5', Captain Kerr said, 'Open fire' and in the control tower the gunnery officer said 'Shoot!'

There came the tiny, tinkly, ridiculous ding-ding of the fire gong, like an overture scored for triangle, for a moment the world stood still, then the guns spoke with their terrible great roar, the blast knocked one almost senseless, thick clouds of cordite smoke, black and bitter-smelling, clutched at the throat, blinded the vision, and four shells weighing a ton apiece went rocketing out of the muzzles

* The distance between the West London Air Terminal and Heathrow Airport or a little less than that between Central Park South and La Guardia.

at over 1,600 miles an hour. To Busch in the *Prinz Eugen*, *Hood*'s gun flashes appeared as 'great, fiery rings like suns', and Jasper beside him called out 'Damn it, those aren't cruiser's guns, they're battleships,' just as *Bismarck*'s second gunnery officer Lieutenant Albrecht was telling Schneider the same. Now it was *Prince of Wales*'s turn, Esmond Knight in his air defence position was deafened by the crash of the forward turrets, felt the breath squeezed from his body, was unable to see for the smoke. As it cleared, he saw an orange ripple of fire run down the length, first of *Bismarck*, then *Prinz Eugen*.

In the tightly-shut armoured control position on *Bismarck*'s bridge Lütjens and his staff rocked to the roar of *Bismarck*'s opening salvo. This battle was not of his choosing, for his instructions were to shun any engagement with enemy forces not escorting a convoy, and he had delayed permission to open fire so long that there were some in *Bismarck* and *Prinz Eugen* who thought he was hoping to avoid it. But with the ice to the west of him, the two cruisers to the north, and Holland's force to the east, there was no escape; and in that situation his orders were to fight all out.

Now the shells were in the air, like flights of arrows, and men on either side, counting the seconds until their arrival, asked themselves anxiously where they would fall. Some believed they were directed to them personally, had their name on them as the saying went, felt the first stirrings of panic. 'He's fired,' came the agitated voice of a petty officer on *Prinz Eugen*'s bridge, and Captain Brinkmann said quietly, 'Keep calm, man. Of course he's fired. Now let's see what comes of it.' With a shriek and a roar the shells fell, great geysers of water leapt in the air, high as Hiltons, white as Daz. *Hood*'s shells landed in the vicinity of *Prinz Eugen*, but not dangerously so, *Prince of Wales*'s were a thousand yards short of *Bismarck*; but the shells of *Bismarck* and *Prinz Eugen* were deadly accurate, they enveloped *Hood* in a curtain of splashes, the men of *Prince of Wales* saw it with horror and relief.

If Admiral Holland's plan of the night before had worked, and he had come upon Lütjens unseen, he might already have won a great victory. But now everything had gone sour on him, he had the worst of every world. By steering at this angle he was denying his

83

own force the maximum of fire-power and yet giving the enemy more to aim at than necessary. He had reduced his initial superiority in heavy guns of eighteen against eight to ten against eight, which was about to be reduced to nine against eight, as one of *Prince of Wales*'s forward guns had a defect which would render it inoperative after the first salvo. Further, while the British fire was divided between *Bismarck* and *Prinz Eugen*, the German fire was concentrated on *Hood*. It would have helped if *Norfolk* and *Suffolk* had closed up on *Bismarck*, worried her from the rear, drawn the fire from her after turrets: this was Holland's intention, and orders to Müllenheim-Rechberg in *Bismarck*'s after control to keep his eyes fixed on the two cruisers show that Lütjens was expecting it. But Holland had failed to give Wake-Walker the necessary orders, the opportunity was lost.

There were other handicaps. The Germans had what sailors call the weather gauge, which meant the British ships were steaming into wind, the spray drenching the lenses of the forward turrets' two 30-foot rangefinders, necessitating use of the smaller rangefinders in the control tower instead. And by keeping *Prince of Wales* close to him, making her conform to his movements rather than let her vary her course and speed, Holland was making it easier for the Germans to rangefind, more difficult for the British ships to observe each other's fall of shot.

The shells went to and fro, east and west. One from *Hood* landed just ahead of *Prinz Eugen*, the water rose in a tall, white column and, falling, drenched fo'c'sle and upperworks, smeared the lenses of periscopes and telescopes that jutted out from the armoured control position on the bridge. Other splashes rose on the port bow, and Captain Brinkmann ordered the helmsman to steer towards them, knowing that salvoes never land in the same place twice. Then he opened the heavy door, went outside with Friebe to see through dry binoculars. *Prinz Eugen*'s first salvo had been a little short, now she was firing her second. Twenty seconds went by, Brinkmann saw the white fountains shoot up, some short, some over – a straddle – and then a flame leapt up on *Hood*'s boatdeck amidships. 'It's a hit,' shouted one of Jasper's crew excitedly, 'the enemy's on fire.' Busch saw the fire as 'a glaring blood-red rectangle which began to emit thick fumes', Captain Leach in *Prince of Wales* as 'a vast blow-lamp', Captain Phillips in *Norfolk* as 'a glow that pulsated like the appearance of a setting, tropical sun'.

On *Hood*'s bridge the fire was reported by the torpedo officer as being caused by a shell-burst among the 4-inch anti-aircraft ammunition. Able Seaman Tilburn, one of the 4-inch guns' crews, was ordered with others to put the fire out, was about to do so when ammunition in the ready-use locker started exploding, so they all lay flat on the deck. Then another shell, or perhaps two, hit *Hood*, killing many of the gun crews now sheltering in the aircraft hangar; and part of a body, falling from aloft, struck Able Seaman Tilburn on the legs.

Now Holland decided, whatever the risks to *Hood*, that he could no longer afford to keep half his gun-power out of action. He had already made one small alteration back to port, and to bring the after turrets of both ships to bear, he hoisted the signal for another. While some on *Prince of Wales*'s bridge were looking at the fire in *Hood*, and others had their eyes fixed on the enemy, one man's telescope had never wavered, despite the smoke and confusion of battle, from the flagship's yardarm. 'From *Hood*, sir,' shouted the Chief Yeoman of Signals as the flags went up, 'Two Blue. Turn twenty degrees to port together.' Captain Leach and Lieutenant-Commander McMullen heard the news with joy: now at last the four-gun after turret with its frustrated crew would be brought into action.

The executive signal came down, the two ships began to turn. Then the incredible happened. When Schneider in *Bismarck* saw the fire on *Hood*'s boatdeck, he ordered an immediate broadside, and presently, and for the fifth time in four minutes, *Hood* was hidden by a curtain of shell splashes. But at least one shell of that broadside made no splash: it came plunging down like a rocket, hit the old ship fair and square between centre and stern, sliced its way through steel and wood, pierced the deck that should have been strengthened and never was, penetrated to the ship's vitals deep below the water-line, exploded, touched off the 4-inch magazine which in turn touched off the after 15-inch magazine. Before the eyes of the horrified British and incredulous Germans a huge column of flame leapt up from *Hood*'s centre. One witness in *Norfolk* said it was four times the height of the mainmast, another that it 'nearly touched the sky'. Busch saw it as a red and white funnel-shaped glow, Esmond Knight as a long, pale red tongue, Lieut-Commander Havers in *Suffolk* as a stick of red rhubarb, Lieutenant Schmitz, the war artist in *Prinz Eugen*, as in the shape of a sinister fir-tree. It was followed by a thick mushroom-shaped cloud of smoke which to Lieut-Commander Towell in *Prince of Wales* had the appearance of steam, but which Esmond Knight described as 'dark yellow, like the smoke from a gorse fire'. One of the oddest things about the explosion was that it made no noise. On *Hood*'s bridge Midshipman Dundas and Signalman Briggs heard nothing unusual, and Esmond Knight said, 'I remember listening for it and thinking it would be a most tremendous explosion, but I don't remember hearing an explosion at all.' As the smoke welled upwards and outwards bits and pieces of *Hood* could be seen flying through the air – part of a 15-inch gun turret, the mainmast, the main derrick. Captain Brinkmann noticed the ship's shells exploding high up in the smoke, bursting like white stars. To Esmond Knight it seemed the most famous warship in the world was blowing up like a huge Chinese Christmas cracker.[1]

In all disasters, however unexpected and dramatic, there is often a moment, maybe no longer than a fraction of a second, when those about to die comprehend dimly that something unusual has happened, that things are not as they should be. On *Hood*'s bridge, after the great flame had shot up, there was time for Signalman Briggs to hear the officer of the watch report the compass had gone, the quartermaster to report the steering had gone, the captain to order a switch to emergency steering: then the ship fell sideways like a collapsing house. On the boat-deck Able Seaman Tilburn was conscious of a most extraordinary vibration. He saw a man beside him killed, another's side ripped open by a splinter and the guts coming out, went over to the side to be sick, found the deck level with the water. And elsewhere in the ship there were others calmly watching dials or adjusting levers who suddenly were aware that something very strange was happening to them, who, as they were lifted off their feet, and plates and bulkheads collapsed around them, sensed for one terrible, brief moment, no longer than it takes a flash of lightning, that death had come to fetch them.

In *Prince of Wales*, *Bismarck* and *Prinz Eugen* only a handful of men saw *Hood*'s end with their own eyes: the vast majority were below decks and to them the incredible news came on inter-com and by telephone, second hand. Some simply did not believe it. *Prinz Eugen*'s executive officer, Commander Stoos, on duty in the lower command post, hearing his captain's voice announcing the news, said quietly, 'Some poor fellow up there has gone off his head.' In *Bismarck*'s after transmitting station Leading Seaman Eich heard Commander Schneider's joyous shout, 'She's blowing *up*,' and would remember the long drawn out '*uuup*' for the rest of his life. In the after director tower Müllenheim-Rechberg heard it too, and despite orders to stick to the two cruisers, couldn't resist swinging round to see for himself. The smoke was clearing to show *Hood* with a broken back, in two pieces, bow and stern pointing towards the sky. As he watched, he saw the two forward turrets of *Hood* suddenly spit out a final salvo: it was an accident, the circuits must have been closed at the moment she was struck, but to her enemies it seemed a last defiant and courageous gesture.

Now *Prince of Wales*, turning to port to obey Holland's orders, had to go hard a-starboard to avoid the wreckage ahead, and Jasper, through *Prinz Eugen*'s main rangefinder, saw on the far side of *Prince of Wales* a weird thing – the whole forward section of *Hood*, rearing up from the water like the spire of a cathedral, towering above the upper deck of *Prince of Wales*, as she steamed by. Inside this foresection were several hundred men, trapped topsy-turvy in the darkness of shell-room and magazine. Then *Prince of Wales* passed, both parts of *Hood* slid quickly beneath the waves, taking with them more than 1,400 men, leaving only a wreath of smoke on the surface. 'Poor devils, poor devils!' said Jasper aloud, echoing the thoughts of those around him; for as sailors they had just proved what sailors do not care to prove, that no ship, not even *Hood* is unsinkable, and that went for *Bismarck* and *Prinz Eugen* too.

But joy and awe were both short-lived, for the battle was not yet over. Before the blowing up of *Hood*, *Prinz Eugen* had already been ordered to shift her fire to *Prince of Wales* and now *Bismarck* had to make only the smallest of adjustments to find the range too. On *Prince of Wales*'s bridge they saw the burst of black smoke from *Bismarck*'s cordite and the long ripple of orange flashes from her guns, knew this time without a doubt where they were aimed, what they were capable of doing. Yet Captain Leach was not despondent. His own guns had found *Bismarck* with the sixth salvo, straddled and hit. If everyone kept a cool head, they might win a victory yet.

The salvo fell and then there was chaos. A 15-inch shell went clean through the bridge, exploded as it went out the other side, killing everyone except the captain and Chief Yeoman of Signals, and the navigating officer who was wounded. Young Midshipman Ince was among the dead, aged eighteen and full of promise, at his prep school voted the boy with the best influence. On the deck below, the plotting officer, unable to distinguish between hits from *Bismarck* and the firing of *Prince of Wales*'s own guns, was unaware anything had happened until blood trickled down the bridge voicepipe, dripped on to his chart.

This same shell did for Esmond Knight too. He remembered hearing the salvo, 'like a great rushing cyclone', then everything went hazy and he was having a dream about the band playing in Hyde Park, there was a high, ringing noise in his head and he came to, thinking he was dying, feeling a little sad about it, nothing more. He heard the crash of another salvo and cries of 'Stretcher-bearer!' and 'Make way there!' He was conscious of a weight of dead men on him and screams and the smell of blood, and the dreadful thin noise some men make when dying. 'Get me out of here,' he shouted weakly, and strong hands pulled him to his feet. 'What the hell's happened to you?' a voice said, and Esmond turned and looked at him and saw nothing. The man whose delight in life was visual things, painting pictures, watching birds, was already among the ranks of the war-blinded, would now never see the Harlequin Duck or Icelandic Falcon, or anything but dim shapes again.

Now in *Prinz Eugen* there were reports from the hydrophonic detection room of torpedoes approaching, both ships turned to comb, i.e. steer parallel to their tracks. Captain Brinkman even claimed to have seen the tracks, but it must have been imagination, only *Hood* had torpedoes and even if she had fired them before blowing up, they couldn't have run the distance in time. As *Prinz Eugen* swung round, funnel smoke blinded Jasper in the main gunnery control, so Albrecht, the civilian from Siemens and designer of the firing mechanism for the guns, fired the after turrets himself. Now the two German ships turned back, confident, assertive, weaving in and out of *Prince of Wales*'s shell splashes, dancing and side-stepping like boxers who suddenly sense victory in the blood. *Bismarck*'s salvoes thundered out every twenty seconds, *Prinz Eugen*'s every ten, the shell splashes rose round *Prince of Wales* like clumps of whitened trees. Now the British battleship was within range of *Prinz Eugen*'s torpedoes; but just as Lieutenant Reimann was about to fire, she turned away.

For after only another twelve minutes of battle, *Prince of Wales* had had enough. She had been hit by four of *Bismarck*'s heavy shells and three of *Prinz Eugen*'s. The compass platform, echo-sounding gear, radar office, aircraft recovery crane, fore secondary armament director, all the boats and several cabins had been wrecked. The shell that hit the crane landed just as the Walrus aircraft was about to be launched to spot fall of shot, the launching officer's hand was in the air: the wings were peppered with splinters, pilot and observer scrambled out, the plane was ditched over the side to avoid risk of fire. The same splinters that blinded Esmond Knight also pierced a fresh-water tank, loosed a flood of hot water on to survivors of the bridge and men on the signal deck below. One 15-inch and two 8-inch shells hit the ship below the waterline, let in 400 tons of sea water. Another 8-inch shell found its way into a shell handling room, whizzed round several times without going off or hitting anyone, took two men to throw it over the side.

Moreover *Prince of Wales*'s own gunnery was less than adequate. Although Lieutenant-Commander Skipwith, the spotting officer, had observed straddles on *Bismarck* with the ninth and thirteenth salvoes, few salvoes were of more than three guns when they should have been of five. Mechanical defects were developing continuously in the newly-installed guns, and though the Vickers Armstrong workmen in the turrets were doing wonders, they had hardly corrected one fault before another arose. It dawned on Captain Leach that not only was he engaged in a very unequal battle, but if he continued much longer, he might soon deprive the Navy of a valuable ship without inflicting further damage on the enemy. He knew that his Commander-in-Chief was four hundred miles to the south-east with *King George V* and *Repulse*, and that if *Bismarck* and *Prinz Eugen* continued on the same course, would make contact with them early next day. If he broke off action now, joined the shadowing cruisers, over-hauled the guns and repaired the damage, he would be well placed to attack *Bismarck* from the rear when Tovey came in from the east, effect a concentration of fire-power that would force the enemy to divide his.

So after having fired eighteen salvoes, *Prince of Wales* made smoke and disengaged to the south-east. As she turned, the shell ring of Y turret jammed, rendered the four guns in it inoperable. Her casualties were two officers and eleven men killed, one officer and eight men wounded. The time was 6.13 a.m., just twenty-one minutes after Admiral Holland in *Hood* had so proudly led his squadron in to battle.

For most Englishmen the news of *Hood*'s death was traumatic, as though Buckingham Palace had been laid flat or the Prime Minister assassinated, so integral a part was she of the fabric of Britain and her Empire. Admiral Wake-Walker, announcing the tragedy to the Admiralty and the world with his laconic signal '*Hood* has blown up,' felt compelled to classify it 'Secret', as though somehow this might prevent the dreadful news reaching Hitler. Many people simply did not believe it. Cain on watch in the *Electra* thirty miles to the north thought the Yeoman of Signals was trying to be funny, rounded on him fiercely. 'My God, but it's true, sir,' the man replied, his eyes filling with tears. Farther south Commander Baker-Creswell in his destroyer *Bulldog*, which only fifteen days before had captured the U-boat *U.110* and her secret cipher machine, thought there had been a mistake in the name. He had known *Hood* all his naval life, dined in her wardroom in Hvalfjord only two or three weeks before. Beyond him Herbert Wohlfarth in *U.556*, bound for the coast of France, also thought there'd been a mistake, asked U-boat Command for a repeat. In the same area the famous Captain Vian, hero of the *Altmark* affair, whose 4th destroyer flotilla was soon to play its own part in the *Bismarck* operation, said later that he had felt no stronger emotion at any time in the war – and this from a man whom many thought had no emotions. Captain Phillips of the *Norfolk*, who had once been her gunnery officer, was utterly shattered, so was Admiral Somerville, whose flag she had so recently flown. Lofty Earl, who had served in her as a boy and was now quartermaster of the *Glenroy* fighting the battle of Crete, unashamedly broke down and cried.

Abroad too, all over the Empire and in South America and the United States, those who remembered her gliding gracefully into their harbours or lying like a golden jewel there at night, who had entertained or been entertained by her young men, danced beneath white awnings on her quarter-deck to the music of her band, strolled on her decks and seen her power and majesty for themselves, were incredulous and aghast. They remembered, many of them, where they were when they heard the news, just as people today can tell you where they were when they heard of the death of President Kennedy. Señor Gomez, of the London Bar, Gibraltar, who had collected laundry from her many times between the wars, was in a pub in London's Fulham Road, heard it on BBC Radio. 'I think the world has come to an end. I truly think we are finished, señor. If the Germans can sink *Hood*, I say to myself, then there is no more hope.' Others, all over Britain, felt the same. If *Hood* could not stop *Bismarck*, what could? What now lay between her and the destruction of the Atlantic convoys? Later, resolution set in, an urge to avenge *Hood*'s death at all costs, but now before the shock wore off, a question-mark arose in the minds of many, as it had at the time of Dunkirk.

And what of *Hood*'s survivors? Admiral Wake-Walker could not spare *Norfolk* or *Suffolk* to look for them, but *Hood*'s own destroyers were not far off and they were ordered to the spot. A Hudson air-craft piloted by Flying Officer Pinhorn, one of two Coastal Command planes from Iceland that had watched the battle, contacted one of the destroyers, gave her a course to steer. In all four destroyers, preparations went ahead for the reception of shell-shocked and exhausted men: blankets and warm clothing were drawn from stores, hot soup brewed in the galleys, sick-bays made ready for the wounded.

The ships set course southwards in line abreast, several miles apart. After two hours hard steaming it was clear to those in *Electra* that they had reached the edge of the scene. There were patches of oil on the water, a floating drawer full of ratings documents, odd bits of wood, little else. They steamed on at slow speed, saw three Carley rafts not far apart, one man on each: Midshipman Dundas, Able Seaman Tilburn, Signalman Briggs. Was this all then, all that had survived of the great ship's company? Mr Cain remembered how the ship looked at Sunday divisions, line upon line of men mustered on her upper decks 'like a small army'. 'There *must* be more,' said the Engineer Officer, 'there can't be only *three* of them.' But no, that was all. They searched a long time, found other small pieces of wreckage, a marine's hat with the number RMB X738 on it, but nothing human, not even bodies. The rest of the small army, Admiral Holland, Captain Kerr, ninety other officers, more than fourteen hundred men lay a thousand fathoms down, their ship their tomb, there they would lie for ever.[2]

The three survivors were taken on board *Electra*, stripped of their wet clothes, wrapped in blankets. There wasn't much they could say, least of all why they should have survived and others hadn't. Dundas remembered climbing out of the upper bridge window as the ship went over, Briggs left by the starboard door of the compass platform behind the navigating officer and Staff Gunnery officer, noted Admiral Holland was making no attempt to get away. Tilburn had time to get rid of tin hat and gas mask before going over: when he was in the water and the ship rolled on her side, one of the aerials wrapped round his seaboots, threatened to drag him down, so he got out his claspknife and cut off his boots under water. All three agreed that after the roar and confusion of battle the first thing they noticed was the silence. They looked up, saw *Hood*'s bow down to A turret standing vertically out of the water, swam away as fast as

92

they could. Briggs saw oil fuel on fire not far away, was worried as there was oil around him, presently the fire went out. Each found a Carley raft, climbed on to it, paddled towards each other. The other aircraft that had watched the battle, a Sunderland piloted by Flying Officer Vaughan, flew overhead: they waved and splashed the water to attract its attention, but it hadn't seen them, flew away. They tried to hold the rafts together but it was too cold, their fingers became numbed, they drifted apart. Tilburn believed he was going to die, remembered reading how people in extreme cold closed their eyes and never woke up, thought that a pleasant way to go, closed his eyes but obstinately stayed awake. Two hours went by, then *Electra* showed up.

At 9 a.m. the destroyers gave up the search, turned north for Iceland, their crews profoundly depressed by the tragedy of *Hood*, that they had not been with her when she most needed them, that their own part in the chase was now over. And a hundred miles away from them, *Bismarck* and *Prinz Eugen*, closely pursued by *Norfolk*, *Suffolk* and the wounded *Prince of Wales*, continued thundering south.

Part 2

ESCAPE

Nothing is here for tears; nothing to wail
Or knock the breast; no weakness, no contempt,
Dispraise or blame, nothing but well and fair,
And what may quiet us in a death so noble.

Milton: Samson Agonistes

CHAPTER

5

When the crews of *Bismarck* and *Prinz Eugen* were told that *Prince of Wales* (which they mistook for *King George V*, they didn't know *Prince of Wales* was in service) had broken off action and turned away, there was much cheering and shouting, joy at victory and relief at survival: some men left their posts, went on the upper deck to see for themselves. The two gunnery officers came in for much praise: Schneider was the centre of congratulation in *Bismarck*'s wardroom, in *Prinz Eugen* Jasper was called to the telephone from A turret to listen to the crew playing his favourite dance tune on a gramophone. In both ships there was a special issue of cigarettes and chocolates: everyone said the victory was a birthday present for Admiral Lütjens who was to be 52 next day. 'Report hits and casualties,' Lütjens signalled to *Prinz Eugen*, and Brinkmann was happy to signal back, 'None.' (In all ships, German and British, slight damage had been caused by blast from own guns – Commander Busch found his cabin a shambles; broken glass, clothing, papers on the floor, desk lamp and water bottle smashed, the only thing un-damaged the photographs of his English wife and son.) A great jagged splinter from one of *Hood*'s shells found at the base of *Prinz Eugen*'s funnel brought home to her crew how incredibly lucky they had been: as Brinkmann pointed out, one of these slicing through *Prinz Eugen*'s flimsy armour and exploding in the boiler-room would have quickly brought her to a stop.[1]

Bismarck had been less fortunate. She had received three hits altogether, though Müllenheim-Rechberg and others were unaware of any until the action was over. One had carried away the captain's motor-boat amidships, damaged the aircraft launching gear, landed in the sea beyond without exploding. The second had also struck amidships, penetrated the ship's side beneath the armoured belt, destroyed one of the dynamoes, put No. 2 boiler-room and its two boilers out of action, wounded five men by scalding, caused some flooding. The third and most serious hit had struck the port bow about the level of the water-line, penetrated two oil tanks, come out the starboard side without exploding. This hit not only let sea-water into the oil tanks and quantities of oil into the sea, but knocked out the suction valves, cut off from the engines a further thousand tons of oil. Now for the first time Lütjens had cause to regret not having topped up from *Weissenburg* or *Wollin*.

It was this, as much as anything, that determined *Bismarck*'s future course of action. There is evidence that after *Prince of Wales* broke away, there was a difference of opinion between Lindemann who wanted to finish off the damaged battleship, and Lütjens who was determined to press on south.[2] But it is a story that has grown on hindsight, on what many – Hitler among the first – saw later was the most advantageous thing to have done. It is probable that Lindemann did request to continue the action, for his guns had sunk in five minutes the biggest warship (next his own) in the world and severely damaged another. What a triumph to sink that too, then take his victorious ship and crew back home. But Lütjens's orders did not cover this sort of contingency: a spectacular success against the enemy's fleet simply had not been allowed for. Therefore, he must stick to his instructions, the sinking of merchant shipping, encounters with enemy warships to be avoided. Even to have known that it was not *King George V* he was fighting but the raw and untested *Prince of Wales* would not have altered his decision; for to have turned and followed her would have meant exposing the squadron further to her gunfire as well as gun and torpedo attacks by *Norfolk* and *Suffolk* (and possibly other ships lying beyond the horizon), risking the lives of his ships and crews on a venture that had been expressly forbidden.[3]

Meanwhile there was enough to think about with the damage. Because of flooding the bow was down by two or three degrees, there was a list to port of nine degrees, the starboard propeller was coming out of the water. Lindemann ordered counterflooding aft to restore the trim, and maximum speed was reduced to 28 knots. Oil from the damaged tanks continued gushing into the sea, so Lütjens signalled *Prinz Eugen* to drop back, see how much of a wake it was leaving astern. As the cruiser fell back, the battleship came up on her port side, close, so *Prinz Eugen*'s men could see *Bismarck*'s men clearly, saw too the great dark gash on her starboard bow where the shell from *Prince of Wales* had come out. In her wake stretched a broad carpet of oil, all colours of the rainbow, smelling strongly, a tell-tale sign of her presence, like a clue in a boy's paperchase. Brinkmann made his report, *Bismarck* turned sharply to the west, ordered *Prinz Eugen* to take the lead again.

Now *Bismarck* reduced speed a little, collision mats were put down to cover the two holes in the bows, divers were sent to the flooded compartments. Presently the collision mats stopped any more water getting into the ship, though the oil continued to leak out of it. Some officers suggested a big reduction of speed and further counterflooding to bring the bows right out of the water, enable the holes to be repaired by welding; but Lütjens was not prepared to risk the dangers of delay. A civilian technician from Blohm and Voss called Schlüter suggested lightening the bows by cutting loose the anchors and cables, dumping them overboard, but this idea was also rejected. Ordinary Seaman Manthey said the divers had great difficulty working in the flooded compartments, but eventually managed to make temporary repairs, pump out some of the water so the bows began to rise.

But however successful the repairs, it was clear beyond a doubt to Lütjens and his staff that with one boiler-room out of action, maximum speed reduced to 28 knots, serious flooding and loss of fuel and the ship leaving a pathway of oil that could be seen for miles, *Bismarck* could no longer carry out her assignment without dockyard repairs. But to which dockyard should he go? If back to Germany his nearest friendly port was Bergen or Trondheim, both a little over a thousand miles away. But this meant a return through the hazardous passages north or south of Iceland, with the enemy's air forces now fully alerted, and the possibility that further heavy British units were at sea between him and Scapa Flow (the appearance of *Hood* which Group North had reported as being in West Africa and of a *King George* class battleship had proved how little he could rely on his own Intelligence). The coast of France was six hundred miles farther, but meant longer nights and wider seas in which to shake off his shadowers, perhaps entice them over a line of U-boats, top up with fuel from one of the waiting tankers, then steam unmolested to the Normandy dock at St Nazaire. A further advantage of this was that once repairs had been effected, *Bismarck* (with perhaps *Scharnhorst* and *Gneisenau* too) would already be poised on the edge of the Atlantic trade-routes instead of having to renegotiate the perils of a second break-out from Germany. So, three hours after sinking *Hood*, Lütjens signalled Group North, together with a report on *Bismarck*'s damage and the efficacy of British radar, his intentions to release *Prinz Eugen* for independent cruiser warfare and for *Bismarck* to put into St Nazaire.

Because of a faulty aerial or inexperienced radio personnel, neither Lütjens's signal that he had sunk *Hood* nor his later signal about making for St Nazaire reached Germany until early afternoon. There the news of *Hood*'s destruction was seized on joyfully by Dr Goebbels's Propaganda Ministry, and that evening, accompanied by 'We march against England' and other martial airs, broadcast to the nation, spreading as much euphoria (to a people already feasting on news of Luftwaffe victories against the Royal Navy off Crete) as it did gloom in Britain. In the Berlin Admiralty, though, satisfaction at Lütjens's success was tempered by despondency at news of *Bismarck*'s damage and the decision to steer for France. It was not clear to Raeder whether Lütjens intended to make for St Nazaire immediately or after shaking off his shadowers and then oiling in mid-Atlantic. His Chief of Operations, Rear Admiral Schniewind, telephoned Admiral Carls commanding Group North at Wilhemshaven, found that Carls had already drafted a signal recalling Lütjens to Germany. Schniewind pointed out that at noon Lütjens had crossed the line Northern Hebrides-Southern Greenland, passed from Naval Group North's operational control to that of Naval Group West in Paris, so the decision was no longer his. Group West's commander was Admiral Saalwächter, a successful U-boat commander of the first war, clever and congenial, later to die in Russia as a prisoner of war. He told Schniewind he was not prepared to issue a recall himself, and then Schniewind and Raeder discussed whether they should. In the end Raeder decided against it. 'We don't know enough about the actual situation,' Raeder told Schniewind. 'The man who can best judge it is Lütjens. Therefore we must leave it to him.' This view – that the man on the spot knows best – was (as will be seen) in sharp contrast to that of Raeder's opposite number in the British Navy, Admiral of the Fleet Sir Dudley Pound.

Preparations went ahead to cover all eventualities. In Norway Schulze-Hinrichs and his destroyers were ordered from Trondheim to Bergen, U-boats detailed to patrol the Faeroes-Shetland passage, and Air Fleet 5 put on special alert. In St Nazaire balloon barrage equipment, searchlights, heavy and light flak units were ordered to the Normandy dock, and in other French west coast ports escort vessels brought to short notice for steam. Air Fleet 3 and Air Commander, Atlantic, were also alerted, as were U-boat headquarters at Lorient, where Lütjens's old friend, Karl Dönitz, offered to suspend all Atlantic operations, put his entire fleet at *Bismarck*'s disposal. In April in Paris Lütjens had discussed with Dönitz the possibility of *Bismarck* drawing enemy forces over a concentration of U-boats, and now, with the two cruisers and *Prince of Wales* hard on his tail, Lütjens sent Saalwächter a signal asking for just such a concentration south of Greenland the following morning. Dönitz ordered seven boats to take up position.

The British Admiralty meanwhile, fast recovering from the shock of the *Hood*, were also making their dispositions, and not for the first but almost the last time in the Royal Navy's long and brilliant history were exercising the strength that global sea-power gave it. A hundred and thirty-six years earlier the aged First Lord of the Admiralty, Lord Barham, had set in motion the widely spread dispositions that were to lead to Trafalgar and the defeat of Villeneuve: now his successors put into motion the even wider dispositions which they hoped would lead to the cornering of *Bismarck* and defeat of Lütjens. From Halifax, Nova Scotia, the old battleship *Revenge*, from east of Newfoundland the old battleship *Ramillies*, from north-east of the Azores the cruisers *London* and *Edinburgh*, from west of the Clyde the battleship *Rodney* and her destroyers – all these ships were ordered to break off immediately from patrol or convoy escort or whatever they were doing and steer to intercept the German squadron. From Portsmouth a submarine was sailed to take up position outside the Biscay ports; and so vital did the Admiralty think it not to lose touch with *Bismarck* that they signalled Wake-Walker to remain in pursuit even if it meant running out of fuel: Commodore Blackman steaming north in *Edinburgh* at 25 knots was told the same. And from Washington came word that a squadron of American naval planes based in Newfoundland would search the waters south of Cape Farewell the next morning.

The nearest force to Lütjens now was that of the Commander-in-Chief, Admiral Tovey, who with *King George V*, *Repulse*, *Victorious* and five cruisers was some 360 miles to the south-east. The news of *Hood*'s end had been broken to Tovey by Commander Jacobs, the fleet wireless officer, in a voice loud with emotion. 'All right, Jacobs,' said Tovey calmly, 'there's no need to shout.'[4] Now he and Brind with Commander Robertson, the staff operations officer, were in the plotting-room off the admiral's bridge, discussing quietly what needed to be done. Would the German admiral continue south, break out to the westward after dark, or double back on his tracks to Germany, north or south of Iceland? Tovey felt he must steer a course that covered all three contingencies, so at 8 a.m., while crossing the bows of the homeward bound convoy H.X. 126, so badly mauled by Wohlfarth, Kuppisch and others four days before, he altered course from a little north of west to a little south of it, and three hours later swung a further 20° to port to a course of south-west. As time went by and the *Bismarck* continued steering south-south-west, it seemed to Brind less and less likely that she would double back north, and he urged Tovey to steer a more southerly course. But Tovey, fearing a break-out to the west as much as a return north, maintained the course of the fleet.

Meanwhile, thanks to the dogged persistence of *Suffolk*'s radar operators and *Norfolk*'s look-outs, the shadowing of the German squadron went on. Aircraft from Coastal Command in Iceland had also remained in touch since the battle with the *Hood* (one had flown alongside *Prinz Eugen* for several minutes, found her fire uncomfortably accurate, identified her positively as the *Admiral Scheer*), gave Wake-Walker helpful reports during the early part of the day. As the forenoon wore on *Bismarck* gradually dropped speed while carrying out repairs to the bows, first to 26 knots, then 24, and *Norfolk* on her port quarter found herself slowly creeping up on her beam. *Prince of Wales* in turn had taken advantage of *Bismarck*'s reduction of speed to close the distance between herself and *Norfolk*. Wake-Walker signalled Leach to take station astern, asked how things were: Leach replied he was again ready for action, though still engaged in washing down the bridge to remove the remains of the men killed there.

Soon the visibility deteriorated, *Bismarck* disappeared in the mist, *Suffolk* found herself temporarily out of radar touch. *Norfolk*, followed by *Prince of Wales*, swished along in the mist for some time, now completely out of contact with the enemy. Suddenly Wake-Walker had a hunch, nothing more, that *Bismarck* had altered course to port across his bows, that the range between them was closing rapidly. He ordered Captain Phillips to turn 360° to port – a complete circle – before resuming his previous course, signalled *Prince of Wales* to follow him, thus lengthening the distance from *Bismarck* by three or four miles. Forty minutes later the mist cleared, revealed *Bismarck* only eight miles away, dead ahead. She had in fact altered course to due south – a turn to port of thirty degrees – only minutes after *Norfolk* had started to circle. But for Wake-Walker's intuition the two ships would have closed each other in the mist unseen, met beam to beam a mile or two apart, there *Bismarck* would have blown *Norfolk* out of the water.

For Tovey the news of *Bismarck*'s alteration to the south, i.e. slightly towards him, was greatly encouraging. He and Brind made calculations on the chart, concluded that if *Bismarck* were to maintain this course and speed, they would be in action with her and *Prinz Eugen* early next morning. But what if the Germans put on a burst of speed during the night, zigzagged violently, broke away westwards or to the north? He had only one weapon that could slow *Bismarck* down, make the action more certain – the carrier *Victorious* and her Swordfish torpedo planes. Captain Bovell had told him before sailing that the maximum range he could launch an attack and get his planes back was a hundred miles. If *Victorious* were to leave his flag now, steer a direct intercepting course towards the enemy, she should be a hundred miles from *Bismarck* by evening. He looked out of the bridge windows at where her flight-deck rose and fell in the long swell, at the huge curtain of spray climbing her bows, thought of her young airmen, some of whom had never flown on operations at sea before. Was it fair to baptise them on such a mission, did they have the smallest chance of success? But he thought of *Hood* too and her fourteen hundred dead and what would happen in the Atlantic if *Bismarck* got away. And he knew, as he had always known, that there was no choice. A little after three in the afternoon Tovey hoisted a signal to Rear-Admiral Alban Curteis in the *Galatea* to take *Victorious* and his four cruisers and proceed in execution of previous orders. 'Good luck,' he made to Bovell, and perhaps only Bovell knew how much they needed it. Then he ordered *King George V* and *Repulse* to turn forty degrees to port to a course of a little west of south, so that if *Bismarck* herself continued due south, there would be no danger of what sailors call 'losing bearing', i.e. getting behind her. He and Brind stood and watched *Victorious*, protected by Curteis's cruisers, standing on towards the still distant enemy in a flurry of spray, become a smudge on the south-western horizon, dip and disappear below the world's rim: from that moment she and her young aircrews were seldom out of their thoughts.

Visibility was patchy all day: the mist came and went, at times *Bismarck* was in sight of *Norfolk* and *Prince of Wales*, at others blotted out; but away on the starboard quarter *Suffolk* had regained radar contact and held it firmly.

In the forenoon morale on board *Bismarck* remained high. It was true they had been unable to shake off the shadowing cruisers despite frequent alteration of course, but that was only a matter of time; and if reinforcements arrived, they would deal with them as they had dealt with *Hood* and *Prince of Wales*. Search aircraft from Iceland that appeared and disappeared were a nuisance, but so long as the cruisers were in contact, they were to be expected. Few doubted they would shake off the enemy during the night, top up with fuel from one of the waiting tankers, make good the damage, then go on to attack allied shipping. Information in big ships circulates slowly; and to Müllenheim-Rechberg and others the news that *Bismarck* was to make for St Nazaire and *Prinz Eugen* was to operate independently came as a complete surprise.

In the early afternoon Lütjens signalled to Brinkmann his plan for the breakaway. During a rain squall *Bismarck* would make off to the west: *Prinz Eugen* was to maintain present course and speed for three hours, then steer for either of the tankers *Belchen* or *Lothringen* south-west of Greenland, replenish her tanks and proceed independently on cruiser warfare: the executive code-word for the movement was to be – an ironic touch – 'Hood'.

This was the first news Brinkmann had had that the two ships were to part company, for Lütjens had not informed him of his signal to Group West about St Nazaire. Puzzled, Brinkmann imagined the object of the manoeuvre was for one of the two ships to get clear of the shadowing cruisers (he assumed *Bismarck*, as *Prinz Eugen* with her superior speed would have a better chance of shaking them off later). He remained completely in the dark as to Lütjens's intentions for *Bismarck* after she had got clear, whether to operate her also independently or, because of the damage, make for Germany or France. The most likely explanation for this is that Lütjens had assumed *Prinze Eugen*'s wireless office had picked up his signals to Group West. But a more communicative admiral would have checked.

Before Brinkmann had time to query the situation there was an air-raid warning as another plane from Iceland made contact. Soon after a rain squall came up, *Bismarck* signalled 'Hood', and sheered off to the west. Twenty minutes later she was back in station, having sighted (and been sighted by) *Suffolk* shadowing by radar thirteen miles away on the starboard quarter.

And so the chase continued south; and at about this time Admiral Wake-Walker, batting along in the *Norfolk* ten miles astern, received from the British Admiralty a very disturbing signal.

The operations room of the British Admiralty was situated in a large, new, ugly concrete building, called the Citadel, adjacent to the old Admiralty building in Whitehall, London, close by the War Office and Nelson's column in Trafalgar Square, and just up the road from Downing Street and the Houses of Parliament. This was the heart and centre of the whole British naval war effort. There was a big map of the world on one wall, one of the Atlantic on another, and pins and flags showed the constantly shifting positions of our warships and convoys, as well as enemy surface craft and U-boats, sighted by aircraft or fixed by intelligence or radio direction finding. It was to this room that Tovey spoke on the green telephone from his flagship at Scapa. It was here that information and intelligence of all kinds, from ships, shore establishments, embassies, monitoring posts and agents all over the world flowed in; from here that operational instructions, commands, advice and situation reports to ships at sea went out. It was manned by fifteen or twenty officers and men who, ever since receiving Captain Denham's signal of *Bismarck*'s departure, had been at full stretch. The officers most concerned with important decisions at this time were Captain Edwards, Director of Operations; Captain Daniel, Director of Plans; Rear-Admiral Clayton; Commander Denning and Lieutenant-Commander Kemp of Naval Intelligence. Above them in the naval hierarchy were Rear-Admiral Power, Assistant Chief of the Naval Staff, Vice-Admiral Sir Tom Phillips, Vice-Chief of the Naval Staff, and the head of the Navy, Admiral of the Fleet Sir Dudley Pound, First Sea Lord. Any important operational signal going out from the Admiralty to the fleet at sea either originated from Pound or else had his approval.

Of all the admirals involved in the *Bismarck* operation it was

Dudley Pound about whom opinion was most divided.[5] He had had a distinguished career, been flag captain of the battleship *Colossus* at Jutland, but was now a sick man, had only become First Sea Lord because other, more senior officers had been even iller than himself. He had a tumour of the brain that was eventually to kill him, also a disease of the hip that caused him pain and insomnia. Before the war, when Commander-in-Chief, Mediterranean, he was sometimes to be seen pacing the deck of the flagship in the dead hours of night: the Fleet Medical Officer thought him unfit to command in time of war but couldn't bring himself to tell the Admiralty. He was not really fit to be a wartime First Sea Lord, with all the strains of office: pain and loss of sleep at night meant that he sometimes dozed off at daytime meetings. But he was flattered by the Prime Minister's trust in him; and Churchill liked him because he was often amenable to his wishes.

Those who worked with Pound at the Admiralty at this time speak of him with affection, tell of his courtesy and patience and long hours of work. But with those subordinate to him at sea and abroad, it was a different matter. It may have been irritability due to poor health, or impotence with Churchill that made him flex the muscles of office, but there are too many instances of his disciplining or threatening to discipline senior officers for what he considered dereliction of duty; like his impulsive inquiry into Admiral Somerville's conduct in the action off Cape Spartivento and his summary dismissal of Admiral North from Gibraltar for failing to stop a French squadron passing the Straits, an error that had nothing to do with North, was entirely the fault of Whitehall.

But his most besetting sin was what sailors call 'back-seat driving', constantly going over the heads of appointed admirals, trying to run operations from Whitehall, thinking that he knew best. 'He was neither a great tactician nor a great strategist,' wrote Tovey 'but unfortunately he believed he was.' Tovey's staff officers, like Brind and Bingley and Lloyd, speak feelingly of the stream of instructions that came pouring down the line from him in London whenever the Fleet was in harbour, and which added to their work rather than eased it.

As the day of the 24th wore on, as morning gave way to afternoon and the German squadron continued unmolested southwards, each mile bringing them nearer the shipping lanes – and in particular troop convoy WS8B – it seemed to Churchill and others in high office a strange thing that Admiral Wake-Walker should be content to let *Prince of Wales* trail along in *Bismarck*'s wake, make no effort to re-engage and slow her up. Now Pound of all people knew from the maps in the operations room the exact situation – indeed his staff had sent out a helpful situation report that morning informing British ships in the area of each other's whereabouts. He knew *Victorious* was on her way to launch a torpedo attack, that *King George V* and *Repulse* were also closing the enemy, could be expected to make contact next morning. He also knew, for it was his job, of the virtues of concentration, of Nelson's great dictum, 'Only numbers can annihilate,' indeed was about to signal *Ramillies* not to engage *Bismarck* unless she was already engaged with other ships. Nevertheless, and doubtless because of Churchill's prodding, he sent a signal to Wake-Walker *asking what his intentions were about* Prince of Wales *re-engaging*.

Wake-Walker received the signal in the late afternoon, was much shaken. The more he looked at it, the clearer the implication was; that the Admiralty would not have asked his intentions about *Prince of Wales* re-engaging if they did not think that was what she ought to be doing, and that he, not having ordered it, was lacking in offensive spirit – a charge on which commanders in wartime are understandably sensitive. He drafted and tore up several replies before signalling that he did not consider *Prince of Wales* should re-engage until other heavy ships made contact or failed to, adding he doubted whether she had the speed to force an action. Tovey, hearing this exchange of signals in *King George V*, was as pleased with Wake-Walker's reply as he was angry at the Admiralty's inquiry. Wake-Walker was doing what he wanted in keeping *Prince of Wales* in touch, but out of battle, until his arrival, and he had no desire to risk further damage to her, or the cruisers losing contact. He decided that if the Admiralty sent any further such signals, he himself would break wireless silence to tell them Wake-Walker's conduct was entirely in accordance with his wishes.

Later the Admiralty sent *Norfolk* and *Suffolk* a signal congratulating them on their shadowing, urging them to keep up the good work, but by this time the damage had been done. Wake-Walker told his staff he proposed to order *Prince of Wales* to take station ahead of *Norfolk*, and *Suffolk* to close in from twelve miles to the westward to five, so he could manoeuvre his ships as a force. His flag-lieutenant David Kelburn and *Norfolk*'s navigating officer Norman Todd implored him not to move *Suffolk* from where she was, as it would make shadowing more difficult. But the admiral was adamant. He was going to order *Prince of Wales* to creep up on *Bismarck*'s port quarter, attack her from astern, then retire with his force to the eastwards in the hope of luring *Bismarck* towards the Commander-in-Chief. What reason he imagined would induce *Bismarck* to go eastwards, it is hard to say, but that was his story and he was sticking to it: no more Admiralty signals were going to suggest he was lacking in offensive spirit.

In *Prinz Eugen* meanwhile, two miles ahead of *Bismarck* and out of sight of the British squadron, Commander Busch woke in the staff medical officer's cabin from an afternoon sleep. Earlier he had missed the sound of the ship's alarm bells, been roused by the bark of the quick-firing anti-aircraft guns above his head: when he reached the desk, the firing was over, the aircraft was a shadower from Iceland that had strayed a little too near. On the way back to his cabin Busch stopped to talk to the off duty seamen, resting on stacked hammocks in the after passageway, asked them to be sure to wake him if the alarm bells sounded again. He told them the story of the paymaster of a cruiser in the first war who slept through most of an action in the North Sea, only woke when the ship was hit aft, shouted out angrily, 'Yes, for God's sake, come in!'

Now he went on deck, found the sea rougher than in the morning, little heads of foam breaking on the grey swell, nothing in sight but *Bismarck*, black and massive, astern. He climbed to the bridge, found Beck the navigating officer with a sheaf of signals in his hand, cap under arm, the wind ruffling his red hair. Jasper was sucking a boiled sweet from a bag the officer of the watch was handing round, and Brinkmann, smart in his blue battledress, was smoking his usual cigar.

They told him of the *Bismarck*'s unsuccessful efforts to get away, then as he had the next watch, he went to the wardroom for an early dinner. The normal lighting was not on, the place seemed dark and cheerless, sombre as a Rembrandt painting. At one end the deck was littered with the hammocks of the after turret's crew, beyond at the games table officers were drinking, beer playing skat and doppelkopf. At the other end half a dozen officers were sitting at the horseshoe dining table. One or two newcomers had changed into white mess coats, most kept on duty monkey-jackets, ready for action if the alarm bells rang. They picked at the food, pickled herrings and baked potatoes with bacon and onion sauce, ate mostly in silence. Busch sensed an atmosphere of depression. They were all tired and tense, the cruisers had been in touch for nearly twenty-four hours, it seemed they could never shake them off: unconsciously they were listening for the alarm bells which had been sounding on and off all day, shrill and urgent, tearing at frayed nerves, warning of God knows what. The whole of the British Navy was after them, seeking a terrible vengeance: soon other ships would arrive, and even if they disposed of them and escaped damage again, there would be others and then others to take their place. The whine and rumble of the turbine shafts racing beneath them, the vibration of deck and bulkhead, the clatter of cutlery and glasses marathon-dancing on the table, were messages that every minute and metre were taking them farther into the unknown. 'If there's an alert now,' said the shipwright lieutenant, echoing their thoughts, 'it won't be aircraft, it'll be the other thing. And that'll be something to be getting on with.'

Busch went on watch again at 6 p.m., reported on the bridge to Jasper, noticed it was getting misty. Brinkmann, having heard no more from Lütjens about 'Hood', was assuming he had abandoned the idea, was now busy drafting his own proposals. 'To Fleet Commander from *Prinz Eugen*,' he dictated to the signalman, 'Submit either (a) *Bismarck* and *Prinz Eugen* draw enemy across own U-boats. If contact is broken, make for tanker *Belchen*. If contact maintained continue southwards, shifting *Esso Hamburg* and *Spichern* northwards. Join battle if forced by enemy. Otherwise refuel. At some juncture fuel situation must become critical for enemy too. Or (b) Proceed in company direct to *Belchen* or *Lothringen* and refuel in spite of enemy shadowers. If enemy engages, join battle.'

He was about to send this signal to *Bismarck* when the flagship's own signal lamp started winking. '*Prinz Eugen* from Fleet,' shouted the signalman. The message was brief, four letters only flashing across the empty sea. 'Hood,' sang out the signalman, and even as they watched, *Bismarck* swung away to starboard, into the mists, her main turrets already easing round towards the enemy, her anti-aircraft guns thick and erect as bristles, looking to Busch like drawn swords: slowly the mist swallowed her, all but her fighting top sliding down the sky, then that disappeared too.

A long time went by, *Prinz Eugen* drove on southwards, the mist began to clear. From astern they heard the low rumble of *Bismarck*'s guns, saw the yellow and orange flashes, brown cordite smoke welling up the sky. Men came up from mess-decks and washroom, cabin and galley, crowded the guard-rails to see for themselves. Briefly *Bismarck* came into sight on the north-western horizon, still firing, militant and proud, said Busch, wearing a halo of smoke from the salvoes of her turrets. 'There goes our big brother,' said Jasper on the bridge. 'We're going to miss him very, very much.' Like Tovey watching *Hood* glide out of Scapa Flow only three days before, he and the rest of *Prinz Eugen*'s crew, passing out of this story, looked at their country's greatest warship for the last time.

CHAPTER

6

So instead of Wake-Walker initiating the action with *Bismarck* he had planned, *Bismarck* had got in first. When she disappeared into the mist, *Suffolk* was thirteen miles on her starboard quarter, easing her way over towards *Norfolk* and *Prince of Wales*. Captain Ellis had been resting his radar set and its tired crew, now he switched on again. It was just as well, the range started coming down rapidly. When it was at ten miles Ellis put the wheel over to port and increased speed. *Bismarck* emerged from the mist, heading straight for *Suffolk*, fired an opening salvo. The white geysers gushed up silently a thousand yards astern, later ones fell near enough to loosen rivets in the plating aft. *Suffolk* replied with nine broadsides, mostly short, retired behind a smoke-screen when Wake-Walker signalled, 'Do not waste ammunition'. The blast from B turret, firing aft, had smashed all the bridge windows, opened the enclosed, steam-heated bridge to icy winds and spray. *Norfolk* and *Prince of Wales* hurried over, opened fire at *Bismarck* at 15 miles: *Bismarck* fired three salvoes, *Prince of Wales* twelve before two of her guns again went out of action. 'I am sure this opportunity to re-engage must have had a good effect on her', Wake-Walker wrote breezily later. He hoped it had had a good effect on the Admiralty too.

Bismarck turned west, then south: Lütjens had accomplished one task in enabling *Prinz Eugen* to slip away, but if he had had hopes of getting *Bismarck* clear too, they were soon disappointed: Argus-eyed *Suffolk*'s radar never lost touch. Wake-Walker formed the squadron

10. *'One saw nothing but an agony of water, grey-green or blue-black, spume-tossed, marble-streaked . . .'* H.M.S. **Sheffield** *on patrol in the Denmark Straits*

11. *'. . . Flying Officer Suckling . . . made a run over the fjords, opened the shutter.'* **Bismarck** *in Grimstad Fjord, from 25,000 feet up, May 21st, 1941*

12. 'the two ships . . . entered the quiet waters of Korsford.' **Bismarck** and **Prinz Eugen** still camouflaged, in Norwegian waters

13. **Bismarck** leaving Grimstad Fjord

in line ahead, *Suffolk* leading, *Prince of Wales* supporting her in the centre, *Norfolk* in the rear. At first he thought of stationing them on *Bismarck*'s starboard quarter 'in order', as he put it, 'to push her to the eastwards' (how or why he thought he would accomplish this he never explained) then discarded it for the port quarter, the side on which *King George V* and *Repulse* would eventually engage. This line ahead formation was not the best for shadowing, as David Kelburn and others again pointed out, for it left no ships on *Bismarck*'s other side; but having been about to attack *Bismarck* himself, then been attacked by her, he felt the need to keep his ships together as a fighting force – even if it meant some sacrifice in efficient shadowing. But he assured *Prince of Wales* he did not intend her to engage *Bismarck* again until Tovey's arrival in the morning.

And so things continued as before, except that now the Admiralty sent a signal warning of U-boats, and Wake-Walker ordered the force to zigzag together, the port runs taking them away from *Bismark*, the starboard ones back towards her. In *Bismarck* there was much satisfaction that *Prinz Eugen* had got away so cleanly, was over forty miles away, beyond the southern horizon: all that remained now was for the flagship to slip away during the night. The optimism spread with the arrival of a signal from Saalwächter sending congratulations on the sinking of *Hood*, saying that preparations for *Bismarck*'s reception were going ahead at St Nazaire and Brest, advising Lütjens to shake off the enemy by withdrawing temporarily to a remote sea area. By steering south-south-west for the U-boat patrol line half-way between Greenland and Newfoundland, this is just what he was doing.

And then later, came the announcement on the German wireless network to stand by for a special naval announcement. They knew this was not another of Dönitz's U-boat triumphs, it could only refer to them. Word was sent down to the wireless office to plug in the network to the loudspeaker system, tune the set carefully to minimise hissing and crackling, for they were a long way from home. Everywhere on board, and in *Prinz Eugen* too, in mess-deck and turret, engine-room and control position, men stopped their chatter, put down cards, roused themselves from sleep, crowded round the speakers so as not to lose a word. First came the familiar voice of the announcer: 'This is Berlin,' and those who knew Berlin, like Busch, remembered it, and those who didn't, imagined it, brave and beautiful. Then came a band playing the naval anthem, stirring enough on its own, but in this context, as an overture, overwhelming. The music ended, there was a brief pause, then the announcer read the despatch from the Supreme Command, how the battleship *Bismarck* on a mission in the Atlantic had sunk the pride of the British Navy, the great battle-cruiser *Hood*, was now proceeding on further operations. And throughout *Bismarck* officers and men from Lütjens down to the humblest able seaman were in a turmoil of pride, for this was their victory that was being celebrated, it was to them alone, in the wild Atlantic and two thousand miles from home, that the whole German nation was paying homage. And later from the nightly request concert in the big hall of the Deutschlandsender in Berlin, crowded with war wounded, arms workers, nurses, they heard Heinz Gödecke's familiar voice announcing a request for the *Bismarck:* '*Komme zurück.*' 'Come back!' In *Prinz Eugen* there was disappointment that she (because of security perhaps) had not been mentioned on either occasion, that families would not know of their share in the battle. 'True,' said one man, 'but at least they won't have to worry about us either.'

Yet this was the last good news in *Bismarck* for some time. For the fleet engineer officer, Thannemann, and the ship's engineer officer, Lehmann, had been doing their sums, and now they reported to Lütjens the seriousness of the fuel situation. The problem was this: If *Bismarck* continued on her present course, drew the shadowers over the U-boat line, she would have ample fuel to reach *Belchen* or *Lothringen*, even to run down to *Spichern* or *Esso Hamburg* near the Azores. But say she was prevented from reaching any of her oilers, say the U-boats failed to torpedo the shadowers and she herself was unable to shake them off (and for over twenty-four hours now, in snow-storms and rain squalls, daytime and dark, they had shown an amazing capacity for hanging on) then they would be marooned in mid-Atlantic with insufficient fuel to reach France. True, the shadowers might soon have fuel problems of their own, but they couldn't bank on it, and anyway others might be coming to take their place. If on the other hand they abandoned the U-boat patrol line, made for France now, there would be adequate reserves for the journey, providing nothing unforeseen happened. Looked at in that light there could be no choice. Just before 10 p.m. Lütjens signalled Group West: 'Impossible to shake off enemy owing to radar. Proceeding directly to Brest because of fuel situation,' and ordered Lindemann to come round from south-south-west to due south. There was no dry-dock at Brest big enough to hold *Bismarck* but it was 100 miles nearer than St Nazaire, they would get oil for the tanks and land-based air cover that much sooner.

Meanwhile, unknown to Lütjens, the *Victorious* and her escorting cruisers were slowly closing from the eastwards. Captain Bovell had hoped to be within 100 miles of *Bismark* by 9 p.m., fly off his striking force then, but Lütjens's diversion to the west to allow *Prinz Eugen* to slip away had opened the gap and by 10 p.m. he was still 120 miles away. This was beyond the maximum operational range he had laid down, but the weather was deteriorating hourly with low cloud, rain squalls and a rising north-wester, and though it would be light until after midnight (ship's clocks were four hours ahead of local time) the longer departure was postponed, the greater the difficulties of the planes finding the enemy, returning safely to the ship.

There were to be nine aircraft in the attack, ancient Swordfish biplanes, 'Stringbags' the Navy called them, looked like survivors of Richthofen's Circus, cruising speed 95 mph and that was pushing it. Each carried a crew of three, pilot, observer, rear gunner, and an 18-inch torpedo slung below the belly. The squadron was divided into three sub-flights led by Eugene Esmonde, the squadron commander, Percy Gick, a former instructor at the Torpedo School, and 'Speed' Pollard (so called because of his lethargy), all regular R.N. officers: these were the only men of experience, the others were mostly reservists, some had never been in a carrier before. Earlier the twenty-seven of them had been briefed by Commander Ranald, the flight operations officer, shown silhouettes of the mighty *Bismarck*, had explained to them the method of attack. Now, dressed in bulky flying jackets with little red lights and whistles attached, they sat about in the crews' rest-room, smoking cigarettes, thumbing through dog-eared magazines. Few could concentrate on anything but what lay ahead. Soon they would be required to take off from this swaying bucket, fly over a hundred miles in decreasing visibility to look for a moving target that might alter course at any moment, find it, attack it, survive its devastating fire power, return in darkness to *Victorious*, land in darkness too. The more one looked at it, the more ridiculous it seemed. Asked in the mess how they regarded their prospects, they put on a bold front to keep up their spirits, said absurd things like 'A piece of cake!' and 'No trouble at all', which convinced nobody, not even themselves: if asked, they would have offered no odds at all on their chances of survival.

Soon after 10 p.m., at about the time that Lütjens was deciding about Brest, orders came down from the bridge for the squadron to go. The nine planes were squatting at the end of the slippery flight deck like a covey of damp partridges. The deck staff started engines, the crews clambered in and fixed the straps. The *Victorious* turned to starboard, into the north-west wind, reduced speed from 28 to 15 knots. The first plane trundled down the flight-deck, took off, then the second, presently the whole squadron were airborne without mishap. They formed up on Esmonde, turned away from the ship, set course south-west. As they were swallowed up in a rain squall Captain Bovell wondered if he would ever see any of them again.

Some thirty miles ahead of *Bismarck* when she turned to her new course, a solitary vessel with grey upperworks and a yellow mast, pushed her way slowly through the evening drizzle and swell. She was the United States Coastguard Cutter *Modoc*, 1800 tons, from 1922 until the war part of the North Atlantic International Ice Patrol: for the past three days she had been searching for boats and survivors from torpedoed ships of the H.X. 126 convoy attacked by Wohlfarth and his fellow U-boat commanders on 20th May.

Although it was to be another seven months before America entered the German war, she had already shown where her sympathies lay; with the country of which she had once been a part, whose language she shared, whose institutions had been models for her own. In March President Roosevelt declared that the defence of Britain was vital to the defence of the United States, authorised the Lend-Lease Act which gave to Britain millions of tons of desperately-needed food and weapons of war. In April, when the first food ships left, he pledged American responsibility for the defence of Greenland, and it was to relieve her sister-ship *Northland* as part of the Greenland Survey Expedition that *Modoc*, commanded by Lieutenant-Commander H. Belford, U.S.C.G., sailed from Boston on 12th May.

Eight days later the two ships met, there was an exchange of mail and a conference between the captains. *Northland* departed for Boston but within hours received wireless orders to cancel her return and with *Modoc* to search for survivors from H.X. 126. *Northland* steamed off in the direction of the sinkings, two days later sighted bodies in the water, three boats and a raft, all empty, later met a British destroyer and armed trawler, part of the convoy's escort, which had already picked up 120 survivors. All this time there was a westerly gale blowing, so *Modoc* made a long cast to the eastwards to search for boats that might have drifted down-wind. On the way she sighted two rafts and a boat, all showing signs of recent occupation.

On 24th May about 6.30 p.m. by *Modoc*'s clocks (which were one hour behind local time and five hours behind the British fleet) she was steaming slowly north-westwards. Earlier in the day she heard by radio of the sinking of the *Hood*, and a chance meeting between *Northland* and the British corvette *Arabis* (which was taking in *Norfolk*'s shadowing reports) revealed that *Bismarck* was continuing south. It seemed unlikely the chase would come her way, but earlier when she and *Northland* had entered the war zone, they had hoisted outsize United States Coastguard ensigns, illuminated themselves by night, broadcast their positions every hour, to avoid possible mis-understandings.

It was a dull, grey evening, with the wind coming from ahead, the spray falling like light rain on the fo'c'sle as the bows breasted the swell. Lieutenant Bacchus, officer of the watch, and look-outs on *Modoc*'s bridge swept their glasses from beam to beam. For days now they had seen nothing but tossing seas and low, grey clouds, endured the long, slow rolling of the ship, suffered an eternity of fatigue and boredom: some of the men, from the ports and villages of New England, understood why they were there, this was their bailiwick, but to others, with names like Krankel and Bledroth and Unter-meyer, from Kansas and Milwaukee and the sunny cities of the Pacific coast, it seemed a kind of off-beat assignment. Their war was to come.

Then in an instant boredom vanished. There swam into the lenses of the port forward lookout's binoculars, as there had swum into the lenses of Able Seaman Newell's binoculars only the night before, the outlines of a giant battleship. It was the *Bismarck*, speeding south. She herself must have sighted *Modoc* at about the same time, but gave no indication of it: from Group North she had received fre-quent reports of *Modoc*'s movements, was fully expecting her.

From below decks in *Modoc* men swarmed up to see *Bismarck* for themselves, were electrified as others had been, at the power and massiveness and beauty of her. They had heard of the *Hood* before today, what sailor hadn't, some had even seen her, yet that very morning this very ship, her huge guns trained fore and aft, had taken only five minutes to sink her. How many other vessels would she soon be sending to the bottom? They had heard that she herself was unsinkable, looking at her they could well believe it.

This glimpse of *Bismarck* as she sailed by on her day of triumph had smashed the grey monotony of their trip like a brick through a frosted window, was something to chew over and talk about until they got home, tell later to families and friends. It was enough, Heaven knows, they weren't asking for more, but they got it. From the low clouds above them, there dropped like leaves in autumn eight of the craziest-looking planes you ever saw, each with two wings and struts, two fixed wheels and a single propeller, things the Wright brothers or Blériot might have flown an age ago. The planes sped off towards the *Bismarck*, from the battleship's huge upperworks the orange and yellow flak burst like fireworks, some, in Belford's words 'whizzed dangerously close to our bows'. Next in hot pursuit of *Bismarck* came speeding two cruisers and another battleship. As *Modoc*'s men watched them approach, they saw with horror the battleship's guns being trained on them: Wake-Walker, less well-informed than Lütjens, had mistaken *Modoc* for *Bismarck*, hoisted the signal to open fire. Fortunately *Prince of Wales*'s answering pendant jammed, by the time it was cleared the mistake had been seen. The guns turned away in search of *Bismarck*, and a much shaken *Modoc* sped off into the mists to continue searching for the fellow countrymen of those who had so nearly blown her out of the water.

Yet if *Modoc* had been surprised by the appearance of Esmonde and his flock (less one, which had erred and strayed), they were no less surprised by her. Flying from *Victorious* at 85 m.p.h., they had found *Bismarck* by radar an hour and a quarter later, gone back into cloud to make their attack, failed to relocate her, made for *Norfolk* to get their bearings. From here they streaked off in the wrong direction, so David Kelburn seized a bridge signal lamp and re-directed them: Esmonde's plane flashed back 'O.K.' Up they went into cloud, soon got another radar echo, dived down to attack *Bismarck*, found to their astonishment *Modoc* instead. It was an unfortunate error, for it alerted *Bismarck*, took away all surprise: Esmonde's ailerons were hit when still four miles away.

In *Bismarck* they watched the approach of the Swordfish with amazement and admiration. 'It was incredible to see such obsolete-looking planes,' said Müllenheim-Rechberg, 'having the nerve to attack a fire-spitting mountain like *Bismarck*.' But attack they did. Esmonde's sub-flight came in low on the port beam, dropped their torpedoes at half a mile range: a minute later Gick's three planes attacked on the port bow, Gick himself was unsatisfied with his run-in, turned and came in again against an inferno of fire. In *Bismarck* the din was terrific, with shells and bullets from fifty guns including the main armament firing in an unbroken stream: one gun got so over-heated it had to be cooled with a fire hose. On the bridge Leading Seaman Hansen at the wheel was so deafened by the noise he couldn't hear Lindemann's helm orders, decided himself when to throw the wheel over to comb the torpedo tracks. He was successful with all planes but one. While Esmonde and Gick were attacking from the port side, Sub-Lieutenant Lawson of the Reserve crept round to the starboard side where he was silhouetted against the sunset, dropped his torpedo, zoomed up to the clouds. Once more Hansen threw the wheel over, this time too late. Seconds later one of the shadowing Fulmar monoplanes which had left *Victorious* after the Swordfish observed a huge column of water shoot up amidships on *Bismarck*'s starboard side, followed by a burst of black smoke from the funnel.

Miraculously not one of the Swordfish was shot down or even badly damaged. One reason was that *Bismarck*'s frequent keeling over as she continually altered course made it extremely difficult for the lighter guns to stay on target. And Gick, remembering the black shell-bursts ahead of him, thought the German gunners, not believing that any warplane could fly so slowly, had allowed too much deflection.

But now they had to find their way back to *Victorious*, still nearly a hundred miles away. On the carrier's bridge Captain Bovell and Commander Ranald waited anxiously, watched the night close around them: it was far darker than the night before, for they had come 500 miles south, were now on the latitude of Aberdeen; and to add to their worries the aircraft homing beacon had broken down. At about 1 a.m. when the aircraft were due back, Captain Bovell had a signal projector switched on, swept it slowly through all points of the compass. But the ship entered a rain squall, visibility became zero, the aircraft failed to see the signal lamp, flew on and past. 1.15 came, 1.30, 1.45. Now Bovell really began to worry, for soon the planes would be out of fuel. It was getting on for 2 a.m. when Esmonde sighted a red lamp signalling from Admiral Curteis's bridge, and Bovell and Ranald, crazy with relief, heard the sound of approaching engines. *Victorious* turned into the wind and one after the other the pilots, including three who had never made a night landing before, somehow or other reached the deck: the engine of one plane, empty of fuel, cut out at the moment it was pulled up by the arrester wires. Gick's air gunner, Petty Officer Sayer, got out half-frozen: a shell splash from one of *Bismarck*'s 15-inch guns had knocked the flooring from under him, so that he was suspended above the sea; all the way back he kept complaining on the inter-com, 'Bloody draughty back here.'

There was no sign of two of the Fulmars, so Bovell kept his signal projector sweeping hopefully. But it was a beacon for U-boats and an hour later Admiral Curteis ordered him to switch it off. Bovell, caring only for his lost children, pretended he hadn't understood, kept the light going. A second signal was sent, more peremptory: Bovell, not wanting a court-martial, had no option but obey. Later he was to learn that both planes had come down in the sea and that, amazingly, the crews of both had been picked up by passing ships.

The night wore on, the main forces slowly converged. From *King George V*, steering south-west at 28 knots with *Repulse* and destroyers, Tovey wirelessed to Wake-Walker that he hoped to meet the enemy about 9 a.m., and to *Repulse* whose armour was even flimsier than *Hood*'s, he signalled to keep 5,000 yards outside him and not to engage until the flagship had opened fire. For the men of these ships action was now only a few hours away, as it had been the night before for the men of *Hood* and *Prince of Wales*. Like them, they felt the cold hand of fear on the skin, wondered when the time came how it would go for them, well or ill. But with this difference: yesterday the *Bismarck* was an unknown quantity, the British sailors believed they could give as good as they got; today *Hood*'s fourteen hundred dead and the ravaged *Prince of Wales* were eloquent witnesses of what *Bismarck* could do. And in *Prince of Wales* herself, despite the favourable odds and Wake-Walker's wishful thinking that battle would do them good, men who had been through it once the day before steeled themselves to go through it again: some remained alert at their posts, watchful and brooding, remembered what had passed, imagined what was to come; others, tired out, dozed, want-ing to be fresh in the morning; and many who had never prayed before, asked to be allowed to live.

Because of the brush with *Modoc*, Wake-Walker temporarily lost touch with *Bismarck*, didn't sight her again until an hour after the torpedo attack when she appeared eight miles away. *Prince of Wales* fired two salvoes, *Bismarck* replied with two, none accurate, then contact was lost again in the gathering dark. *Suffolk*, though, con-tinued to hold *Bismarck* by radar.

In *Bismarck*, to help morale and justify the piles of empty shell cases which lay like anthills about the ship, all sorts of extravagant claims were made about damage to the Swordfish. Lieutenant Doelker, Manthey's divisional officer, told him 27 aircraft had attacked altogether, two waves of torpedo planes and one of bombers, that five had been shot down. The ship's loudspeaker system confirmed it, adding the cryptographers had decoded enemy wireless signals saying that only one of the attacking planes had regained its carrier. Whether these claims were inventions or imaginings, it is impossible to tell. On occasions like these men believe what they want to believe, see what they want to see.

The torpedo had done little damage. Although set to run at 31 feet where it would tear out the ship's bowels, do the maximum injury, it was what's called a surface-runner, struck the armoured belt just below the water-line, according to Ordinary Seaman Manthey did no more than scratch the paint. The explosion went upwards, not inwards, the blast lifted some men standing near the aircraft catapult off their feet, smashed Chief Boatswain Kirschberg's skull against the hangar and killed him, broke three airmen's legs. Kirschberg was *Bismarck's* first fatal casualty, his death caused depression among the crew, for he was one of the senior ratings, a character, very popular: they sewed his body in sailcloth, put it in one of the boats. The three airmen were carried to the sickbay, had their legs set in plaster, joined the stokers of No. 2 boiler-room scalded after the hit there by one of *Prince of Wales's* shells.

Yet if the torpedo damage was negligible, there was much concern about No. 2 boiler-room and the forward oil tanks, where the earlier damage had been aggravated by the high speed twisting and turning as Hansen combed the tracks. No. 2 boiler-room was now completely flooded, had to be abandoned, forward the collision mats and caulking had been displaced, the water poured in, the ship again went down by the bows. Speed was reduced to 16 knots to allow divers to go down and reset the collision mats, bring in more pumps. An hour later, sufficient repairs had been made to allow an increase to 20 knots: this was within a knot of the ship's 'most economical' speed, i.e. the highest speed at which the precious fuel would last longest.

For Lütjens and his staff two things had become paramount: to abandon the somewhat leisurely course they were steering (it veered between south and south-south-east), down the middle of the Atlantic, cut away direct for France as soon as possible; and secondly, and even more important, escape the shadowing cruisers. The attack by the Swordfish meant there was an enemy carrier within a hundred miles: other planes would be back in the morning for certain, and while luck had seen them through one attack, it might not in another. Also, Lütjens had heard from Group West earlier that evening of Force H's departure from Gibraltar for 'an unknown destination'; and he guessed that unless he could give the cruisers the slip, it would be only a matter of time before *Ark Royal's* planes also found him.

Fortunately for Lütjens a means of escape now came to hand. As the night went on, it became evident to him and his staff from the hydrophone office (which was listening to the strength and bearing of the shadower's screws), from the rangefinders, and also perhaps from the radar, that not only were there no British ships on the starboard side, but that those on the port side were continuing the zigzag observed earlier, at times coming to within twelve miles of *Bismarck*, at others increasing the distance considerably. If *Bismarck* were to turn sharply to the west and increase speed by a few knots when the British ships were going away from her, would the amazing antennae with which they seemed to be equipped notice the movement, would they follow her round as they had done on every occasion when she had tried to escape before?

There was everything to be gained, nothing to be lost by trying; and soon after 3 a.m. Lindemann ordered the helmsman to put the wheel over to starboard. Slowly the ship began to describe a huge loop, through west and north-west to north, through north and north-east to east, three hours later crossed her own wake and that of her shadowers, steadied on a course of 130°, almost due south-east, pointed at the north-western corner of Spain, south-western corner of the Bay of Biscay – pointed too, though Lütjens was not to know it,

123

at the ships of Force H thirteen hundred miles away, battling north-wards into a north-westerly gale, and at that very moment taking in a signal from the Admiralty: 'Cancel my signal ordering Force H to join Convoy WS8B as escort. Steer to intercept *Bismarck*.'

The zigzag that Wake-Walker had ordered meant altering course up to thirty degrees either side of the mean. To have kept to this so that *Bismarck* was within radar range on the port (outward) leg would have meant the squadron getting dangerously close to her when on the starboard (inward) leg; so it was agreed that *Suffolk* should temporarily lose radar contact when on the outward leg, regain it ten or fifteen minutes later on the inward leg. As things turned out it would have been better if Wake-Walker had accepted the U-boat risk, zigzagged just a few degrees either side of the mean line of advance, better still if he had ordered *Suffolk* back to her well-tried position on *Bismarck*'s starboard quarter. But Pound's signal still nagged at him, he felt it essential to keep his ships together.

The crews of *Norfolk* and *Suffolk*, the captains and bridge officers especially, were near to exhaustion. In *Norfolk* Wake-Walker and Captain Phillips had been kept going by the ship's doctor on Benzedrine and black coffee, now they agreed to split the night watches between them. In *Suffolk* Captain Ellis had no one similar to delegate authority to, was spending the fourth consecutive night on his bridge without sleep apart from catnaps: in addition he was lashed by gouts of wind that tore through the frames of the smashed bridge windows and drenched by showers of spray. The radar operators, themselves tired beyond tears, kept singing out the bearings and distance of the enemy in the flat, even monotones of an Anglican priest reciting matins. It seemed as though they had been doing it since time began, would go on doing it for ever. Tiredness, constant repetition, over-confidence had made them automatons, dulled them to the idea of anything new: at 2.30 a.m. and again at 3, they reported echoes of *two* enemy ships, not knowing *Prinz Eugen* had gone.* When at about 3.30 a.m. they failed to pick up *Bismarck* on

* These signals, when deciphered by German cryptographers ashore, led Group West into thinking *Bismarck* and *Prinz Eugen* were still in company.

the inward leg, at first no one thought greatly of it. They had lost and found her several times during the past 33 hours, soon they would find her again. But time passed and passed, and though *Suffolk* increased speed and kept on towards the west where she believed *Bismarck* had gone, there was not a sign or whisper of her. She had vanished as completely as if she had never been, and at 5 a.m. Ellis signalled to Wake-Walker: 'Have lost contact with enemy.'

CHAPTER

7

To Bovell in *Victorious* the news of *Suffolk*'s loss of contact was particularly galling, for if the three other Fulmars he had sent up during the night had done their job, they would still be in touch; and he had planned to launch a second Swordfish attack at 5 a.m. But the Fulmar observers simply didn't have the experience: they couldn't navigate to work the radio sets properly, and their signals, said Bovell, 'revealed a complete lack of knowledge of enemy reporting'. He was lucky to get the planes back to the ship.

But all was not lost. *Bismarck*'s last reported course had been 160° or south-south-east, which seemed to Bovell a clear indication that her destination must be France, and if so, she had either made some westing before turning south-east, or swung right round and cut back across her wake. He signalled Curteis for permission to fly off seven Swordfish at first light to search towards the east and south-east, and Curteis, who shared his conclusions, approved. The aircraft were got ready and lined up on the flight deck for departure at 7.30 a.m. Then at 7.16 a signal was received from Tovey ordering *Victorious*'s aircraft and escorting cruisers to search, not towards the east and north-east, but towards the west and north.

Tovey had been asleep in his bridge cabin when *Suffolk*'s loss of contact signal arrived, went at once to the plotting-room, was joined by Commodore Brind. Now Tovey knew as well as anyone that if *Bismarck* was still bound for France, the eastern to southern sector was where to find her. To assume she was continuing for France was a reasonable conjecture but not a certainty. There were other possibilities; that the damage she had received was so serious that she was returning to Germany by one of the northern passages; or alternatively that it was so slight that once she had lost the shadowing cruisers, she could steer north-west to the coast of Greenland to repair it, oil from a waiting tanker, go on to attack allied shipping. Ideally Tovey would have liked to cover all points of the compass, but he had not the ships or aircraft. If one of the three routes had to be discarded, it was clearly the one to France: *Bismarck* in Brest or St Nazaire might mean that he had failed to sink her but there she would be bottled up like *Scharnhorst* and *Gneisenau*, a target for bombers, temporarily out of harm's way; but *Bismarck* loose on the Atlantic trade-routes did not bear thinking about. So he ordered a search between south-west and north-east to a depth of a hundred miles: this would cover both a break-out to the west or a return to Germany by the Denmark Straits.

At 8 a.m. that morning the situation as God saw it was as follows. *Bismarck* was now east of all three British forces: north-east of Admiral Tovey's force (which had passed about 100 miles ahead of her at around 4 a.m.) south-east of Admiral Curteis's force (which had crossed her wake at around 6 a.m.) and due east of Admiral Wake-Walker's force. She was steering south-east at a speed of 20 knots while all the British ships were steering in a westerly direction, i.e. away from her. *Prince of Wales*, no longer needed to protect *Norfolk* and *Suffolk*, was on her way to join the Commander-in-Chief: she would take the place of *Repulse* which, very low in fuel and with prospects of an immediate action gone, was about to leave for Newfoundland to oil, and would search in that direction *en route*.

Four hundred miles to the south Captain Reid in *Ramillies*, thinking *Bismarck* was bound for an oiler near the Azores, altered course to the north-west; and east of *Ramillies* Commodore Blackman in the cruiser *Edinburgh* was also steering north-west along the track of *Bismarck* when last seen. Both these ships were on a parallel course to *Bismarck* and would (if all three continued it), pass well to the westward of her.

But 350 miles south-east of *Bismarck*, on the line of her course to

Brest, was the old battleship *Rodney*, which, it will be remembered, with four destroyers was escorting the troopship *Britannic* across the Atlantic before going to Boston to refit. The day before she had detached one destroyer, the *Eskimo*, to take *Britannic* on alone: the other three, *Somali*, *Tartar*, *Mashona*, had had to drop astern because of the weather, were now catching up. The *Rodney*, named after the famous admiral who defeated a French fleet off Dominica in 1782, was another oldish ship, built in 1927, 35,000 tons, nine 16-inch guns in three turrets. In both her and her sister ship *Nelson* turrets and superstructure were bunched together to save space, economise in armour plating: as a result they looked truncated, as if the designer had forgotten to add a proper stern. At this time *Rodney* was urgently in need of refit. One engine-room had recently broken down twice, leaving her dependent on a single propeller. Her maximum official speed was 23 knots, but she hadn't attained it in years. She had 500 passengers on board, drafts for the West Indies, the Falklands and Halifax, and her upper deck was stacked with crated stores for the refit.

Rodney's captain was Frederick Dalrymple-Hamilton, a big, tall Scot, owner of a property in Wigtownshire. When he first heard *Bismarck* was out, he formed a small operations committee; the commander and navigator, a Captain Coppinger who was taking passage to America, an American lieutenant-commander called Wellings, returning home after a spell as Assistant Naval Attaché in London, himself in the chair. They met in the charthouse two or three times a day, discussed the latest moves and signals, advised what action *Rodney* should take. After *Bismarck* was lost, they agreed that if she was bound for France, they would be excellently placed to intercept her, had best stay put and await events.

One other thing Dalrymple-Hamilton needed to do, inform Tovey and the Admiralty where he was. He was loath to make a radio signal that might be picked up by German D/F stations and passed to *Bismarck*, but it was essential. Early the day before a message from the Admiralty had told him to steer a certain course to close the enemy which he ignored as it was wildly wrong: as a result the Admiralty's latest broadcast situation report had placed *Rodney* some

4. Left 'companionable when you got to
know him, well read, very able,
intensely ambitious.' Vice-Admiral
Lancelot Holland, Commanding
Battlecruiser Squadron

5. Right 'top of his term as a cadet,
chain-smoker and coffee-drinker, blond
hair sleeked back.' Captain
Ernest Lindemann, Commanding
Officer, **Bismarck**

6. 'a big, congenial man, full of humour
and vitality.' Vice-Admiral Sir James
Somerville (right) and Captain Loben
Maund on the flight-deck of **Ark Royal**

17. *'There were exercises in towing and being towed . . .'* **Bismarck** and **Prinz Eugen** *in the Baltic. Note* **Bismarck's** *beam*

18. *'A tall, impressive looking man, very technically minded.'*
Rear-Admiral Frederick Wake-Walker on the bridge of **Norfolk** *while pursuing* **Bismarck** *and* **Prinz Eugen,** *May 23rd, 1941*

200 miles from where she actually was. So for the first and only time in the entire operation *Rodney* signalled briefly her position, ships in company, intentions.

Of the seven Swordfish which Captain Bovell had flown off at 7.30 that morning to search to the north and west, six returned to *Victorious* four hours later. But of 5H, piloted by Sub-Lieutenant Jackson, observer Sub-Lieutenant Berrill, air gunner Leading Airman Sparkes, there was no sign. *Victorious* called for a long time, the look-outs scanned the horizon, nobody answered, nothing came. Bovell felt the loss keenly, for 5H was manned by one of his best crews. Later, he wrote of its observer to the Admiralty:

'Sub-Lieutenant David Berrill failed to return to *Victorious* only a few hours after he had taken part in the attack against *Bismarck*. A year ago he took part as an observer in the bombing in broad daylight of the enemy gun emplacements behind Dunkirk. Of the ten aircraft sent on this operation five were shot down, and those that returned were well battered. A month later he was turned upside down in a Swordfish at night in a field while returning from a bombing raid. Some months afterwards he went into the sea in the back of a Swordfish over the side of H.M.S. *Furious* and again later on he went over again. I have never seen him dismayed under any circumstances . . . '

The events which Captain Dalrymple-Hamilton and his committee had decided to wait for were not long in coming: they were not what they expected and were to have equally unexpected results. In *Bismarck* that morning, Lütjens thought he was still being followed. 'One battleship and two heavy cruisers maintaining contact,' he signalled Group West at 7 a.m., although the last British contact with him had been four hours earlier. Why Lütjens thought this, it is hard to say. It could be that the strength of the wireless signals made by Wake-Walker at the time gave the impression of being nearer than they were; that the radar pulses from the British ships, though much too far to reach *Bismarck* and bounce back, were yet causing interference on her radar scan (assuming it was working again);[1] or simply that Wake-Walker's ships had been with him so long, had become so much a part of his life and times, that he and his staff had become brain-washed, mesmerised into thinking they must still be there. Whatever the reason, it was in this belief that at 6.54 a.m. and again at 7.48 a.m. he transmitted to Germany a long signal, about the efficiency of British radar, the engagement with *Hood*, damage to the oil tanks, the unreliability of *Bismarck*'s own radar – a thing he would not have dreamt of doing if he had thought he was alone, as only two days before Group North had sent a signal warning of the efficiency of British Radio Direction Finding.

In the event *Bismarck*'s transmissions were picked up by various D/F stations scattered about Britain, and the bearings passed to the operations staff at the Admiralty. They could hardly believe their luck, this was the sort of miracle they had been hoping for, the information that would give *Bismarck*'s position, show what direction she was steering. In the Admiralty Lieutenant-Commander Peter Kemp plotted the bearings on a gnomonic chart (the kind suitable for radio waves which follow the great circle of the earth): they were a pretty woolly set, the proximity of the D/F stations to each other and their great distance from *Bismarck* resulting in almost parallel lines, no bearings from Gibraltar or Iceland to give a nice 'cross-cut'; but they showed *Bismarck* to be south and east of her last reported position.

Kemp showed this to Rear-Admiral Jock Clayton, his immediate superior, suggested the position be radioed to Tovey immediately. Clayton said not to send the worked-out position, only the D/F bearings. Kemp protested it was hardly right to expect the C-in-C to do the Admiralty's homework for them in the middle of an important operation, but Clayton explained that before putting to sea Tovey and his Radio Intelligence Officer, Lieutenant-Commander Guernsey, had separately asked for bearings only and not a worked-out position: Tovey had two newly equipped D/F destroyers with him and hoped that one or both would provide a cross bearing, enable him to pinpoint where *Bismarck* had been.

So Kemp sent the bearings only and they reached the flagship soon after 10 a.m. But what Kemp and others at the Admiralty didn't know was that Tovey no longer had any destroyers, D/F or other-wise, with him: they had all left for Iceland at midnight because of shortage of fuel (of the two equipped with D/F, one had broken down with boiler trouble soon after leaving Scapa and returned to base, the other's D/F was out of action). Next, the bearings were plotted wrongly in the flagship; and as a result showed *Bismarck* to be, not south-east of her last reported position, as Kemp had found her and as she really was, but *north* of it; and the only deduction to draw from this was that she had reversed course, was returning to Germany by the Faeroes-Iceland gap.[2] Accordingly at 10.47 a.m. Tovey broadcast this position to the fleet, and *King George V*, *Prince of Wales*, *Victorious*, Curteis's cruisers, and *Suffolk* all turned north-east. Wake-Walker in *Norfolk* away to the south, knew there were other cruisers covering the Faeroes-Iceland gap, none except *Sheffield* to the south, so steered as though *Bismarck* was making for France; so did *Edinburgh* and *Rodney*. *Ramillies*, doing all of 19 knots, also turned north-east, but she would never catch up, and soon the Admiralty ordered her to find *Britannic* and escort her to Halifax.

When the Admiralty operations staff heard what Tovey was doing, they didn't quite know what to make of it. Earlier Captain Charles Daniel, the Director of Plans, and Captain Ralph Edwards, the Director of Operations, had been sent off to make separate assess-ments of where they thought *Bismarck* was bound. They came back an hour or so later with the same answer – France. So at 10.23 a signal was sent to Tovey, Somerville and Wake-Walker and at 11.08 to *Rodney* to act on that assumption, and at 12.44 p.m. the Flag Officer Submarines was ordered to sail six submarines to form a patrol line in the Bay of Biscay. Yet nothing was certain. Tovey would not have turned the fleet towards the Faeroes-Iceland gap without good reason, and the best reason was that one of his D/F destroyers had provided the cross-bearing which had shown *Bismarck*'s position more accurately than their own rather uncertain fixes. The best thing to do was wait and see. All the most likely routes were being covered, and in addition three Catalina flying-boats of Coastal Command were sent off to search, first from the south-east *Bismarck*'s most likely track to France, then, continuing north, her likely track to the Faeroes-Iceland gap.

At 10.54 a.m. however the Admiralty obtained another D/F fix on *Bismarck*, which confirmed her general movement towards France: this time they broadcast the plotted position and it was received in the *King George V* at 2.01 p.m. Again at 1.20 p.m. a further fix of an enemy transmission was obtained, made on U-boat wavelength but with the strength of a surface ship: this also fitted in with *Bismarck*'s passage to France. Although it seemed strange to Tovey that *Bismarck* should start transmitting on U-boat wavelength (he was in fact right, the ship transmitting was a U-boat) it was, if true, further evidence that the enemy was making for France.

At 3.48 p.m. therefore Tovey ordered the flagship to come round to east-south-east. But soon after this he intercepted a signal from the Admiralty to *Rodney*, cancelling her earlier orders to steer for France, telling her to conform with Tovey's movements towards the Iceland-Faeroes gap. Why this signal was ever sent, when Admiralty opinion had been hardening in favour of France all day, is a mystery. One writer[3] says Captain Edwards told him it was made at the insistence of Winston Churchill who himself believed *Bismarck* was returning to Germany. Another explanation is that it was thought essential for *Rodney* and *King George V* to join forces so as to have local superiority.[4] The signal made no difference to *Rodney* whose course of north-east was right whichever of the two courses *Bismarck* was steering. But to Tovey it was totally baffling. Concluding that the Admiralty were now favouring the Faeroes route, yet with all other evidence pointing to France, he gave orders for *King George V* to come round to port and steady on 080°, a compromise course between the two destinations.

And so, all that morning and part of the afternoon, Tovey and Lütjens were steering away from each other, the one north of east, the other south-east, with the distance between them gradually opening.

In Brest dockyard, at a little before 8 a.m. on this same Sunday 25th

132

May, Lieutenant Jean Philippon of the French Navy was on his way to the Combined Navy Office where he had the forenoon watch. He was a lean, spare man with black hair, a strong hawklike face, and percipient eyes. When war broke out Philippon was first lieutenant of the submarine *Ouessant*, which arrived in Brest in February 1940 for a long refit. She was out of action when the Germans overran France and as the Panzer troops entered the town, Philippon and his fellow officers scuttled her.

For the German Navy Brest was a jewel beyond price, an advance base for submarines and surface ships on the very edge of the Atlantic battle-field; and in the wake of the occupying forces there came as admiral commanding the port the most famous of Germany's first war U-boat aces, the legendary Lothar von Arnauld de la Perière, holder of the Kaiser's highest award for gallantry, a man of Huguenot origins, amiable character and impeccable French. His mission was to persuade the French Navy, under the terms of the Franco-German Armistice of 24th June, 1940, to collaborate with him in the administration and running of the dockyard. Luck was with him. The port's two admirals, Traub and Brohan, had already been removed to an unknown destination. The next senior officer was Captain le Normand, an old friend of de la Perière, they had both commanded submarines in the same waters in the first war, later got to know each other as captains of cruisers. Le Normand didn't much care for being commandant of a collaborationist dockyard, but seeing in it the means of conserving the installations for France, as well as saving many sailors from the miseries of a prisoner of war camp, he accepted. The French Navy Office in the dockyard was converted into a Combined Navy Office, with de la Perière's staff on the upper floors, Le Normand's on the lower. Lieutenant Philippon was chosen by Le Normand for his staff. He told Le Normand that he would not work directly for the Germans, so he was put in charge of the dockyard's gardens.

All through the late summer and early winter of 1940 Philippon looked after the gardens diligently, but by the end of the year, when there were no more flowers to tend or vegetables to grow, he was finding his duties, or lack of them, increasingly irksome. Nor was it easy to stomach the sight of German naval officers and men strutting about the yard, German ships and submarines entering and leaving the port. On a New Year visit to his home at Puynormand, he confided his frustrations to the family doctor, an old friend, said how he longed to do something for France. The doctor listened carefully, then before Philippon left, hinted darkly that he might expect a visitor soon. Within a few days the visitor came, the famous 'Colonel Rémy', who was to head the most successful of all the French resistance groups. Would Philippon act as an agent for the British Admiralty, observe what he could in the dockyard, ship movements, garrison strength, new construction, bomb damage? Philippon was in a dilemma, he hated the British Navy for what they had done to the French fleet at Oran, yet his duties at the gardens allowed him to go anywhere without raising suspicion, and it was a challenge, not just to help the British but his fellow country-men who had rallied to the Cross of Lorraine overseas, an oppor-tunity to serve France. He accepted. *Bien*, said Colonel Rémy, and did he know of a good radio operator for his messages, a man that could be relied on? Philippon remembered Bernard Anquetil, a former quartermaster of *Ouessant*, now living quietly at Saumur, 250 miles away, gave Rémy his name.

And so it was arranged, and Lieutenant Jean Philippon of the French Navy adopted the code-name 'Hilarion' and became a spy for France. He gave his messages to a brave youth named Paul Mauger, code-name 'Mimi', whom Rémy had recruited at Nantes. Mimi took the messages by train to Saumur, there Anquetil trans-mitted them by radio to England.[5]

At first Philippon sent routine stuff, but this changed with the arrival of *Scharnhorst* and *Gneisenau* in March. With his own eyes Philippon saw *Scharnhorst*'s worn-out boiler tubes being hoisted out of her onto the quay, knew this meant three months repairs, sent word accordingly. He missed *Gneisenau*'s move from No. 8 dock when the unexploded bomb fell in it on 4th April, but after Flying Officer Campbell's brilliant attack on her two days later, his news of it reached London within 48 hours and the further news that she would be out of action for six months, within a week. And every week he sent reports of the damage that British air-raids were doing to the town, if not to the dockyard and ships.

At the beginning of May Philippon got word that the German Navy was putting up *ducs d'Albe* or big mooring posts at Lanvèoc and near Ile Longue, with anti-torpedo netting all round them. He went to look at them, concluded they must be for ships of 35,000 tons or over; *Bismarck* or *Tirpitz*, he thought, perhaps both: once again Mimi took the train to Saumur.

And now, at eight o'clock of this Sunday morning, 25th May, Philippon entered the Combined Navy Office to take over the duty watch from his friend Jan. The night before he had heard on the radio of the sinking of the *Hood*, so he knew *Bismarck* and *Prinz Eugen* were out.

'Be on your guard today,' said Jan, 'the Boches are in a bad mood'.

'Why?'

'I don't know, but something's up. They seem rattled.'

A German lieutenant from de la Perière's headquarters upstairs came in, asked Jan to order the harbour tugs to raise steam immediately, said they were wanted at Lanvèoc and Ile Longue for inspecting the anti-torpedo netting.

There was some further conversation which Philippon didn't hear, then the German left.

'What's up?' he asked.

'The *Bismarck*'s expected Wednesday. The whole port's getting ready to receive her. There's quite a panic.'

Philippon tried not to show his intense interest, asked Jan if he'd mind keeping watch a little longer, as he'd left something at home. He knew there was an express about to leave for Paris, hurried to the station. There was no time to find Mimi, so he scribbled in a code that Rémy had supplied for emergencies, *Bismarck expected Brest Wednesday, Hilarion*, put it in an envelope and wrote a Paris address. Then he gave it to a startled passenger, said it concerned a sick child, was a matter of life and death, and the passenger, glad to be of service, promised to deliver it in person.[6]

And on this same Sunday 25th May, Herbert Wohlfarth and the

crew of *U.556*, still far out in the Atlantic, were also making their way towards France, their present mission completed.

After the attack on Convoy H.X. 126, they had one torpedo left. Presently they sighted a straggler from the convoy, the 5,000 ton *Darlington Court*. Wohlfarth ordered an attack but on the way in, his navigator Sub-Lieutenant Souvad said: 'Captain, why waste our last torpedo on this little ship? Why not keep it for something better on the way home?' Wohlfarth considered the matter, decided, as he put it, that the certainty of a sparrow now was better than the possibility of a pigeon later. But when they reached the firing position, something went wrong, they had to break off and come round again. Once more Souvad suggested it might be better to keep the torpedo, but Wohlfarth had made up his mind. When they reached the firing position a second time, he fired. The torpedo hit the straggler amidships and she began to settle. Souvad turned *U.556* for France, and Wohlfarth radioed to Dönitz his position, course and expected time of arrival.

And now on this Sunday morning came a signal from Dönitz to Wohlfarth. It was a signal that made all the crew happy, lifted their morale. 'Hearty congratulations on your successes' it ran. 'The Führer has been pleased to approve the immediate award to you of the Knight's Cross of the Iron Cross.'

In three days, thought Wohlfarth, they would be at their berth at Lorient. And then they would have a party.

And on the morning of this same Sunday 25th May, soon after transmitting the signal that should have brought British forces racing towards her, but which paradoxically had the effect of sending them farther away, *Bismarck* received a message from Group West. 'Last enemy shadowing report was at 0313. Type of enemy signals now being sent indicates shadowing vessels have been shaken off.' And so the dulled, radar-shocked minds of Lütjens and his staff realised at last that the hounds had finally lost the scent, that *Bismarck* was alone on the ocean. And officers and men who had been at action stations for thirty-six hours were able to stretch themselves, allowed to go in turn to their messes, wash and shave, get a bite of hot food.

Müllenheim-Rechberg welcomed the opportunity to what he called run round a little, visit the bridge to get the latest information, meet other officers, exchange views and compare notes. And later that morning a little ceremony took place when Lütjens, who as a Commander-in-Chief in the field was empowered to grant immediate awards, decorated Leading Seaman Hansen with the Iron Cross for his brilliant handling of the ship during the attack by *Victorious*'s Swordfish.

There was another cause for celebration in *Bismarck* that morning, one that had nothing to do with the present operation. It was the admiral's birthday. He was fifty-two. His staff officers and the crew, through Commander Oels, wished him many happy returns. There was a signal from Raeder which said: 'Heartiest congratulations on your birthday. May you continue to be equally successful in this coming year,' and another from the Führer, briefer, for he was worried about the damage the ship had suffered, had premonitions about loss of prestige: 'Best wishes on your birthday. Adolf Hitler.'

But the admiral himself was not sharing the general joy, not allowing himself any wishful thinking. There were still nearly a thousand miles to go, and Dr Externbrink and his colleagues held out no prospects of misty or foggy weather on the route to France. Lütjens knew, from the volume of enemy traffic being picked up by the wireless office, from the reports being sent by Group West, that the British Navy were straining every nerve to find him, that the worst was still to come. At noon, in grey mood, he addressed the crew over the loud-speaker system for the first time since leaving the Baltic. In clipped unemotional tones he thanked them for their birthday wishes, for their part in the victory over the *Hood*. And then, because it was not in his nature to do otherwise, he spoke of the dangers and difficulties that lay ahead. 'The British are massing their forces to destroy us, and we shall have another battle with them before we reach home. It may well be a question of victory or death. If we have to die, let us take with us as many of the enemy as we can.'

A more imaginative admiral would have considered the effect of such words on morale. It was almost as if Lütjens wanted to infect the crew with his own fatalism, share with them the euphoria of a truly Wagnerian end. Captain Lindemann said a few words afterwards, tried to make amends with news of aircraft and U-boats that were on the way, but the damage had been done. 'I was at my action station in the after control tower,' said Müllenheim-Rechberg, 'and so didn't hear the speech myself. One of my petty officers came and told me about it. "The admiral says we haven't a hope, sir, the whole British fleet is after us and they're bound to find us." The younger sailors got very depressed.' The engineer officer Junack, after an early lunch in the wardroom, went on watch below, got news of the speech there, found the men equally disheartened. Theo Klaes, loader at one of the flak batteries, heard the older men of the battery's crew agree that if the normally silent Lütjens were prepared to say as much, the situation must be really bad. And according to Junack morale was further shaken by the sight of some officers, including those on the admiral's staff, wearing life-jackets under their uniforms, when ship's orders stated they were always to be kept in their containers.

Meanwhile the crew were sent to special defence stations, four hours action stations, four hours lighter duties, four hours rest. It was a strenuous routine but it kept people occupied, prevented them brooding. Under Commander Lehmann the boiler-room staff were busy all day, as they had been the previous day, in changing the feed water from the boilers. The flooding of No. 2 boiler-room meant that salt water might have got into the feed system and if so, would corrode the boiler tubes. The matter was so serious that all four fresh water distillers and an auxiliary boiler had to be brought into use, and it wasn't until Sunday evening that the danger was finally removed.

Lehmann can hardly have had a moment to himself that day, for he was also supervising the building of a dummy funnel. Someone had suggested that British aircraft pilots, unaware that *Prinz Eugen* had parted company, would not be looking for a ship on her own: a second funnel might delude them into thinking *Bismarck* was an American or even a British warship, especially if they prepared English signals. The funnel, made of wood with a plating round it, was prepared by the ship's carpenters. It was quite impracticable: it could not have been put up without getting in the way of the after-bridge and after flak control, and high winds or violent manoeuvring by *Bismarck* would soon have flattened it. Lehmann jokingly said that when it was finished, it should be filled with pipe-smokers who would puff smoke out of it, and Manthey remembers the non-duty watch being piped to stand by for dummy funnel smoking. Later in the day, as the weather gradually worsened, the idea was abandoned. But it had given the crew something to talk about, it was a booster for morale, and perhaps in the end that was all it was ever supposed to be.

The day wore on, the wind increased in strength, the sea rose, a rising sea from the north-west. It was a sea that carried *Bismarck* along with it, flung her stern to this side and that, induced a horrid corkscrewing motion that for many of the younger members of the crew, some of whom had only finished shore training six weeks before, brought on agonies of seasickness. But there were compensations. As afternoon gave way to evening and evening to night without further signs of the enemy, the hopes which had taken such a buffeting from the admiral's speech that morning began to recover. The talk on the mess-decks that evening was that the admiral was wrong, they were going to make it after all.

Tovey meanwhile continued steaming east-north-east, increasingly puzzled by the contradictory signals reaching him, increasingly wondering where *Bismarck* had gone. During the afternoon the mistake in plotting the morning D/F bearings had been discovered, so apart from the Admiralty's signal telling *Rodney* to conform to his movements, all indications now were that *Bismarck* was making for France. If this was the Admiralty's appreciation too, why had they not signalled him? At 4.30 p.m., unable to contain his misgivings any longer he signalled the Admiralty: 'Do you consider the enemy is making for the Faeroes?' He had hoped for an immediate reply, but in those days it took a long time for signals to be coded, transmitted, received, decoded, answered, coded, sent back and decoded once again. An hour and a half passed, Tovey decided he could wait no longer, ordered Captain Patterson to turn south-east, signalled Whitehall accordingly.[7]

But he turned alone, for most of his ships were desperately short of fuel. *Norfolk* had already altered course for Iceland, passed *Prince of Wales* heading for the Faeroes gap. *Prince of Wales* went on for an hour or two, then also steered for Iceland. *Suffolk* (after searching to the south-west all day) turned south-east briefly, thought better of it and steered for Scapa. *Victorious* had enough fuel to continue, but Admiral Curteis's escorting cruisers were getting dangerously low, and with U-boats on the alert, he did not dare let her go on alone. That night her aircraft made a final search to the south-east of the morning's D/F position, sighted nothing.

In the Admiralty meanwhile opinion was hourly hardening in favour of France, it looked more and more as if the flagship had wrongly plotted the morning D/F position; and at about the time that Tovey signalled he was turning south-east, they signalled *Rodney* for the second time that day to assume that *Bismarck* was making for France. Once again she did nothing but continue on her present course, as it still covered both eventualities.

Now that France seemed certain, Wake-Walker in *Norfolk*, en route to Iceland, was in an agony of indecision, torn between his instincts to continue the chase and fear of running out of fuel. In the end instincts won. He ordered Captain Phillips to turn south-east, go on to 26 knots. Presently he sighted *Prince of Wales* again, still steering for Iceland, signalled 'I am going towards Brest.'

Now the two main adversaries, *Bismarck* and *King George V* were steaming roughly the same course, south-east towards the Bay of Biscay, but with *Bismarck* some 150 miles in the lead. *Rodney* continued steaming slowly north-east in the hope of sighting the enemy as she crossed his presumed line of advance. Having reached it without sighting him, she too turned towards the Bay. Neither of the two adversaries knew where the other was, each side, as it waited for news, made dispositions to help.

Group West in Paris sent signals to *Bismarck* about preparations being made. Ships 13 and 24 were being provisioned and fuelled for eight days and would sail immediately, three destroyers would escort *Bismarck* for the last lap across the Bay: Air Fleet 3 was being put at the Navy's disposal, long range aircraft would operate up to 25° West, reconnaissance planes up to 15° West, bomber formations to 14° West. At St Nazaire buoys were in position and lights operating, pilots had been arranged: a berth was being prepared in La Pallice Roads, but should the situation demand it, Lütjens should consider putting into a Spanish port. A further U-boat patrol line was being formed, but *U.74* was unseaworthy because of damage and *U.556* out of torpedoes. Approaching this area *Bismarck* was to fly a blue pendant so that U-boats might not mistake her for a British ship: Dönitz, passing this information to U-boats, added that *Bismarck* was probably camouflaged (no one had thought to tell him the camouflage had been painted over at Bergen). If shadowers were still in touch, Lütjens was to signal his position and maximum speed (to this he wisely made no reply) but in any event he was to signal his position when crossing 10° West. Raeder and Schniewind, not knowing *Bismarck*'s fuel situation, still thought she would be wiser to withdraw temporarily into the Atlantic, debated whether to order it, in the end agreed only Lütjens could decide.

The British too were making their dispositions. In the unlikely event of *Bismarck* making for the Mediterranean, *Rodney*'s sister ship *Nelson* was ordered to sail from Freetown to Gibraltar, the submarine *Severn* was told to take up offensive patrol in the Straits: like Lütjens, her commanding officer was given discretion to enter Spanish territorial waters. At Coastal Command plans were made for aircraft patrols along *Bismarck*'s presumed track to Brest, starting at first light; and the Royal Air Force made the first of several mine-laying sorties to the roadsteads of Brest and St Nazaire. But the most pressing need for Tovey that night, as he himself signalled the Admiralty, was for destroyers; for every mile that *King George V* steamed south-eastwards was taking her, unescorted, into U-boat waters. In the Admiralty operations room they looked at the chart, saw the only destroyers within hailing distance were those escorting the troop convoy WS8B, *Cossack*, *Zulu*, *Sikh*, *Maori*, and the Polish destroyer *Piorun*. Earlier this precious convoy had been deprived of

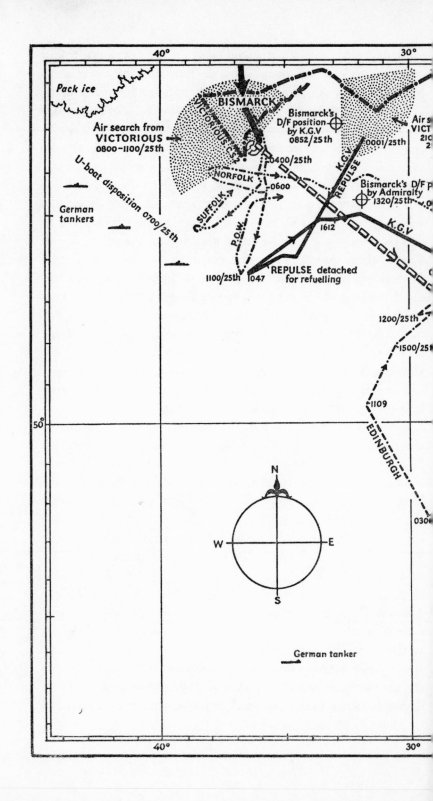

Pack ice

Air search from
VICTORIOUS
0800-1100/25th

U-boat disposition 0700/25th

German
tankers

BISMARCK

VICTORIOUS C.S.

Bismarck's
D/F position
by K.G.V
0852/25th

0400/25th

0001/25th

Air s
VICT
210

NORFOLK

0600

SUFFOLK

P.O.W.

1100/25th   1047

REPULSE detached
for refuelling

K.G.V

REPULSE

Bismarck's D/F p
by Admiralty
1320/25th

1612

K.G.V

1200/25th

1500/25

1109

EDINBURGH

030

N

W   E

S

German tanker

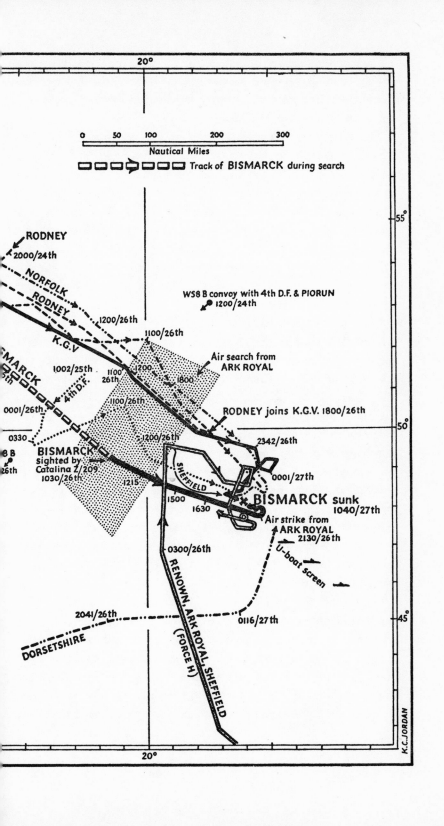

20°

```
0      50    100        200        300
|——————|——————|——————————|——————————|
            Nautical Miles
```

▭▭▭▭▷▭▭▭▭ Track of BISMARCK during search

—55°

RODNEY
2000/24th

NORFOLK

RODNEY

1200/26th

K.G.V   1100/26th

WS8 B convoy with 4th D.F. & PIORUN
1200/24th

Air search from
ARK ROYAL

1002/25th

1100/26th   1200   1800
4th D.F.

0001/26th   1100/26th   RODNEY joins K.G.V. 1800/26th

0330   1200/26th   —50°

B B   2342/26th
26th   BISMARCK
       sighted by   0001/27th
       Catalina Z/209
       1030/26th   1215

                        SHEFFIELD
                        1500
                        1630   BISMARCK sunk
                                                1040/27th
                                    Air strike from
                                    ARK ROYAL
                        0300/26th   2130/26th

                                    U-boat screen

                        RENOWN, ARK ROYAL, SHEFFIELD (FORCE H)

2041/26th   0116/27th   —45°

DORSETSHIRE

20°

K.C. JORDAN

Victorious and *Repulse:* if its destroyers were taken too, all that was left to guard it was one solitary warship, the anti-aircraft cruiser *Cairo*. But there were no U-boats near, and in the circumstances it was a risk that had to be taken.

The officer commanding these destroyers was Captain Philip Vian, a hard, ruthless, dedicated sailor (though privately he could be quite humble and shy) who like all great commanders in war never failed to seize opportunities offered him. The year before he had become a national hero when he took *Cossack* into a fjord of then neutral Norway, rescued from the German supply-ship *Altmark* 300 British merchant sailors captured by the pocket-battleship *Graf Spee* and being taken as prisoners to Germany. In a flat period of the war, the cry of the *Cossack*'s boarding party, 'The Navy's here' had echoed like a peal of bells round England.

Vian received the Admiralty's signal in the middle of the night: *Cossack, Sikh, Zulu,* to join *King George V, Maori* and *Piorun* to make for *Rodney*. Vian formed his division in line abreast, set course east-north-east at 27 knots; the same north-westerly sea that was pushing *King George V* and *Bismarck* towards Brest, hit Vian's destroyers on the beam, made them yaw violently from side to side, lean over so far it sometimes seemed they would never come back: the spray came over fo'c'sle and bridge in solid sheets, smacked against oilskins and sou'westers, blinded look-outs and officers of the watch, went gurgling and chuckling along the bridge scuppers. Men had to hold on to stanchions and rails to avoid injury: two of the ships were thrown so savagely off course that they accidentally changed places in the line, were lucky not to collide. 'Reports reached me', wrote Vian laconically, 'of men being hurt and in one case of being washed overboard, but there was nothing to be done.'

On the bridges of *King George V, Rodney* and *Bismarck*, more comfortable because enclosed, more stable because of their size, officers stood on the gratings of compass platforms, faces reflected in the dim lights of compass bowls, bracing tired bodies to the motions of the ships: each watched intently his own ship's head, listened to the leisured ticking of the compass repeater, heard it stop as the ship answered the helm, start again as the bows began the long haul back

19. 'a small, blue-eyed twinkly man, liked good food and company . . . deeply
religious.' Admiral Sir John Tovey with Captain Jack Leach on the
quarter-deck of **Prince of Wales**

20. *'Bismarck's* salvoes thundered out every twenty seconds.' A time exposure photograph — giving the impression of it being night instead of day — of *Bismarck* engaging **Hood** in the Denmark Straits. Taken from **Prinz Eugen**

21. *'. . . taking with her more than 1,400 men, leaving only a wreath of smoke on the surface* **Hood** blows up, 6 a.m May 24th, 1941. Taken from **Prinz Eugen**

to the course. Others stood silently scanning the dark horizon with binoculars, seeing nothing. At intervals hot cocoa or soup came round. Sometimes a bell or buzzer sounded, the wireless office had a signal ready, the radar was being switched off for repairs, the engine-room wanted to check revolutions. Communication ratings with earphones on heads and nothing to do warded off sleep by frequent testing. 'Bridge-A Turret' they chanted. 'A Turret-Bridge' came the answer. 'Testing. One, two, three, four, five. Five, four, three, two, one.' In *Bismarck* the test word was 'Bismarck', 'Bismarck' given and sent back.

To most now, British and German, it seemed that the long day's night was almost at an end, that the great chase was all but over. Just before midnight Tovey signalled the Admiralty that he might have to reduce speed to economise on fuel, while in *Bismarck*, cruising at 20 knots, they had about enough to reach Brest. And men's thoughts turned, as those of sailors do at the end of a voyage, to how it might be when they reached harbour. In just over forty-eight hours *Bismarck*'s young crew, most of whom had never been outside Germany, would find themselves in France, and because of the damage, the ship would stay there some time. What would life in Brest or St Nazaire be like? Would they live on board or ashore? Would the locals be hostile or friendly? Was French food everything it was said to be, what was the form about girls?

Rodney's crew were having similar thoughts. Soon they would be resuming their interrupted journey to Boston and the long-promised refit; unlike *Bismarck*'s crew they had no doubts of the welcome that awaited them. American hospitality to British servicemen had already become legendary (it was, many Americans felt, the least they could do for those then holding the front line). There would be invitations to stay in American houses, trips to New York and into the countryside; things to eat they hadn't seen for months, steaks that covered the plate, as many eggs as they wanted, lashings of butter and cream. In the shops they would buy scent and silk stockings for girl friends; and above all, there would be lights: street lights and car lights, lights blazing from the windows of houses and shops.

Even the men of *King George V* could afford a few daydreams. Normally they would expect to take the long road back to Scapa, where the rain rained and the wind blew, and sheep and seabirds were their only companions. But the point of Scapa as a base was to guard the sea-routes from Germany into the Atlantic. Now that *Bismarck* had broken out, was about to join *Scharnhorst* and *Gneisenau* in France, would their presence not be required rather nearer the Biscay ports? At Plymouth, say, where there were pubs and cinemas and girls, and London only a few hours away by train. There was a lot to be said for Plymouth.

So ran the thoughts of some sailors as in their seaborne castles they were buffeted through the night across the long Atlantic. Others, below decks, in the small privacy of bunk or hammock, dreamt of other things. Some, with intensity, of homes and families. Some, the imaginative ones, who had been most afraid when battle seemed imminent, now saw themselves as heroes, wove new battles in which they rescued men from steam-filled boiler-rooms, alone on the bridge helped their dying captain con the ship safely back to harbour. And others, because they were young and randy, thought of sex; and as the waves smashed like hammer blows against the sides and rolled them this way and that, and in the darkness the duffel coats and oilskins swayed and rustled on their hooks, and the air droned through the ventilating pipes, conjured wild fantasies, took off, for a few moments obliterated all awareness of their environment, the boring enemy and his beastly war. Most, sooner or later, slept; but some, in *Bismarck* mostly, lay half the night in agonies of seasickness, retching until it seemed they must choke, not caring if they lived or died.

And then dawn broke over a wild grey sea that was empty of other ships and a sullen grey sky that was empty of planes. In *Bismarck* it was nearly twenty-four hours since Lütjens had made his Death or Victory speech, they were four hundred miles nearer port, of the enemy there was still no sign.

Hopes that had been rising all night rose to a new peak, perhaps even Lütjens secretly shared them. But they were not to last. In the dead of night, about the time that Captain Vian and his destroyers were taking leave of Convoy WS8B to join the fleet, a Catalina aircraft of Coastal Command, No. Z of 209 Squadron, was racing in the darkness across the trout-filled waters of Lough Erne in the north-west of Ireland. The co-pilot was an American serviceman, Ensign Leonard B. Smith, wearing the uniform of the United States Navy – a fact known then to very few. The plane rose gracefully towards the stars, circled once over the sleeping countryside, set course south-westwards across Donegal Bay and Eagle Island towards the open sea.

Part 3

DEFEAT

But only agony, and that has ending;
And the worst friend and enemy is but Death.

Rupert Brooke

CHAPTER

8

When on the late afternoon of the 25th the Admiralty operations staff sat down to plan the air patrols for the following day, they were somewhat despondent. Despite extensive searches by several aircraft along the most likely tracks to France and the Faeroes, nothing had been sighted: this was no reflection on the skills of the pilots, rather on the minuteness of ships in the immensity of the ocean. In the weather being experienced in the North Atlantic just then, they could pass within five miles of *Bismarck* and not see her.

The staff completed their proposals, the duty captain telephoned them to Captain Charles Meynell, the Navy's liaison officer with Coastal Command at their headquarters at Northwood. Meynell took them along to Air Marshal Sir Frederick Bowhill, Coastal Command's Chief. Bowhill concluded that, so far as *Bismarck*'s direct course to the French ports was concerned, they were perfectly adequate. But would *Bismarck* steer direct for the French ports? Bowhill had been a seaman himself, twenty-two years in the Merchant Service and Royal Navy, had been round the Horn under sail, in the first war commanded the seaplane carrier *Empress*. His trained seaman's mind told him (what was not evident to Admirals Pound or Phillips) that a direct course for the French ports was unlikely, that it would take *Bismarck* unnecessarily close to British airfields, result in her making a night landfall on a rocky and treacherous coast. If he was the German admiral, he told Meynell, he would steer a more southerly course, point the ship towards the north of

Spain, only turn east when near the latitude of the French ports. There should be an extra patrol to cover this area. Meynell agreed, telephoned the Admiralty operations staff for approval. They agreed, provided it did not interfere with the more northerly patrols already accepted; and Catalina Z of 209 squadron was the aircraft chosen to execute Bowhill's wishes.

Ensign Leonard ('Tuck') Smith was twenty-six, a farmer's son from Higginsville, Missouri. As a lad he'd always wanted to fly, made model aeroplanes powered by rubber bands. After graduation and a year of boredom in a Chicago insurance firm, he joined the naval reserve in 1938, trained as a pilot at Pensacola, Florida. When the European war broke out he was second pilot and navigator in a squadron of Catalinas, or PBY's, based at Sand Point Naval Air Station, Seattle.

Early in 1941 Smith's commanding officer called some of the pilots together, told them the U.S. government was lend-leasing the British PBY's and volunteers were needed to go over to England and teach the British pilots how to fly them. Smith volunteered, was sent to Washington, D.C., where he and sixteen other pilots got a different sort of briefing from the Chief of Naval Operations· 'Boys, we're going to war soon with Germany and Japan. But we haven't fixed the date yet, so we want you to go over there and learn all you can about it.' The volunteers flew to Bermuda where the Consolidated Aircraft Co., which built the Catalinas, was delivering them to pilots of British Ferry Command. On the morning of 4th May 1941, they all embarked: in addition to Smith the party included Ensign Carl Rinehart who had trained with him at Pensacola and Lieutenant Jimmy Johnson who had already clocked 1,500 hours. Three thousand miles and twenty-four hours later, at about the time that Hitler was inspecting *Bismarck* and *Tirpitz* in Gotenhafen, they became waterborne in Greenock, Scotland.

The Americans went to London for a few days' acclimatisation, then nine of them, including Smith and Johnson, flew to Lough Erne to join Coastal Command as 'Special Observers'. 'The C.O. there,' said Johnson, 'informed us he was sending nine of his co-pilots on leave, so we became full crew members, which was quite humorous.' Johnson became co-pilot of Catalina M of 240 squadron, Smith of Catalina Z of 209 squadron. The remaining eight Americans, including Carl Rinehart, went to Oban on the west of Scotland as 'Special Observers' to 210 squadron.

Smith's fellow crewmen in Z/209 came from all over England, Sussex, Newcastle, New Barnet, Liverpool. The captain was Flying Officer Dennis Briggs, who had recently flown in the first Catalina to take part in the Battle of the Atlantic, even survived a crash in it. 'It was the blind leading the blind', said Smith. 'Briggs had had plenty of operational flying but knew little about Catalinas. I knew something about Catalinas but had no experience of operational flying.'

Smith found the patrols similar to those from Seattle, but longer and more arduous: the plane carried 1,750 gallons of petrol so could remain airborne for up to twenty-eight hours. The crew took their meals with them, meat and eggs and vegetables, cooked them on a little Primus stove as they went along. They were very cramped: the noise and vibration were continuous, many plugged earholes with cotton wool to lessen the din. Each crew member did three hours at a stretch, then took an hour off in one of the four bunks aft. Fourteen days after Smith's joining, they had a very exciting trip: they just missed a mountain on the way out, were fired on by escorts of the convoy they had been sent to protect, had a small fire on board on the way back.

That was on 24th May, the day *Hood* was sunk. The following evening they learned that *Bismarck* had escaped and were told they were to join in the search for her. They went to bed early, were roused at 2 a.m. on 26th May, dressed in kapok-lined flying-jackets and fur-lined boots. At the briefing for the mission no one showed much enthusiasm or belief in its success: patrolling over convoys at least gave something to engage the attention, but this looked like being a long trip with, as the song said, nothing to see but the sea. In the operations room an officer bet a sergeant twenty cigarettes that Z of 209 would not find *Bismarck*.

For three hours the plane flew steadily south-westwards, then dawn broke and to those on watch came the pleasant smell of frying bacon and eggs. Some, having eaten it, wished they didn't have to wait so long for lunch. They flew on for another three hours and at 9.45 a.m. reached the area of search. Here the plane was put into automatic control, Smith moved into Briggs's seat, Briggs took over as second pilot. It was a hazy morning with poor visibility and a very rough sea. About half an hour later, flying below cloud at 500 feet, Smith pointed ahead and said, 'What's that?' Briggs looked and saw about eight miles away, at almost maximum visibility, a dull, black shape, which gradually took on the contours of a large warship. Hardly able to contain his excitement, he ordered Smith to take a closer look while he moved to the wireless table to write a signal to base. Smith banked to starboard, went up into cloud, meaning to curl round to a position astern of the ship, but he slightly misjudged it, a few minutes later at 2000 feet the clouds parted and there was *Bismarck* on the beam, less than 500 yards away. Now there was no need to question her identity: she disclosed it on her own. There were shell bursts all round them, the nasty rattle of shrapnel hitting the hull. The barrage was so fierce that a crew member off duty was knocked out of his bunk, and the rigger, washing up breakfast things in the galley, dropped two plates. Smith took violent evasive action, jettisoned the plane's four depth charges to gain height, went on to full speed. ('Never been so scared in my life,' he said afterwards). Briggs, trying frantically to finish his message and get it off before being shot down, saw *Bismarck* from the corner of his eye as one great winking flame, watched her keel over to port as she turned to starboard under helm to avoid being hit.[1]

'One battleship bearing 240° five miles, course 150°, my position 49° 33′ North, 21° 47′ West. Time of origin, 1030/26.'

It was the signal for which the navies of two nations had been waiting, the one with hope, the other with fear. In Germany it was decoded within minutes, passed to Raeder in Berlin, Saalwächter in Paris. They had to accept the inevitable, at least had the compensation of knowing where *Bismarck* was (690 miles from Brest – though when Lütjens's own signal reached them, there was a discrepancy in the position given of about 70 miles – Briggs was 25 miles out,

Neuendorff, who hadn't had a sight for days, nearly 80). On the British Admiralty operations room chart it could be seen how narrowly *Rodney* and her destroyers had missed *Bismarck* the day before – *Rodney* and her destroyers by 50 miles, *Edinburgh* by 45 miles – while that very morning Vian's flotilla had crossed her wake only 30 miles astern. At the Admiralty and in the fleet at sea (and at Coastal Command too where Bowhill was giving himself a small pat on the back) relief at *Bismarck*'s rediscovery was tempered by the knowledge that unless she could somehow be slowed down, *King George V*, 135 miles to the north, *Rodney*, 125 miles to the north-east, would not be able to catch up.

But perhaps *Bismarck* could be slowed down? Vian with his five destroyers and twenty-six torpedoes knew where his duty lay, altered course towards the enemy without asking permission, went on to full speed. Captain Benjamin Martin in the cruiser *Dorsetshire*, with eight torpedoes, escorting a convoy 600 miles to the south-ward, handed over escort to the armed-merchant cruiser *Bulolo*, also without permission, steered at 26 knots to get between the enemy and Brest. Perhaps both of them remembered Nelson's dictum: No Captain can do very wrong if he lays his ship alongside that of an enemy.

Yet the man to whom the news of *Bismarck*'s rediscovery was most urgent, who had the best means for slowing her down, was the commander of the force nearest to her. Vice-Admiral Sir James Somerville, with *Renown*, *Ark Royal* and *Sheffield*, steering north, had crossed ahead of *Bismarck*'s track earlier that morning, was now only just over 100 miles away, between *Bismarck* and Brest.

Vice-Admiral Sir James Somerville was one of the Navy's characters, a big congenial man, full of humour and vitality. He had no pretensions to intellect, peppered his conversation with four-letter words, was a devotee of the dirty joke. (There could have been no better recipient for the signal that Admiral Cunningham sent him when, a K.B.E., he was made a K.C.B.: 'Congratulations, but isn't twice a knight at your age rather overdoing it?') He maintained, says his biographer, 'a schoolboyish approach to all things, a youthful zest and sense of fun combining with an uninhibited simplicity of expression ... an unconscious urge to be the centre of the stage and act the unorthodox admiral at all levels ... these were important ingredients in his make-up as a leader ... and brought him enemies as well as friends.'

During the Spanish Civil War Somerville was Rear-Admiral commanding Mediterranean destroyers. In the 1936 civil war his flag-ship *Galatea* was lying in Palma, Majorca, along with the German pocket-battleship *Deutschland*, flying the flag of Rear-Admiral Carls, and the Italian destroyer *Malocello*. All three were there to protect the interests of their country's nationals, but when the Republicans announced intentions to bombard the port, they were asked to leave. As senior officer, Somerville took the three ships to sea, manoeuvred them as a squadron. The Republicans didn't bombard Palma, and on return Somerville signalled 'the International Squadron' that their station-keeping and manoeuvring had aroused his warmest admiration. Admiral Carls, in halting English, replied: 'When all the ships of these three navies would be joined in a squadron like that, one day, it would be very good in many ways.' Now, five years later, Carls, commanding Group North at Wilhelmshaven, was the admiral who had sent *Bismarck* on her way.

In 1938, when Commander-in-Chief East Indies, Somerville had an attack of T.B., was invalided home and out of the Navy. But when war broke out he was passed fit by a Harley Street specialist, was soon knocking at the Admiralty's door. As a radio specialist he was given a job in the Admiralty's signal division concerned with the development of naval radar; and as a result, says his biographer, 'an effective surface warning set reached our warships many months, if not years, before it would have done otherwise.' So *Suffolk*'s success in shadowing *Bismarck* and *Prinz Eugen* was due partly to Somerville.

His next job was to assist Admiral Ramsay at Dover with the evacuation of the British Army from Dunkirk. This involved a trip to France where Admiral Wake-Walker was supervising the evacuation on the beaches, and going many hours without sleep. The way his health stood up convinced the Admiralty he was fit again for sea, and in June 1940, when Force H was formed to fill the naval vacuum left in the Western Mediterranean by the defeat of France, he was appointed its commander. The nucleus of this force was a carrier, *Ark Royal*, and the battlecruiser *Hood*, in which he hoisted his flag at Gibraltar.

Force H's first, most distasteful duty was the bombardment of the French fleet at Oran. It was then employed on various duties in the Mediterranean, sending through supplies and aircraft to beleaguered Malta, going on operations against the Italian fleet. On one occasion, the action off Cape Spartivento in which Admiral Holland had distinguished himself, Churchill expressed unease at what he considered Somerville's lack of offensive spirit and Pound, true to form, set up a Court of Inquiry before Somerville had even returned to Gibraltar. But all was forgotten when Somerville first proposed, then executed brilliantly a dawn bombardment of the docks at Genoa. On several occasions he went up with *Ark Royal*'s aircrews, an act that few other admirals would have done or thought of doing. 'How I hate seeing them go off and wondering how many of the brave lads will return,' he wrote. 'It's on these occasions I think they appreciate I know what conditions are, as a result of going up with them.'

On 23rd May Force H returned to Gibraltar after safely flying off to Malta 48 Hurricane aircraft from *Ark Royal* and *Furious*. That afternoon, while *Bismarck* and *Prinz Eugen*, as yet unsighted, were approaching the Denmark Straits, Somerville, now in *Renown*, took Captain Talbot of the *Furious* for a walk up the Rock. 'We found a little track among the scrub' he wrote, 'and we sat in the sun surrounded by wild flowers . . . it was a small and very welcome bit of peace.'

Early next morning Force H was on its way north. By 4 a.m. on the 25th, at about the time that *Bismarck* was shaking herself free of *Suffolk*'s radar, Somerville detached his destroyers to Gibraltar because of lack of fuel after high speed steaming. The senior officer was ordered when 150 miles clear to signal to the Admiralty Force H's position, and to ask what the situation was regarding *Scharnhorst* and *Gneisenau*. Somerville had taken Force H to sea to look for these ships during their Atlantic cruise in March, was now gravely concerned they might come out to support *Bismarck*. An Admiralty signal had reported them both at Brest two days before, but his sailing orders had stated that if further reconnaissance showed either or both to have left, he would be sent further instructions.[2] There had been nothing from the Admiralty since, so Somerville ordered a Sword-fish search in the direction of Brest at first light next morning. The rest of a rather worrying day was spent communicating with *Ark Royal* about next day's area of search for *Bismarck*. It was arranged that the first patrol should leave at first light.

That night the gale that was pushing *Bismarck* along on her south-easterly course hit Force H hard. At 11.15 p.m. they had to reduce to 23 knots, at 11.40 to 21 knots, finally at 1.12 a.m. on the morning of the 26th to 17 knots. The old *Ark*, 'sunk' by German propaganda so many times but still afloat, seemed to be creaking and groaning in every plate, and her captain, Loben Maund, wondered just how much more punishment she could take: hardly a day passed without his chief shipwright going down to repair loose rivets and cracks caused by a near miss months before: the ship hadn't had a major refit for 100,000 miles, twice recently the stern gland of the centre shaft had blown out. This was not the time or place for it to happen again.

Dawn broke to show a storm-tossed sea, streaked with white foam, waves the height of four-storey houses. Although *Ark Royal*'s flight-deck was 62 feet above the water-line, it was being drenched with spray, there were times when the forward end shipped green seas like a destroyer. Captain Maund sent down two officers inde-pendently to measure by sextant the rise and fall of the stern, they came back with answers of 53 and 56 feet. The wind speed over the deck was fifty miles an hour. Few carrier-borne aircraft had ever operated in such conditions before.

But the times were abnormal too; and on *Ark Royal*'s aircraft now depended whether *Bismarck* could be further slowed down or not. The Swordfish detailed to cover the route to Brest got safely away, and then ten others were brought up from below and ranged in line. With the ship rolling up to 30° to starboard the flight-deck crews had the greatest difficulty preventing the aircraft sliding across the deck. It had been intended to fly off the planes at 7 a.m., but reduction of speed during the night had meant loss of ground, they were now scheduled to leave at 9 a.m. Just before 8.45 Captain Maund turned the ship into the wind, reduced to 10 knots: rolling gave way to pitching, the wind was like a hurricane, the fierce gusts almost tore the flimsy planes out of the deck crew's hands. Across the raging sea on the bridge of *Renown* Admiral Somerville kept his binoculars fixed on them. On the bridge of *Ark Royal* Commander Traill, the flight operations officer, looked down at the first plane due to take off, raised his green flag. He waited for what he hoped was a lull, let the flag fall. The plane gathered speed slowly against the wind, infinitely slowly it seemed to those watching. As it lumbered past, Traill watched the goggled observer read the wind indicator on the side of the bridge, raise a gloved hand thumb upwards. Now, as the ship rose to meet the next wave, the plane was climbing skywards; then, as the wave passed, tearing like the Gadarene swine downhill towards the sea. Everyone held his breath, the plane took off, its wheels ploughed a furrow through the wavetops, then it was airborne and clear. Jerkily, hesitatingly, the others followed, many touched the water as they left, all got safely away. Well, thought Maund, just as Bovell had done two nights before, we've got them away, how do we get them back?

An hour and a half later came Flying Officer Briggs's sighting report, followed soon after by a signal saying he had lost contact. A glance at the chart showed *Bismarck* to be heading straight for the centre of the Swordfish's search area, only twenty minutes later Sub-Lieutenant Hartley in Swordfish 2H sighted her. But he made the same mistake as Admiral Holland, mistook her for *Prinz Eugen*, reported a cruiser. Seven minutes later aircraft 2F under Lieutenant Callander arrived, confirmed Briggs's report of a battleship. Which was it? It was vital to know, for a torpedo attack on a cruiser required a shallower depth-setting. Somerville ordered two more Swordfish with long-range tanks to take off from *Ark Royal* and relieve 2H and 2F.

The other eight Swordfish had already been recalled to the ship to be armed with torpedoes. The *Ark* was now steaming at high speed on a parallel course to (and about 50 miles from) *Bismarck* to make up the ground lost when steering north-west to fly off. Now she turned north-west again in order to land on. The stern was still rising and falling the height of a large house, but between them the pilots and batsman gauged each approach wonderfully, somehow managed to get the planes down on the slippery, skiddy deck. Only one misjudged completely, the stern swished up as he came in over it, smashed the plane to pieces though the crew were unhurt: further landings were held up while the pieces were swept over the side.

During these flying operations *Renown* remained to the east of *Ark Royal* – sometimes because of mist out of sight – in order to keep between *Bismarck* and France. If ordered to attack with *Renown*, Somerville's plan was to do so from astern and upwind, so that *Bismarck* would have to turn and slow up her retreat, also because of the advantages of making smoke. But *Renown* was of the same vintage as and even less protected than *Hood*, and the Admiralty, fearful of Somerville doing something rash and history repeating itself, signalled that *Renown* was only to engage if *King George V* or *Rodney* were themselves heavily engaged. *Sheffield*, though, was not serving any useful purpose, so at 1.15 p.m. Somerville ordered her to steer for *Bismarck*, then 40 miles away, and shadow from astern. He informed the Admiralty and Tovey of this by wireless signal, also *Ark Royal*, who was out of visual touch with the flagship at the time.

This wireless signal reached *Ark Royal* in cipher a few minutes later, but as it was not addressed, only repeated to *Ark Royal*, and as other important messages were waiting to be deciphered (especially those from the shadowing aircraft), it was put on one side. So that when after lunch the crews of the striking force went to the Observers Room for briefing, they were not told that *Sheffield* was on her way to *Bismarck*, would be quite near her by the time they reached the scene. Their instructions were that *Bismarck* was alone on the ocean, that no other ships were anywhere near.

At 2.15 p.m. the Swordfish started coming up on the lifts. Because there was still a faint doubt as to whether the enemy was *Bismarck* or *Prinz Eugen*, the torpedoes were set to run at 30 rather than 34 feet; and they were fitted with magnetic pistols, designed to

22. '... because of flooding the bow was down by two to three degrees ...'
Bismarck after being damaged by **Prince of Wales,** May 24th, 1941.
*Taken from **Prinz Eugen***

23. 'formed to fill the naval vacuum left in the Western Mediterranean by the
defeat of France' Force H: **Sheffield** (top), **Ark Royal** and **Renown** at
sea in company

24 'courageous single-minded, stoical, austere, taciturn as a Cistercian monk.'
Admiral Günther Lutjens, Fleet Commander

trigger off an explosion under the enemy's hull. At 2.40 p.m. engines were started up and at 2.50 p.m. the leader of the flight, Lieutenant-Commander Stewart-Moore in Swordfish 4A took off. Fourteen other planes followed without mishap, formed up and turned south towards the enemy.

An hour passed, Maund and Traill and everyone else in the *Ark* waited anxiously for news. Then a harassed signal officer dashed to the bridge, holding a copy of Somerville's signal about *Sheffield*, just deciphered.

Maund, a calm man, read it, said to the signals officer, 'Make to the striking force, "Look out for *Sheffield*". No, there's no time to cipher it, make it in plain language. Make it now'.

All that morning and early afternoon *King George V* went cork-screwing along towards the south-east, steering a slightly converging course on *Bismarck*, cutting a bit of a corner on the route to Brest. To Tovey and his staff officers, Brind, Bingley, Lloyd and others, gathered round the plotting-room table off the bridge, it was clear from reports of the shadowing Swordfish that little by little they were catching up. But not fast enough. By this time tomorrow *Bismarck* would be inside the range of shore-based air cover and *King George V* would have had to turn back for lack of fuel. If the planned Swordfish attack failed to slow *Bismarck* down, then they must return home with *Hood*'s death unavenged and – despite all the ships and aircraft allotted to the operation – *Bismarck* still at large.

All day signals of *Bismarck*'s position continued streaming in from Coastal Command Catalinas and *Ark Royal*'s Swordfish – the second a good deal more accurate than the first. After losing contact in Z/209 Briggs and his rigger went round plugging holes made by *Bismarck*'s flak, the large ones with rubber pegs, the smaller with margarine from the rations. Briggs spent a couple of hours trying to find *Bismarck* again, didn't succeed, but around 1.30 p.m. he inter-cepted a signal from Jimmy Johnson's plane, M of 240 squadron, that it was in touch. Johnson had lifted M/240 off Lough Erne an hour after Z/209, had sighted Vian's destroyers at noon, *Bismarck* an hour and a half later. Soon Briggs sighted M/240 circling, didn't use an Aldis lamp for fear of attracting *Bismarck*'s attention. Jimmy

Johnson was at the controls, pointed in the direction *Bismarck* was steering, Briggs acknowledged.

Presently Z/209 had to break off to return to Lough Erne, Briggs wanting to get waterborne before dark,[1] but in M/240 Jimmy Johnson and Flying Officer Goolden kept in touch with the enemy all afternoon. Three times they found and lost *Bismarck*, on each occasion the German flak opened up at them, the last occasion at about 5.30 p.m. soon after they had sighted *Sheffield*. 'The loud bursts and puffs of smoke seemed very near,' wrote Jimmy Johnson, 'I thought I could *smell* the acrid smoke, but it was probably my imagination.' At 6 p.m. they too had to return to Lough Erne, but by now Swordfish shadowers from *Ark Royal* were keeping constant touch.

In *King George V* meanwhile Tovey had been receiving Somerville's signals about recalling the Swordfish for arming as a striking force, then of their proposed time of departure, finally of the successful take-off. Now there was nothing to do but wait. It was an agonising period but Tovey was not left brooding for long. 'Ship bearing Red Seven-O,' shouted one of the port lookouts. All eyes on the bridge turned to the port beam, there below the horizon were the unmistakable outlines of a warship's fighting top. Could it be *Prinz Eugen*? The alarm bells were sounded, the guns crews ran to their turrets, the great guns swung round. But now her upperworks were coming into view, there could be no mistaking them. It was *Rodney*, for Tovey and his staff a truly wonderful sight. She had made no signals for over thirty hours, had been told by the Admiralty to steer a variety of courses which could have taken her anywhere, and now, like Aphrodite, was rising from the sea to take her place on the stage at the time when she was most needed.

The course that she and her two remaining destroyers (*Somali* had returned to base to fuel) were steering was only a few degrees off that of *King George V*, so it took a long time for the two ships to converge. When *Rodney* was near, Tovey signalled, 'What is your maximum speed?' and Dalrymple-Hamilton replied: '22 knots'. Tovey wanted to reduce speed anyway to conserve fuel, so hoisted, 'Speed of the fleet 22 knots.' *Rodney* fell in astern of *King George V*, but soon the gap between them began widening. The engine-room staff were doing marvels with *Rodney*'s worn-out engines, down below men were fainting, but it was still not enough. 'I am afraid,' Dalrymple-Hamilton signalled ruefully to Tovey, 'that your 22 knots is a bit faster than ours.'

It was now well after 6 p.m., and Force H and *Bismarck* were only 90 miles away. There was still no news of the Swordfish attack, although the planes had left the carrier over three hours ago, and it couldn't have taken more than an hour and a half at most to deliver the attack. What had happened, why was there no news? At 6.21 p.m. Tovey signalled the Admiralty and Somerville that unless *Bismarck*'s speed had been reduced by midnight, he would have to return to harbour for lack of fuel: *Rodney* could continue until 8 a.m. the next day without her destroyers, then she too would have to return; and in answer to Somerville's offer to join him with *Renown*, he advised him to remain with *Ark Royal*.

Another ten minutes went by, then the blow fell. From Somerville came the briefest of signals, the one they had been waiting for, but not with the news they wanted. 'From Flag Officer Force H to C-in-C Home Fleet,' the message ran, 'Estimate no hits.' That was all. Why no hits? Was it the weather or skilful avoiding action, or *Bismarck*'s flak? – or a combination of all three? Not that it mattered any more; the pursuit had ended, the campaign was over. On the bridge nobody said anything: there was nothing more to say.

When Stewart-Moore's striking force left *Ark Royal* at 2.50 p.m., they went up into cloud, laid off a course to take them to the enemy. Several of the planes had recently been equipped with radar, and after some forty minutes flying they picked up a ship right ahead. The pilots had not expected to contact *Bismarck* so soon, but as they had been told at the briefing there were no other ships near, they knew the contact must be the enemy. They dived down through the cloud, saw the outlines of a warship right ahead, went back into cloud to get into positions for attack.

Ten minutes later Captain Charles Larcom on the bridge of the *Sheffield* saw the Swordfish approaching. He was expecting to see them, having just received Somerville's signal that they had taken off from *Ark Royal*. But there was something horribly familiar about their approach. Instead of flying past him in the direction of the enemy, they were coming at him from different directions, as he had often seen them do *when carrying out practice torpedo attacks on him*. In a flash he realised the pilots had mistaken him for *Bismarck*, rang down for full speed, ordered the gun crews not to open fire. The first plane dropped its torpedo, Larcom put the wheel over to comb the track. A second torpedo fell and an extraordinary thing happened: it exploded in a great fountain of spray as it hit the water. The third torpedo did the same, the magnetic pistols were firing prematurely, and three others exploded in *Sheffield*'s wake. But five or six more were launched successfully, streaked through the water towards the ship. On the bridge Larcom listened to reports of where they were coming from, swung the wheel hard over to port or starboard. Men looked down, watched the ship's bows swing slowly round to run parallel to the tracks, held on hard, not knowing if they would make it. Thanks to Larcom's cool ship-handling they did, not one torpedo hit.

Only three pilots recognised *Sheffield*, refrained from attack. Others saw the mistake as they pulled away, realised the ship hadn't fired: one pilot, penitent, signalled by lamp to Larcom, 'Sorry for the kipper.' That they hadn't recognised *Sheffield* earlier is proof of the power of suggestion, for *Sheffield* had two funnels to *Bismarck*'s one and her lines were as familiar to them as *Ark Royal*'s. Expecting to see *Bismarck*, *Bismarck* was what they saw.

The planes set course for *Ark Royal*, on the way got Maund's signal, 'Look out for *Sheffield*', saw a long way off Vian's grey destroyers careering in from the west. Near the carrier the three planes with torpedoes were ordered to drop them in the sea in case of accident, then, despite some hairy moments, all planes landed safely on. The pilots and observers clambered out despondently, went to the bridge to tell their woeful tale. But Maund was sympathetic, told them they were not to blame, to go down to the wardroom and get some supper, be ready for another attack in an hour's time. In one way the attack on *Sheffield* was a blessing, for it showed

165

the magnetic firing pistols to be faulty: contact pistols with a depth-setting of 22 feet were ordered instead, these would not explode unless they hit the hull. Maund informed Somerville by lamp what he was doing, and Somerville signalled Tovey and the Admiralty: 'Second striking force will leave *Ark Royal* about 18.30.'

But Tovey and his staff were not much cheered. Not knowing about the *Sheffield* incident (for Somerville had wisely decided this was not the moment to publish it) they had little reason to think that a second attack on *Bismarck* would be any more successful than the first. Time was running out fast: now it would require a miracle to slow *Bismarck* down in the five hours that remained before midnight.

In *Bismarck*, apart from the weather which brought continued discomfort to young men who still hadn't found their sea-legs, it had been a day of fluctuating fortunes. There had been a nasty moment at eight in the morning when a lookout high up in the fighting top observed the topmasts of several warships passing from left to right across the northern horizon. This was Vian's flotilla, on its way to join the Commander-in-Chief; thankfully it was soon lost to sight. The arrival of Briggs's Catalina followed by the Swordfish was depressing, for it meant the enemy had found them again and that another carrier, probably *Ark Royal*, was operating not far away. But as the hours wore on, as morning gave way to afternoon and afternoon to evening and there were still no attacks, people began to think there might not be any, that perhaps the carrier was near enough to send shadowers with long range tanks but too far to send planes with torpedoes. And even if the Swordfish did attack, there wasn't much to fear. What was it that Lütjens had said about aircraft torpedoes – ? they were like bee stings that hurt but didn't damage. And hadn't this been proved two nights ago when the torpedo had exploded against the armoured belt, hardly making a dent?

During the day signals kept arriving in the ship from Group West about further preparations to receive her. Expected time of arrival was noon next day;[2] because of the weather it would be necessary to go to Brest rather than St Nazaire or La Pallice, mine-sweepers and anti-submarine flotillas would be operating in the approaches. Reichsmarschall Göring had ordered Colonel Harlinghausen, Air Commander Atlantic, to give *Bismarck* every assistance possible, U-boats on passage had the same instructions from Admiral Dönitz. Group North also signalled that during the afternoon the Luftwaffe had sighted *Rodney* and three destroyers 'nearly 200 miles astern', which showed she was right out of the hunt. All these messages gave a lift to morale, made the crew feel they were as good as home, which they almost were, for in a few hours it would be dark and by dawn next day they would be under protection of German air cover, almost within shouting distance of France.

And then a shadow fell across the sunset, for astern of *Bismarck* where for nearly two days there had been empty sea, were now the dim outlines of a shadowing cruiser. Through the rangefinders she was identified as *Southampton* class. Almost certainly *Sheffield*, thought Lütjens, and if so the rest of Force H, *Ark Royal* and *Renown*, couldn't be far away. Would *Renown* and *Sheffield* attack after dark? From the strenuous efforts the British were making to catch him, Lütjens must have thought it probable, even if they were sunk in the attempt. And was *Ark Royal* waiting for the light to fade before launching a torpedo attack? Either event meant high-speed manoeuvring and *Bismarck* hardly had fuel for that: as it was, steaming at 20 knots, she barely had enough to reach Brest. How Lütjens must have again regretted not fuelling at Bergen or in the Arctic! Had he done so, he could have steamed four or five knots faster during the past thirty-six hours, by now would have been a further 160 miles nearer home, almost out of danger altogether. Well, he could still fight a surface action at speed providing a tanker met him in the morning. 'Fuel situation urgent,' he signalled to Group West, 'when can I expect fuel?'

In Paris Saalwächter was puzzled. He knew *Bismarck* was short of fuel, but surely not as short as all that? He had the signal repeated back to Lütjens, adding, 'Text of message appears defective, as I assume you have sufficient fuel?' But he ordered the tanker *Ermland* to be sailed immediately.

Whether Lütjens intended to reply, we shall never know, for now came the sound that he had been expecting all day. 'Frederiiicke, Frederiiicke, Frederiiicke,' shrilled the alarm bells. 'Attack by enemy aircraft imminent'.

Somerville's hopes of getting the second strike away from *Ark Royal* at 6.30 p.m. were too optimistic. The ship was steaming at 25 knots to make up for ground lost when steering into the wind to fly off: the bows and stern were being flung from side to side by the following sea, so at times the ship seemed almost out of control: to strike down, refuel, rearm and bring up fifteen aircraft in such conditions was not a thing to be hurried. To add to Maund's worries there was trouble with the ship's engines: the lubricating oil of the centre main circulator caught on fire. When reported to Tony Oliver, the senior engineer officer, in his cabin, he replied at once, 'Don't let it stop,' for stopping meant losing one engine and whatever slim chance remained of catching *Bismarck*. Bottles of olive oil were poured over the red-hot parts, salt water hoses played on the engine-casing, and three experienced men put on permanent watch on the circulator.

The leader of the striking force this time was Lieutenant-Commander Tim Coode, with Stewart-Moore as second in command. They and their forty-three fellow pilots, observers and air gunners had no illusions about what lay ahead; but the false attack on *Sheffield* had been helpful, showed them that flying off and landing on in such weather was not as hair-raising as it seemed. Further the stigma of failure they all felt at not having recognised *Sheffield*, the humiliation of having attacked one of their own ships, was something they wanted to expunge. On them now lay all the hopes of the Navy and of England, for if they could not slow *Bismarck* down, no one else could. They feared what was before them, but there was exhilaration too, a challenge to prove themselves, show what the Fleet Air Arm could do.

The weather was as bad as ever, angry seas, cloud at 600 feet, frequent rain-storms which at times blotted out visibility almost entirely. There had been a suggestion the Fulmar fighters should also take off, to create a diversion during the attack, but in these

25. '... his most besetting sin was what sailors call "back-seat driving" '. *Admiral of the Fleet Sir Dudley Pound, First Sea Lord*

26. '*a handsome, square-faced man of 65 ... highly intelligent and approachable.*' Grand Admiral Erich Raeder, C-in-C-German Navy

Overleaf '... standing on towards the still distant enemy in a flurry of spray.' **King George V** (leading), **Victorious, Repulse,** steaming at full speed in pursuit of **Bismarck,** evening of May 24th, 1941

28. 'Incredible to see such
obsolete-looking planes . . .
having the nerve to attack
Bismarck.' A Swordfish
drops its 18 inch torpedo

29. 'The nine planes were
squatting at the end of the
flight-deck like a covey of dar
partridges.' Swordfish ranged
on **Victorious's** flight-deck
readiness to attack **Bismarck**

conditions it was impossible: ironically only the slow, ungainly, out of date Swordfish were operable. At 7 p.m. when *Bismarck* bore 167° 38 miles, Captain Maund turned the *Ark* into the wind, reduced to twelve knots: now the gap between her and the enemy was opening at over thirty knots. Commander Traill stood on the bridge with his green flag, below him the fifteen planes – all the Swordfish, apart from the shadowers, left in the ship – were ranged on the flight-deck, engines roaring. At 7.10 p.m. the green flag went down, Coode opened his throttle, the flight-deck crew with trousers billowing in the slip-stream pulled away the chocks, and for the second time that day Swordfish 5A went trundling down the slippery deck. Coode took off safely into the stormy sky, one by one the others followed.

The planes formed up in line astern, in six sub-flights of two to three planes each. This time, so there should be no mistakes, the pilots had been briefed to make for *Sheffield*, obtain from her the enemy's exact position. They sighted *Sheffield* briefly just before 8 p.m., lost her, didn't pick her up again until 8.35 p.m. Captain Larcom signalled to Coode, 'The enemy is twelve miles dead ahead' (just as Captain Blackwood, 136 years earlier off Cadiz had signalled to Nelson, 'The enemy is coming out of harbour').

Over *Sheffield* conditions were good for attack, with a cloud base of 2,000 feet rising to 5,000 feet. Coode led the striking force upwards with the intention of meeting them above the cloud, there splitting up so as to approach *Bismarck* from different directions, make it more difficult for her to avoid the torpedoes. But unknown to him *Bismarck* was sailing under what meteorologists call a 'front', a wall of cloud reaching to beyond 10,000 feet and extending downwards almost to sea level. The little planes climbed through the grey murk to 6,000, 7,000, 8,000 feet, there was still no sign of it ending. It was clear to Coode there was now no chance of carrying out a co-ordinated attack, that each sub-flight must attack on its own, and he signalled the others accordingly.

As leader of the force his own sub-flight was the first to attack. Down through the grey murk they screamed together, aiming for a position astern and upwind of *Bismarck*. As the altimeter changed rapidly from 8,000 to 5,000 to 3,000 to 1,000 feet without a sign of the cloud dispersing, Coode wondered how much longer he could continue the dive without, as he put it, running out of height. At 700 feet the three planes plus another from No. 3 sub-flight that had accidentally joined them, broke through the cloud to find themselves, not as they had hoped, astern of *Bismarck* but four miles ahead of her, her great bulk lurching through the seas towards them. To attack upwind in this weather would have been suicidal, so the sub-flight banked to port, climbed back into cloud to attack from *Bismarck*'s port beam.

A few minutes later those on the bridge of *Sheffield*, twelve miles astern, saw stabs of light and the brown puffs of bursting shells on *Bismarck*'s port side. The time was 8.53 p.m. The last attack had begun.

All day *U.556* had been steering south-east, like *Bismarck* towards the coast of France, also very low on fuel. From U-boat headquarters she had been receiving messages of *Bismarck*'s position regularly, realised the pursuit was gradually coming her way. Each new signal was received with added interest, for *Bismarck* was *U.556*'s adopted baby, her special child. Across the wild sea there, where *Bismarck* was, hung a picture in her wardroom of *U.556* deflecting torpedoes from *Bismarck*, a promise, sealed with Wohlfarth's thumb print, to guard and look after her in all the oceans, seas, lakes, ponds and puddles of the world.

And then, out of the blue, without any word of warning, came the opportunity to fulfil the promise. In the evening, after supper, a lookout on the bridge reported two big warships right ahead. The officer of the watch sounded the klaxons, the bridge party scrambled below, *U.556* dived. At thirty feet she levelled off, Wohlfarth ordered 'Up periscope'. When it was raised, he looked, looked again, could hardly believe his eyes. The legendary *Ark Royal*, Swordfish aircraft on deck, was making straight towards him. She had no destroyer screen and was not zigzagging. The battleship on her beam (which he mistook for *King George V*, the mistake was understandable in the weather) had no screen and was not zigzagging either. It was the sort of situation U-boat commanders dream about.

'I could have manoeuvred in between the two of them and got them both at the same time,' he wrote in his log, (it was no hollow boast, he was among the most experienced of captains), '*if only I had any torpedoes.*' But they had all gone on ships from the convoy H.X. 126. Why had he not listened to Souvad's plea not to waste the last torpedo on the straggler; why, when he decided to attack the sparrow, could some kind fairy not have warned him of the two eagles that lay ahead? He stood helpless at the periscope as the huge ships passed a few hundred yards from his torpedo tubes, the noise of their screws loud in the hydrophone operator's ears, watched them slowly disappear from sight.

On the admiral's bridge of the *King George V* and in the plotting-room just off it, Tovey and his officers once more waited for news. This time they did not have the approach of *Rodney* to distract them, nor were any more calculations to be made about the enemy's position and theirs: questions of fuel and endurance had long been decided, they knew that in less than three hours, barring a miracle, they would have to turn for home. Everyone was very tired, physically and emotionally, the movement of the ship did nothing to ease it. In the long, following sea the bows yawed sideways like a car in a skid, the spray-drenched quarter-deck which Tovey and Brind so often paced at Scapa rose and fell like a Big Dipper, the ship leant heavily to starboard, stayed there like a determined drunk until the quartermaster, with the wheel hard a-port, eased her slowly back to the given course. Astern, in a light that was now beginning to fade, *Rodney* with her long snout like a giant dachshund's reached towards them, sniffing the air, as though fearful of getting left behind. *Tartar* and *Mashona*, almost lost in the seas and spray, also struggled to keep up, their bridges like bucking horses, their forward mess-decks awash.

In Tovey's plotting-room the officers stood quietly round the plot, holding on to voice-pipes or table edges for support, bracing stomach muscles and knees to meet the motion of the ship. The plot itself was bare, ruler and dividers and rubber tucked away until it was necessary to pencil in the enemy's position for perhaps the hundredth time. But despite the tiredness and the difficulty of keeping upright, people were too restless to stay still: they moved up to the compass platform to chat to the captain or officer of the watch, lit cigarettes and stubbed them out, puffed at cold pipes, started conversations that petered out. Only the admiral seemed wholly cool, in command of the situation and himself, radiating confidence and serenity. It was a confidence that Lütjens, for all his courage, did not have, for it was an outgoing thing, it permeated through the ship to the humblest able seaman, so that those who waited at their action station for news, young men who had never spoken to him, barely seen him, believed that under this man things would be all right, that whatever path he asked them to take would be the right path, that whatever the outcome there would be no regrets. It had been the same with their forbears and Nelson a century and a half before.

And now the buzzer from the wireless office sounded, another signal had arrived. The Fleet Signal Officer unwrapped it, read, 'From the leader of the striking force. Estimate no hits.' It was the final blow, though no less than what they were expecting, miracles were things of the past. And yet to have come so far, to have been robbed like this at the last moment, was a bitter thing. Tovey said nothing, smiled as though his partner had just lost him the match on the last green, which in a way he had.

In *Rodney* too the disappointment was intense, for the men were keyed up, hopeful that after all their great efforts, the enemy would be delivered to them at last. Captain Dalrymple-Hamilton, who believed in keeping his men abreast of developments, addressed the ship's company over the loud-speakers. 'I am very sorry to tell you that we have just received a signal that the second Swordfish attack on the *Bismarck* has been completed, and that there have been no hits. As a result we have lost our last chance of slowing down the enemy and bringing him to action.' The commander asked permission to go from Action to Defence Stations and it was granted. Those who fell out felt intensely weary, like a long-distance runner about to breast the tape, who sees his nearest rival shoot past him.

Although all hope had gone, the squadron steamed on, there was nothing else for it to do. Presently another signal arrived on the admiral's bridge, this time from *Sheffield*. 'Enemy's course 340°,' it said. Tovey looked at it, baffled: 340° was north-north-west or directly towards them. Then he understood. 'I fear Larcom has joined the reciprocal club,' he said bitingly. What he meant was that Larcom had mistakenly judged *Bismarck* to be moving from right to left instead of left to right. It was a not uncommon mistake, especially at long range and in poor visibility, though hardly to be expected from so senior an officer. Poor old Larcom, everyone thought, to make such a balls-up at this time.

But a few minutes later another signal arrived, this time from a shadowing Swordfish. 'Enemy steering due north,' it said. This was even more baffling: the general opinion was that *Bismarck* must have turned a complete circle to avoid torpedoes, was now swinging to starboard to get back on her original course. A few more minutes passed, in which no one knew quite what to think, then a further Swordfish report confirmed *Sheffield*'s estimate of a course of north-north-west. And then *Sheffield* reported again, this time a course of north.

Now there was no doubt about it, something very serious had happened to *Bismarck*, very serious indeed. Tovey and his officers looked at each other with incredulity and joy.

Coode and his four planes dropped out of the cloud on *Bismarck*'s port beam, levelled out, pointed their noses ahead of the enemy's bow to give the necessary deflection. The whole of *Bismarck*'s port side anti-aircraft armaments burst into life, tracer bullets like billiard balls, red, green, orange, white, came towards them in long, slow arcs, small calibre shells exploded all round them. They tried to remember the simple rules for attack they had learned at training school, drop torpedoes at a speed of 90 knots at a height of 90 feet at a distance of 900 yards, but in this inferno of fire it was hard to think of anything. Sub-Lieutenant Dixon-Child's plane was hit by splinters but kept going, turned away to port, downwind. The observer of the plane from No. 3 sub-flight, attacking a little after the others, thought he saw a column of water shoot up abaft *Bismarck*'s funnel but couldn't be sure: Edmond Carver, observer of

Coode's plane which had reached a position on *Bismarck*'s port bow, saw nothing. He and Coode hung around some time in the low cloud and rain, saw no other attacks, assumed they were the only ones to find the target, made to *Ark Royal* before turning for home, 'Estimate no hits', the signal that was passed on to Tovey.

But the three planes of No. 2 sub-flight, led by Lieutenant 'Feather' Godfrey-Faussett (so called because of his bulk), were now coming in from starboard. They'd climbed to 9,000 feet without leaving cloud, found ice forming on the wings, turned to attack from there. Godfrey-Faussett went tearing down on a firm radar bearing, came out of cloud on *Bismarck*'s starboard beam to find only one plane, Sub-Lieutenant Kenneth Pattisson's, still with him, the other, piloted by Sub-Lieutenant Tony Beale, nowhere to be seen. He and Pattisson went into attack, saw *Bismarck*'s starboard side erupt into smoke and light, watched the coloured bullets curve towards them, heard the shell splinters tearing at the flimsy canvas covering the fuselage. But they pressed home the attack and as *Bismarck* combed the torpedo tracks, thought they saw one hit.

While this attack was in progress, four of the five planes from No. 3 and 4 sub-flights, came out of cloud astern of *Bismarck* and attacked from the port quarter. Now the enemy's port side flak opened up again and one of the planes, caught in a pattern of shell bursts, was shot through and through with splinters: the pilot and air gunner were both wounded but the plane kept flying and with the others dropped its torpedo, though none claimed any hits.

Tony Beale meanwhile had come out in clear air above the clouds, found no one there, returned to *Sheffield* to be redirected. His observer, Sub-Lieutenant Friend, made by lamp as he had done on many a practice occasion, 'Where is target?', to which Larcom replied, 'Enemy bears 340°, 15 miles' – an almost pointed reminder, thought Friend, that he too should have said 'enemy' not 'target', that this time it was the real thing.

Beale climbed towards cloud again, but before reaching it spotted *Bismarck*, worked his way round to her port bow. Friend thought how wicked she looked with her huge humped back, no clear break in her upperworks as in British ships. Beale turned, made a long, brave upwind attack at 50 feet, dropped his torpedo at 800 yards. Oddly *Bismarck* didn't fire until he had turned away, then, said Friend, 'her decks seemed to explode into crackling flame, the sea was lashed with shot and fragments'. Leading Airman Pimlott, the air gunner, fired back, less with any hopes of damaging *Bismarck* than the sheer impertinent joy of it. Friend watched for signs of a hit, was rewarded by a plume of water rising on the port side amidships. 'Pimlott was dancing a small jig as I excitedly told Beale. By turning the Swordfish quickly, he too was able to see the splash subsiding. Thus, all three of us saw our hit.'[3] One of the shadowing aircraft saw it too.

The two aircraft of No. 5 sub-flight lost each other while diving. The leader, Lieutenant Owen-Smith, who saw shell-bursts near him at 3,500 feet, came out of cloud at 1,000 feet and well astern of *Bismarck*, and while working round to a more favourable position on her beam, thought he saw a large column of water rise up on *Bismarck*'s starboard side, right aft, just as Godfrey-Faussett and Pattisson were withdrawing. He himself withdrew to five miles, came in very low on the beam, wheels almost brushing the wave-tops, released his torpedo at just over a thousand yards: his observer didn't see or claim any hit. The other aircraft of No. 5 sub-flight made two attempts to attack from starboard, found the fire too hot, jettisoned its torpedo and retired.

The two aircraft of No. 6 sub-flight also lost each other. The leader, Sub-Lieutenant Willcocks, attacked from 2,000 yards on the starboard beam without success. The other returned to *Sheffield* for a new direction, flew back to *Bismarck* at sea level, also attacked un-successfully from the same direction.

The attack had started just before 9 p.m.: it was over just before half-past. On the way back to *Ark Royal* some of the planes flew past *Sheffield*, waggled their wings, the pilots waved. On *Sheffield*'s bridge they waved back, gave a cheer, less for any success achieved than relief at seeing them in one piece.

Hardly had the last plane disappeared from *Sheffield*'s view when *Bismarck*, emerging from a patch of mist, was seen turning to port. As those on *Sheffield*'s bridge looked at her, a ripple of flame ran down her port side, followed by a burst of black smoke. Their first reaction was surprise. It was, says one writer, as though stung to fury by the air attacks on her, *Bismarck* was seeking revenge on the only British ship she could see. The salvo fell over a mile short, someone made a disparaging remark about her shooting. But *Bismarck* had not sunk the *Hood* in six minutes for nothing. Once more the orange flashes rippled down *Bismarck*'s side, once more the black cordite fumes drifted away on the wind. Captain Larcom gave a drastic alteration of course to avoid the shells now on their way towards him, the ship answered to the helm. On the bridge, and among the anti-aircraft crews in exposed positions on the upper deck, they waited: ten seconds, twenty, went by, each long as a prayer. At thirty seconds the sea on either side erupted with a shattering roar, long white pillars rose beside them, as high, they seemed to some, as Nelson's column. The salvo was a straddle: splinters from one shell raked *Sheffield*'s upperworks, inflicted fearful wounds among the anti-aircraft guns crews. Twelve men were hit altogether, five seriously, later three died: Larcom put the wheel over again, went on to full speed and ordered smoke. Another four salvoes fell dangerously close before the smoke blotted *Bismarck* out. Larcom noticed that in that time the enemy had maintained his course, sent out the signal that was to so puzzle Tovey, 'Enemy steering 340°'.

Sheffield worked round to the west to open the range. When the smoke cleared, Larcom saw *Bismarck* far away, still steering to the north, sent another signal to Tovey. Then she was lost to sight. The radar was ordered to get a range and bearing on her, but now came a report that a splinter had put the radar apparatus out of action. This meant that even if *Sheffield* did sight the enemy again, she would not be able to shadow after dark. The last of the shadowing Swordfish would also soon have to break off, and then, deprived of its eyes, the Fleet would lose contact with *Bismarck* altogether. In the night she would slip away unobserved, by dawn be safe inside Luftwaffe air cover.

So ran Larcom's thoughts, and within minutes a beneficent Providence had acted on them. 'Ships bearing Red One Five,' shouted a lookout, and there, coming to join the fray at the moment they were most needed, were Vian's five destroyers. They made a brave sight as they steered eastward at high speed, at one moment riding the crests of the long swell, the next all but their topmasts hidden in the troughs, yawing and rolling so that it seemed they must be pushed right over, the spray falling over them like rain. 'Where is the enemy?' signalled Vian, and Larcom gave him an estimated bearing and range. The little ships didn't pause in their pursuit, swept on and past *Sheffield*, fanning outwards, disappeared to the east. Forty minutes later and just as the last Swordfish had left for *Ark Royal*, the Polish *Piorun* on the port wing signalled 'Enemy in sight'.

Ark Royal's striking force meanwhile had all landed safely on, though it had taken them over an hour and many attempts to do it. Three planes had crashed on landing, were complete write-offs: Swanton's 4C was found to have 175 separate holes in it, though he and his wounded airgunner both survived. The remaining planes were taken below for refuelling and arming in readiness for a dawn attack, and Somerville signalled that after that, all torpedoes would be expended. The crews were taken off for independent de-briefing, as a result of which Maund signalled to Somerville and Tovey, 'Estimate one hit amidships' and half an hour later, 'Possible second hit on starboard quarter'.

It was a correct estimation, so far as anyone can tell. The hit amidships was on the port side, exploded against the armoured belt like the one from *Victorious*, injured a few men standing above it but did no damage: it was probably caused by the torpedo of Sub-Lieutenant Beale.

But the hit on the starboard quarter was another matter. Leading Seaman Herzog was loader at one of the 37 mm flak guns on the starboard side aft, when he saw two planes coming towards him (almost certainly those of Godfrey-Faussett and Pattisson). He noticed how low they were, wheels almost touching the wavetops, and how bravely they pressed home their attack, coming so near that at full depression the 37 mm gun could no longer bear. At full speed *Bismarck* started turning to port. To Herzog it seemed that one of the planes was pointing amidships, the other farther aft. They dropped their torpedoes, Herzog saw them clearly, and turned away. *Bismarck* went on swinging to port.

Then came the explosion. Herzog was thrown against other members of the flak crew, as he went down saw a wall of water shoot up on the starboard side aft. An ammunition handler in the magazine of Bruno turret, right toward, felt a tremor run through the ship 'as though she had been pushed backwards'. Gerhard Junack down in the engine-room, saw the deck-plates rise and fall 'at least a metre', while Mechanician Klotzsche on duty at damage control described the ship as 'making a movement like an accordion'.

The ship was turning to port at high speed when the hit came, on the bridge Lindemann ordered the wheel to be centred. She refused to answer to it, went on swinging to port, began to heel sharply to starboard. In the after transmitting station Ordinary Seaman Alfred Eich saw on the engine-room indicator the ship was doing 28 knots, while the compass repeater showed she was steaming in a circle. In the after control tower Müllenheim-Rechberg looked at the rudder repeater, saw the wheel was jammed at 15° to port. Farther and farther *Bismarck* heeled to starboard, farther than ever before, so some thought she would capsize: they looked at one another with disbelief and fear, and one man voiced their thoughts, 'She's sinking'.

But Lindemann ordered a reduction of speed and though the ship still went on circling, she presently eased to a more or less even keel, headed into the wind. *Sheffield* came into sight to port and Schneider ordered main armament salvoes. He saw them straddle, *Sheffield* disappear behind smoke. Presently a report reached the bridge of the torpedo damage. The torpedo had struck right aft, at least twenty feet down, breached the steering gear compartments, flooded them: the three propellers were unharmed, but the rudders were jammed at 15° port. Water was also coming into the ship from where the after hydrophones had been destroyed and into the port engine-room up the shaft tunnel that led to the propellers. Ordinary Seaman Blum, on damage control duty, remembered the time in the Baltic when they'd practised damage to the steering gear compartment, how he'd had to feign dead. He remembered too his lieutenant saying then, 'The chances of such a hit are a hundred thousand to one against.'

The first thing to do was try and free the jammed rudders, which meant getting men into the flooded steering compartments, so the ship was put at slow speed into the wind, on a course of between north and north-west, which in the tumultuous seas gave her the least motion; and on the loudspeakers came the pipe, 'All divers report aft'. It was going to be a long and difficult business, for it meant first entering the flooded main steering compartment to unclutch the motor, then going into the flooded hand-steering compartment and coupling that up.

Before the work was begun however Admiral Lütjens did a strange thing. Believing the rudders were beyond repair and the ship doomed, anxious to secure his own passport to Valhalla, he signalled Berlin with typical brevity: 'Ship unmanoeuvrable. We fight to the last shell. Long live the Führer'.[4] Such heroic exultation at such a time cannot have done much to help the morale of the admiral's staff officers nor of the wireless room operators who, because of frequency problems, took nearly two hours to pass it to Group West. Elsewhere in the ship morale was high. 'We had great trust in our captain and what he could do for us,' said one man, 'and so remained full of hope'.

Presently two engineer officers, Lieutenants Giese and Richter, came aft with the carpenter's party. They shored up the bulkhead above the steering compartments, stopped the leak from the broken hydrophonic gear and got the water out of the port engine-room. Commander Lehmann with two stokers in diving suits meanwhile had reached the armoured hatch leading to the main steering compartment. They opened it. At once the sea-water came surging and gushing into the passageway, then as the stern rose the level in the compartment dropped dramatically, the water was sucked back into the sea. The stern fell again like a lift out of control, banged against the trough, the water came surging upwards and quickly the armoured hatch was secured and battened down. No diver could possibly get down there, let alone move about and work.

The little group came up on the quarter-deck, Herzog watched them from his station at the 37 mm flak, saw them joined by the captain and two midshipmen. The captain didn't stay long, then the others began arguing. Herzog said Lehmann seemed the only calm man among them. Someone suggested a diver going over the stern, reaching the rudders that way, but they were positioned right under the stern counter, there was nothing for a diver to cling to, in that seaway he would be sucked right down or smashed to pieces against the side. Others volunteered to blow off the rudders with explosives – give their lives in the process – but even if a man could get near them, he would almost certainly damage the propellers as well; and once they were out of action, the ship would be completely impotent.

So all that remained was to see if the ship could be steered south-east by propellers alone. Back on the bridge where it was almost dark Lindemann tried every combination of telegraph orders he could imagine: half ahead port, stop centre and starboard; half ahead port and centre, slow astern starboard; full ahead port, half ahead centre, stop starboard. But whatever he tried, the result was the same; for a while the ship's head pointed more or less in the direction he wanted, then the 15° of port rudder brought the bows slowly back into the wind, towards the north-west and danger, away from safety and home. There was not a thing wrong with the engines or main armament; but this absurd 15° of port rudder made the ship helpless as a babe.

And now came further troubles to try the sore-pressed *Bismarck*. From the control and information posts about the ship reports reached the bridge that the destroyers they had sighted earlier were now surrounding them, manoeuvring into position to attack. Müllenheim-Rechberg in the after control tower recognised them uneasily as Tribals, the ships that a year earlier had sunk his own destroyer, *Erich Giese*, at Narvik. Was history about to repeat itself, were they going to be successful again?

CHAPTER

10

On *Bismarck*'s course of north being trebly confirmed, Tovey at once altered south towards her. The two flagships were closing at a mean rate of over 30 knots, he thought there might be a chance of action before the light went. But when Somerville's signal reported the critical torpedo hit on the starboard quarter, and Vian also reported he was in touch, he told his staff he would postpone attack until morning. 'I shall never forget,' said his secretary, Captain Paffard, 'the horrified look on Daddy Brind's face'. Brind feared, as all the staff did, that *Bismarck* would repair her damage, slip away in the night. But Tovey knew what he was doing: with rain squalls bringing visibility down to under a mile and a forecast of a pitch black night, it was impossible to say where anyone was and the conditions gave him no advantage; and he trusted Vian to maintain contact. All the same, said Paffard, 'it was a decision that must have taken tremendous moral courage.'

Tovey radioed Somerville to take Force H twenty miles south of *Bismarck* so as to be clear of his approach, while he hauled off to the north-eastwards so as to remain between the enemy and Brest: before dawn he would run down to the south-westwards to engage *Bismarck* against the sunrise with the advantages of sea and wind. Then he went to his sea-cabin, wrote a message for the ship's company and handed it to Captain Patterson.

To K.G.V.

The sinking of the *Bismarck* may have an effect on the war as a whole out of all proportion to the loss to the enemy of one battleship.

May God be with you and grant you victory.

J.T. 26/5/41

In *Rodney* they had fallen out action stations after thinking the Swordfish attack had failed, now General Quarters was sounded on the bugle, and men who had gratefully turned in to warm hammocks, scrambled out again, pulled on sea-boots and duffel coats, grabbed tin hats and lifebelts, stumbled in the darkness and wet towards their action stations. All over the ship there was the sound of running feet on deck and ladders, the clanging of hatches, the dull thud of the closing of watertight doors. When the news came they were not going to be in action that night, the men were allowed to doze at their stations, the communications ratings took it in turns to stay awake. The captain came on the loud-speakers again, told them *Bismarck* was damaged, that they and *King George V* would engage her at dawn. All over the ship men cheered to know that they would be avenging the *Hood* after all. Then the chaplain came on: 'Almighty God, most merciful Father, we make our address to thy Divine Majesty that Thou wouldst take the cause into Thine own hand, and judge between us and our enemies', echoing the thoughts of Christian soldiers down the years, what Raeder in Berlin and many in *Bismarck* must have been praying for too.

To the north of *King George V*, Wake-Walker in *Norfolk* was still trying desperately to catch up. Captain Phillips had reduced speed earlier to save fuel, but with the news of the Swordfish attack he went on again to full speed. To the southward the cruiser *Dorsetshire* was coming up at 28 knots. The cruiser *Edinburgh* had turned for home before hearing that *Bismarck* was crippled, at once reversed course towards the enemy, but her fuel reserves were very low and when action was postponed until morning Commodore Blackman once more turned for Londonderry. Somerville, meanwhile, having received Tovey's message that he would postpone attack until morning, signalled to *Ark Royal*: 'At what time will striking force take off? With any luck we may finish her off before C-in-C Home Fleet arrives'. To which Maund, remembering *Sheffield*, wisely replied: 'Not until such time as aircraft can differentiate between friend and foe'.

Astern of *Rodney* the destroyers *Tartar* and *Mashona* kept station on the battleship and each other. For four days now they had had a continual buffeting, so that one officer was to write afterwards that it seemed in looking back 'like one long twilit day punctuated by meals that would scarcely stay long enough on the table to be eaten'. But they were glad they had stayed, would now be in at the kill. In *Tartar* was an army officer, what sailors call a pongo, a friend of one of the lieutenants: he had joined the ship for a few days' leave, a spot of sea breezes, had not thought to get landed in this. Not knowing the rules and being unoccupied, he had got a little tiddly after dinner, went on deck, gave the wild night his repertoire of pongo songs. Commander Skipwith, when he heard of it, ordered him below. His name, oddly, was Lutyens.

Now the third and last Coastal Command Catalina carrying the third and last American 'Special Observer' to sight *Bismarck* that day arrived on the scene. Catalina O of 210 squadron, captain Flight-Lieutenant Hatfield, co-pilot Ensign Carl Rinehart, had left Oban soon after noon, nearly twelve hours later through a break in the clouds observed *Bismarck* beneath them, turning at slow speed. They went into cloud to get nearer, take a closer look, but like Tuck Smith earlier in the day misjudged it, came out of cloud right over her. Carl Rinehart watched the tracer bullets, blue, green, red, and white rising towards him. 'It was like driving through a snowstorm at night, when the flakes look as if they're going to hit the windscreen, then at the last moment go to either side.' He pulled the wheel one way, Hatfield the other, but both pushed forward the throttle and managed to get clear.[1]

Tartar and *Mashona* were Tribals of the Sixth Destroyer Flotilla, *Cossack*, *Maori*, *Zulu*, *Sikh* of the Fourth. They were the Navy's newest and biggest destroyers, completed just before the war, with their flared bows and long, sleek lines as elegant and powerful-looking as *Bismarck* herself. And those appointed to command them were all seasoned men, the cream of the Navy's destroyer captains.

As in the fading light Vian and his five commanders closed in towards the elusive *Bismarck*, he had formulated what he thought his duty to be. 'Firstly,' (as he wrote to Tovey later) 'to deliver to you at all costs the enemy, at the time you wished. Secondly to try to sink or stop the enemy with torpedoes in the night if I thought the attack should not involve the destroyers in heavy losses'.

The first thing was to take up shadowing positions, cast a net round *Bismarck* from which she would not easily escape: one destroyer on each bow and quarter, *Cossack* shadowing astern. As *Piorun* and *Maori* steered to the northward to reach a position on *Bismarck*'s bows, Schneider opened fire on them. This made Commander Plawski in *Piorun* very annoyed, he and his fellow Poles had many scores to settle with the enemy, it was from their beloved and now ravaged country, from the port they knew as Gdynia and which the Germans had arrogantly renamed Gotenhafen, that *Bismarck* had just come. So he ordered the quartermaster to steer towards *Bismarck* and at a range of just under seven miles he opened fire with his little 4.7 inch guns. For the next half-hour *Piorun* and *Bismarck*, the one 1,700 tons the other 50,000, kept up a spirited exchange. Although the Poles knew it unlikely they were doing any damage, the thought that they *might* be gave immense satisfaction. When one of *Bismarck*'s salvoes straddled his ship, the nearest shell bursting only 20 yards away, Plawski concluded honour was satisfied, made smoke and turned away. During this manoeuvre Plawski lost touch with the other destroyers and *Bismarck*, never sighted the enemy again.

At 11.24 p.m., half an hour after sunset, Vian ordered his ships to take positions for a synchronised torpedo attack. This was easier ordered than done. Steaming downwind it was possible to move at speed, but into it, the way *Bismarck* was going, 18 knots was the maximum without those on the bridge being drenched with spray, unable to see the enemy or where they were going. Further, despite the darkness of the night and *Bismarck*'s wounds, she was soon ranging accurately on the destroyers. The British believed this was by radar, and it may have helped, but Müllenheim-Rechberg saw them clearly through the powerful rangefinders.² At 11.42 p.m. when *Bismarck* was still four miles away, Vian saw her silhouetted in the light of her own gunfire, fifteen seconds later heard the song of her shells, large and small: they burst all round, splinters shot away the wireless aerials, *Cossack* turned away.

A few minutes later it was the turn of Commander Graham in *Zulu*. He too saw the white flashes of *Bismarck*'s guns stabbing the night, heard their thunder, sensed upheavals in the sea all round, as though a cluster of underwater geysers had suddenly erupted. To Sub-Lieutenant James Galbraith in the gunnery control tower the *Bismarck* looked enormous, almost as though they were on top of her; and as well as the roar of her main armament he heard the sharp vicious cracks of the 15 cm anti-personnel shells as they burst alongside in a shower of splinters. Another salvo followed, the glare from the enemy's gun flashes lit up the long, white columns of the preceding salvo, already collapsing in the wind, vast white miasmic ghosts. This salvo and a third straddled: splinters tore into the gunnery control tower, severed Galbraith's wrist, wounded two ratings.³ Graham turned away. Half an hour later Commander Stokes in *Sikh* shadowing astern, saw *Bismarck* alter course to port, let loose a salvo at him; and he also moved away.

Now, because of the darkness of the night, the frequent rain squalls and *Bismarck*'s accurate fire, all Vian's destroyers had lost touch with the enemy. When at half-past midnight *Cossack* fell in with *Piorun* and then *Zulu*, neither where they were meant to be, he knew there was no possibility of a synchronised attack, signalled by wireless for ships to attack individually as opportunity offered.

Maori was the first to go in, having sighted the enemy again at 1 a.m. steering north-north-west. Commander Armstrong crept up on her port quarter at 25 knots, zigzagging continuously: when he was abeam at a range of two and a half miles, she opened fire, so at 1.21 a.m. he turned in and fired all four torpedoes. At the time of the attack *Bismarck* was altering to north-east, no hits were observed.

Commander Graham in *Zulu* was not far away, still looking for

Bismarck, when the flashes of her salvoes at *Maori* lit her up. Like Armstrong he raced up to her port quarter, and when he was abeam fired a starshell to light the target: as it burst over her at 1.37 a.m. he fired two torpedoes at two miles, and she at once opened fire. Graham had hoped to cross her bows to attack from the other side, but the fire was too hot. As *Zulu* withdrew, those on her bridge and upper deck looked hard at the enemy to see if they could observe a hit. At the expected time they were rewarded, first by 'a bright glow that illuminated the water line of the ship from end to end', seconds later by 'a very vivid glare between the bridge and the stem', which was claimed as a second hit – though neither was indicative of a successful torpedo attack.

Three minutes later, at 1.40 a.m., Captain Vian in *Cossack* launched his attack. He had been stealing up on *Bismarck*'s disengaged side, taking advantage of her preoccupation with *Maori*, to get into position. At a range of three miles he fired three of his four torpedoes. At the expected time flames were seen to blaze up on *Bismarck*'s fo'c'sle, and this was claimed as 'an unmistakable hit'. A few minutes later *Zulu* reported *Bismarck* stopped, further evidence it was claimed of the destroyers' success.

Commander Stokes in *Sikh* was out of touch to the southward when his three consorts attacked, but on getting *Zulu*'s report, he closed the enemy at speed, and at a distance of three and a half miles fired all four torpedoes. In his excitement the rating pulling the torpedo levers allowed no proper time-lag between them and there-fore they gave no 'spread'; but the *Sikh*'s engine-room staff reported hearing an underwater explosion at the time when one might be expected, and so *Sikh* too claimed a possible hit.

In fact none of the torpedoes from any of the ships hit. It would have been surprising if they had. In normal conditions then the range at which a torpedo was considered to have a reasonable chance of hitting was a mile to two miles. Here they had been fired at ranges that varied between two miles and three and a half in condi-tions that were extremely abnormal, waves fifty feet high, a pitch black night, an enemy whose course and speed was erratic, whose gunfire was precise. At any other time cooler heads would have scoffed at the notion of flames on the fo'c'sle (almost certainly a burning starshell which Müllenheim-Rechberg records having landed there) or glows the length of the waterline (probably an enemy salvo) as being proof of success. Underwater explosions would have been a better guide, yet the only ship hesitantly to claim hearing this was *Sikh*, and she fired from three and a half miles.

The claims were made in good faith; but the wish fathered the thought. Vian and his officers and men had been through much, believed that on them much depended: the Fleet Air Arm had scored hits on both their attacks, it would be intolerable for them not to do the same. Such thoughts were not conscious, but when men have experienced great strain, as these had, brought themselves to within a whisker of death, they see things their eyes are reaching to see, that will justify the risks taken, prove to themselves and the world that it has all been worthwhile.

Bismarck lay stopped for the next hour or so, wallowing heavily in the waves. Soon after 2.30 a.m. she got under way again, moving slowly north-westwards. Vian got a signal from Tovey to illuminate the enemy with starshell every half hour: the admiral was to the north-eastwards of *Bismarck*, didn't want to bump into her in a rain squall on his run down to the westwards before dawn. The destroyers complied, but *Bismarck* opened such an accurate fire they had to withdraw. At 3.35 a.m. *Cossack*, having moved to the northward of the enemy, closed in to fire her last torpedo. Vian, taking his ranges from an improved radar set just off the bridge, saw on the scan a series of small echoes racing towards him, was told by the operator they were *Bismarck*'s shells (which, he said, with all the Navy's genius for understatement, 'induced some unpleasant moments'). At a range of two miles he fired his torpedo, this time claimed no hit.

By about 4 a.m. all the destroyers had lost touch with *Bismarck*, though they guessed she could not be very far away. At 5 a.m. Vian signalled *Piorun* by wireless to return to Plymouth, as he knew she must be very short of fuel. Plawski and his crew, still searching for *Bismarck* to the south-east, were dreadfully disappointed. Unlike the British who considered the enemy as a scourge to be eradicated, a boil to be lanced, the Poles hated them with a deep, personal loathing, for their brutal conquest of Poland, for making them exiles from their own land. Further, they had ten torpedoes to the Tribals' four, which gave them a far better chance of hitting: all they wanted was to get in really close to *Bismarck*, pump every one of them into her. To have come so near to getting their own back as this, then be denied it, was almost unbearable. For an hour Plawski ignored Vian's order, continued searching for *Bismarck*, then with bitter regrets turned for the Channel.

At 5.50 a.m. *Maori* sighted *Bismarck* again, slowly zigzagging north-west. *Sikh* also sighted her emerging from a rain squall forty minutes later. It was almost full daylight, and just before 7 a.m. at a range of four and a half miles *Maori* fired her last two torpedoes: no hits were observed.

The four destroyers took station in four sectors round the crippled battleship. Vian had done what he had promised to do; hung on to the enemy through the night to deliver him to his Commander-in-Chief in the morning; and now he sat back to wait for Tovey's arrival.

The events of that long night in *Bismarck* are difficult to record with any certainty; for by now most of the crew were near exhaustion, and later when some came to recall them, their memories were confused by subsequent events, horrors that were yet to come.

In big ships news travels slowly, unless there is an announcement from the bridge; this is especially so at action stations when men are immobile at their posts, cut off from one another. The whine of the turbines may take on a higher or lower pitch indicating an increase or decrease in speed, course may be altered this way or that, but the general assumption is that the captain on the bridge knows his business, and if there is something to tell them, they will be told. In *Bismarck* it had been broadcast there had been a hit affecting the rudders; but it was known that men were working on it, they had faith in each other and their ship, and with many hours of darkness still ahead there was every reason to suppose the damage would be made good and they could then continue home. Meanwhile there was an action to be fought with British destroyers, instruments to be watched and tended, shells brought up from below, guns to be trained and fired: there was no time to speculate or brood, energies were needed elsewhere.

On the bridge though, as the night went on, the seriousness of the situation became increasingly apparent. Reports from aft indicated that all attempts to free the jammed rudder had failed, that nothing more could be done: in the wireless room the growing strength of enemy signals (and whatever of their contents the cryptographic team were still able to obtain) made it clear the final reckoning could not long be delayed. It was what Lütjens had been expecting all along. 'To the Führer of the German Reich, Adolf Hitler,' he signalled just before midnight, 'We fight to the last in our belief in you, my Führer, and in the firm faith in Germany's victory'. Hitler replied from the Berghof two hours later, 'I thank you in the name of the German people.' and he also sent a message, perhaps at Raeder's prompting, to the *Bismarck*'s crew. 'The whole of Germany is with you. What can still be done will be done. The performance of your duty will strengthen our people in the struggle for their existence.' There were other messages of encouragement and farewell. Raeder signalled, 'Our thoughts are with you and your ship. We wish you success in your hard fight,' Admiral Carls in far away Wilhelmshaven, 'We are all thinking of you with faith and pride', Saalwächter in Paris, 'Best wishes. Our thoughts are with our victorious comrades.' Later, to strengthen resolve for the battle ahead, Lütjens signalled Raeder, 'Propose award of Knight's Cross to Commander Schneider for sinking of *Hood*'. Hitler was in his study when his adjutant brought him the message, nodded approval. Two hours later *Bismarck*'s crew heard on the loudspeaker Lindemann's voice read out Raeder's personal signal to Schneider: 'The Führer has awarded you the Knight's Cross for sinking the battle-cruiser *Hood*. Hearty congratulations'.

These messages were double-edged: they were designed to help morale but they underlined a situation in which help for morale was needed. From Group West came signals of more practical encouragement. All available U-boats were steering for *Bismarck*, the ship should transmit beacon signals for them on 852 metres and 443 kc's. Three tugs were on their way to take *Bismarck* in tow, the *Ermland* had sailed with supplies of fuel, and squadrons of bombers – 81 aircraft, some remember being said – would be reaching the ship by dawn.

Other cheering announcements came about the ship's success against enemy forces. Earlier it had been broadcast that the flak crews had shot down seven of *Ark Royal*'s Swordfish. now came the announcement that one of the destroyers had been sunk and two others were hit and burning: Ordinary Seaman Manthey remembered seeing with his own eyes one destroyer burning on the starboard beam. In fact none of the Swordfish had been shot down, and the destroyers had not been hit by *Bismarck*'s shells any more than *Bismarck* had been hit by the destroyers' torpedoes. But the claims, like those of the destroyers, were made in good faith: the Germans, no less than the British, saw what they wanted to see. The guns' crews cheered when these reports reached them, during lulls in the fighting sang.

And yet as time went on and the course and speed of the ship remained the same, there was a smell of death in the air and some began to talk openly about what few dared to think; that with every hour that passed, the gap between themselves and *Rodney* and other enemy battleships was slowly but inevitably closing. In one engine room a man went berserk, wanted to stop the ship: Junack had to telephone for a guard to take him to the doctor for sedation. In another, Werner Lust found some former *Karlsruhe* artificers very nervous, they had been sunk before. He himself dozed, on and off, despite threats of court-martial. Up top some of the flak crews, with nothing to do, gathered round Chief Petty Officer Wienand. They liked Wienand, he was always patient, never shouted at them. He talked of his home in Hamburg, and his wife and their plans for the future. He pulled out a wallet and in the light of the destroyer's starshell showed his companions his wife's photograph. 'Isn't she pretty?' he said, and then: 'If I don't survive, I want one of you to go and see her and tell her my last thoughts were of her'. Most of his audience were unmarried and one said, things weren't so bad, U-boats and bombers were on the way to rescue them. 'Yes, I know all that,' said Wienand, putting the picture back in the wallet, 'but I don't really believe it any more. It all sounds too good to be true'. It could be said of Wienand, as it was of Lütjens, that he wanted his men to face reality: that way they would cope better when the time came.

There were others who, when the main destroyers' attack was over and there was little to occupy them, increasingly felt the same, officers especially, those who had knowledge of the signals going backwards and forwards, knew the reality of the situation more than most: Müllenheim-Rechberg, sitting in the after control tower with one or two officers of the prize crews, said he felt 'like meat on the slab waiting for the butcher's chopper'. It was bad too for those whose work was over, who had no part to play in the coming battle; the flak crews, most of whose ammunition was now expended, Dr Externbrink and his fellow meteorologists, the merchant navy captains and the prize crews, the pilots and observers of the Arado aircraft, cooks and cobblers, tailors and stewards, the bandsmen whose instruments lay unwanted in their lockers. From exhaustion these and others, all over the ship, slept: the guns' crews in their huge turrets, the supply teams at the ammunition hoists, stokers and engine-room staff below, doctors and sickberth attendants in the sickbay. Lying in cots there were the stokers who had been scalded when *Prince of Wales*'s shell burst, the airmen whose legs had been broken by the explosion of *Victorious*'s torpedo, a man recovering from an emergency operation for appendix. On the tables near them saws and scalpels, rubber gloves and syringes, cotton wool and bandages and ampoules of morphia hinted at the frightfulness to come.

Some, as they dozed, had nightmares, as Esmond Knight had had before the battle of the Denmark Straits, saw weird shapes, heard screams and cries, imagined the battle had already begun, woke sobbing: others dreamed of home and those they loved, saw them with a fierce intensity, believed they were close to them, at home in Germany in May; waking, they remembered, felt fear again in the gut.

But because they were so young, most weren't ready to die, didn't even want to contemplate the idea of their own deaths it was so horrible, they thought of things to give them hope. They had sunk the *Hood* in six minutes, hadn't they, the biggest warship in the world, and what they had done once, they could do again: bombers and U-boats were arriving in the morning, they would soon sink the British ships or at least prevent them from attacking; and any moment now it might be announced that the rudders had been repaired and they could slip quietly away, by nightfall be safe in France. With such thoughts young minds comforted themselves as they waited hopefully for a seachange. But there was no change nor news of any: the turbines kept their plaintive, low-pitched whine, the water slopped against the sides, the plates groaned and creaked as the bows rose and fell, and with each hour that passed hopes got progressively fainter. Then they asked themselves whether if things became really bad, the admiral might not give orders for scuttling, as Langsdorff had done in the *Graf Spee*, and if so, whether the British would pick them up. (Some said the British shot their prisoners.) And a few applied their minds to something they had never applied it to before, a subject that interests mostly the old and middle-aged, whether there is a life after death.

At about 5 a.m., the order was piped on the loudspeakers: 'Prepare ship's aircraft for launching'. Lütjens, who had few doubts about the fate of the ship in the face of the opposition now massing, wanted the ship's log saved so that Raeder might have a true record of the voyage, details of the actions, to draw conclusions for the future: he also wanted to send home the film of the sinking of the *Hood* taken by the cameraman Dreyer, accounts of the battle written by the war correspondent Hanf.

The hangar door was opened by the deck crew, one of the aircraft lifted by crane on to the launching rails, pushed to one end and linked to the catapult gear. A pilot and observer were detailed, went to change into flying gear. They could hardly believe their luck, they were going to escape from this hellship, they wouldn't have to die after all, in less than four hours they would be in France, drinking fresh coffee, munching newly-baked rolls, telegraphing home. As

30. 'on May 10th flew to Lough Erne to join R.A.F. Coastal Command with the title of "Special Observer".' Lieutenant James Johnson, U.S.N. (Left) and Ensign Leonard B. Smith, U.S.N. (Right)

31. 'Vian's grey destroyers came careering in from the west.' A flotilla of Tribal destroyers in line ahead

32. *'shell splashes high as Hiltons, white as Daz'.* **Bismarck** *under attack by* **King George V** *and* **Rodney,** *9 a.m. - 10 30 a.m., May 27th, 1941*

33. *'bombed them all day, at noon sank* **Mashona** *with the loss of one officer and forty-five men.'* **Tartar** *stands by to rescue survivors from* **Mashona,** *May 28th, 1941*

they made their way to the launching rails, they were aware of envious eyes on them, of being looked at as creatures from another world. The ship's log was brought down from the bridge, with the cans of film and Hanf's copy put in a waterproof bag, stowed inside the plane. There were other messages to take too, for when men heard they were going, they scribbled little notes on any scraps of paper they could find, sent loving thoughts to mothers or sweethearts, pressed them into the airmen's hands.

The two men climbed in, the engine was started, allowed to warm up. When it was ready for take-off, word was passed to the bridge, Lindemann did what he could to bring the ship broadside to the wind. It wasn't easy, as she turned the wind and sea caught her, rolled her heavily from side to side. With engine racing at maximum revolutions the pilot found himself now looking down at the foamy sea, next moment up at the blackness of the sky. Like Ranald and Traill before him, the flight operations officer tried to judge the best moment for take off. When the windward side, on its way up, was level with the leeward, he gave the signal to launch; and the catapult gear operator pressed the lever that would send the Arado shooting 120 feet across the length of *Bismarck*'s beam and away into the night.

Nothing happened. The plane stayed on the rails, engine racing. Once again the officer gave the signal, once more the lever was pressed, once more the plane stayed still. Now an inspection of the gear was made and it was found the compressed air pipe was badly fractured, a splinter from one of *Prince of Wales*'s shells, the one that had carried away the captain's motor-boat, had torn a great hole in it, put the catapult mechanism out of action.

The experts were called, said it was not possible to repair it, at any rate at this time and place. So the engine of the Arado was switched off, the pilot and observer who a few moments ago had been so full of joy, climbed heavily out, the ship's log was taken back to the bridge, the cans of film and copy returned to Dreyer and Hanf. The aircraft, now useless and a fire risk, was allowed to run down the rails and into the sea. The pilot and observer walked wearily to the changing-room, removed their flying gear, rejoined the ranks of those about to die.

After *Ark Royal* and *Renown* had passed him, Wohlfarth steered on the surface for where he believed *Bismarck* to be. At 11.30 p.m. he sighted one of Vian's destroyers, dived, at 90 feet heard the screws pass over him. At midnight he surfaced, saw in the distance the flashes of *Bismarck*'s guns, was astonished to find that by his reckoning she was sixty miles from her given position, sent a signal to U-boat Command giving her true position for the benefit of the Luftwaffe and other U-boats, sent out D/F signals for German shore stations to fix. Not far away Lieutenant-Commander Eitel-Friedrich Kentrat in the damaged *U.74*, hastening towards the scene, altered course when he got Wohlfarth's signal, for U-boats had a reputation for giving accurate positions; it was, Kentrat said, their daily bread.

Without torpedoes and being as low in fuel now as everyone else, all that Wohlfarth could do was keep in touch with *Bismarck* and send out regular transmissions. Once again he had been given the opportunity to fulfil his promise to protect *Bismarck* in the seas and oceans of the world, once again he was unable to do so. As he watched the fierce flashes of her guns and the starshell over her as she fought for her life against Vian's destroyers, he remembered all the happy times they had had together, the day in the Baltic when his little gun had shattered *Bismarck*'s target and Lindemann had been so understanding about it, the convivial evenings ashore in Hamburg and Kiel. 'It is a terrible thing to be so near,' he wrote in his log, 'and unable to do anything'.

He remembered too the signal he and Lindemann had exchanged about getting a Knight's Cross in the Atlantic together. He had got his two days before, and surely, when *Bismarck* reached port, Lindemann would get one too. But would *Bismarck* reach port? He had heard some of the signals coming over the air, had himself plotted her course towards the north-west, knew how serious the situation was. What if *Bismarck* were to sink before lack of fuel made him turn for home, and her crew found themselves in the water? He could take a hundred at most in his cramped submarine, but what of the other 2,000, would he have to leave them swimming in the water? And should he try and rescue some of the senior officers, like Lütjens and the staff, men in a position to report on what had happened? It was a dilemma he never had to resolve. 'Bismarck still fighting', he wrote at 4 a.m., 'Seas getting higher'.

Another two hours went by, the flashes of Bismarck's guns became more distant and sporadic, he lost her turbines on the hydrophones. With his lack of fuel he couldn't chase after her, but now in the dawn light Kentrat in U.74 hove in sight, guided by his beacon signals. Kentrat couldn't attack either because of damage caused by a depth charge attack, but he had sufficient fuel, could take over duties as observer and reporting ship. The two boats closed to within hailing distance, Wohlfarth indicated the direction in which Bismarck had gone. He wished Kentrat luck, then with heavy heart pointed the bows of U.556 towards Lorient, slid beneath the waves. Relying on most economical use of diesels and motors, he reckoned he had just about enough fuel to reach France.

Hitler was at the Berghof that evening, entertaining guests in the big hall, watching the latest newsreels. Since the sinking of the Hood, Raeder had been in touch by telephone, keeping him abreast of events. After hearing of the torpedo hit by Victorious, Hitler telephoned Göring to ask for bombers to attack the carrier, Göring replied she was far beyond their range. When Bismarck was picked up again by Ark Royal's aircraft, he got on to Göring again, the answer was the same.

Now the telephone rang once more. It was Raeder to tell him about the hit on the rudder. He took the news calmly, said his Luftwaffe adjutant, Colonel von Below, though when told that the ship was unmanoeuvrable, he remarked with some bitterness, 'Why is our Air Force not able to do that sort of thing to the British?' Later a teletype message came from Raeder saying that gale force winds were preventing the despatch of light forces and tugs and adding that if a press notice was thought desirable, it should read: 'The battleship Bismarck on entering the Bay of Biscay had another brush with enemy forces and was hit by a torpedo aft' – a clear indication that Raeder believed that nothing more could be done, wanted to prepare the nation for the blow that was to come.

The guests left by side doors, Hitler took von Below to his study. He became increasingly depressed, says von Below, fretting about the effect of the loss of the ship on German prestige. Perhaps his mind went back to the happy day of the launching three years before when he had stood on the podium with the old Chancellor's granddaughter, and the crowds cheered and the sun shone and Europe was at peace. When Lütjens's signal about fighting to the last shell arrived, he dictated his replies to von Below, perhaps at Raeder's prompting. At 3 a.m. Luftwaffe headquarters rang to say the first planes had taken off to search for the ship and attack the British forces, though at the extreme limit of their range. Hitler dismissed von Below and went to bed.

While Hitler slept, Raeder and Schniewind at the German Admiralty in Berlin accepted the ship was now beyond aid, turned their minds to the fate of the crew. At 5 a.m. Schniewind put through a call to the German naval attaché in Madrid, Captain Meyer-Döhner, to ask the Spanish naval authorities to send a hospital ship, merchant ship, or warship to the area 'to render assistance'. Later Captain Meyer-Döhner called back to say the cruiser *Canarias* and two destroyers would leave Ferrol in five hours' time, the British naval attaché, Captain Hillgarth, would not be informed until the ships had sailed. When Hitler heard of this request, he took Raeder to task, said it was harmful to national prestige.[4]

She lay there wallowing in the unrelenting seas, like a great, wounded, sullen bull. The *picadors* had done their work, thrust their darts deep into flank and shoulders, taken half her power from her. Now she waited for the arrival of the *torero*, for the last trial of strength whose result was a foregone conclusion. But if she had to die, as bulls did, then she would die bravely and with dignity, that too was determined.

The destroyers had retreated out of range, were half-way to the grey horizon, so a partial stand-down was piped to allow men to stretch cramped limbs, get some refreshment, walk about. Most stayed put: some, deep in sleep, never heard the pipe, others were too worn out to move. 'Look out for friendly aircraft, look out for friendly submarines,' chanted the loudspeaker hopefully, but this too went ignored, nobody believed it any more. Records were played to stop people brooding. One man remembered hearing *'Warum ist es am Rhein so schön?'* - 'Why is it so lovely by the Rhine?'

Müllenheim-Rechberg left the after control, made his way to the wardroom where soup was being served, took a little to warm him, exchanged a few desultory remarks with others as unshaven and bleary-eyed as himself. Then he went to the bridge, entered the armoured conning tower. Eich had been there a little earlier, seen the captain congratulating Schneider on his Knight's Cross: Lindemann was smoking as usual, but otherwise seemed relaxed, Eich was impressed by his composure.

But things had changed when Müllenheim-Rechberg arrived. There was very little activity going on. Dr Externbrink, Commander Neuendorff and others of the admiral's staff and bridge watch were stretched out asleep. Müllenheim-Rechberg observed Lindemann's steward pouring out his coffee – the steward whom Lindemann had recruited from his favourite Hamburg restaurant, who had been happy to join *Bismarck* because she seemed so large and safe. He noticed Lindemann was wearing an inflated lifebelt, went over and saluted: Lindemann looked at him dully, didn't return the salute, which Müllenheim-Rechberg thought strange as he had once been his aide. 'He looked like a man doomed to destruction', Müllenheim-Rechberg wrote afterwards, 'dead tired, waiting patiently for the end'. He moved to the chart table, saw the drunken course the ship had been steering through the night, a picture that was self-explanatory. Then he went aft, back to his post, and on the superstructure passed Lütjens and Commander Ascher, the staff operations officer returning to the bridge: Müllenheim-Rechberg saluted, the admiral saluted back.

There is further evidence that the once cool Lindemann's nerves had frayed, that his reserves of endurance were exhausted. Down in the engine-room Commander Lehmann had asked Gerhard Junack to relieve him for a while on the engine-room platform. There had

197

been no engine-room orders for some time, but now they rang down from the bridge: 'Stop engines'. At about this time Lütjens's last signal, 'Send U-boat to save war diary' was sent, so it seems likely the admiral had asked for the ship to be stopped for any U-boat near to come alongside. But to stop the engines abruptly and leave them stopped was risky, they could seize up, so Junack picked up the bridge telephone, asked permission to keep the engines turning over slowly. The exasperation of the captain's reply surprised him: 'Oh, do what you like! I've finished with them'. It was as though Lindemann's will had broken, that after his superhuman efforts of the last five sleepless days and nights, the brilliant way in which he had sailed and fought his ship, his mind was no longer capable of answering to the situation.

At a little after eight o'clock an enemy cruiser was reported on the port bow. Lütjens and Ascher raised their glasses, recognised an old friend, the cruiser *Norfolk*, which they had first seen in the Denmark Straits three and a half days before. Now, after 36 hours' solitary high-speed steaming she had arrived on the scene in the nick of time, as the final curtain was about to go up. She flashed her light at *Bismarck*, then veered away. A rain squall swept over *Bismarck*, and when it had cleared, her officers on the bridge saw with tired eyes two battleships dead ahead. One was *King George V* class, the other, as expected, *Rodney*. Lütjens and Netzbandt had seen *Rodney* from the bridge of *Gneisenau* only ten weeks earlier, when one night after they had sunk several ships on the H.X. convoy route, her long silhouette had suddenly become visible against the light of the blazing *Chilean Reefer*. Then Netzbandt had put *Gneisenau*'s wheel over, gone on to full speed, they had melted into the night. There was no use trying that today: now *Rodney*'s turn had come and she and her consort stood relentlessly towards them. Schneider took up his position in the gunnery control tower, non-duty officers were piped to the big charthouse, throughout the ship the alarm bells were sounded for the last time.

By one in the morning Tovey and the battle-fleet had got as far to the north-east as he wanted, turned and ran down the reciprocal bearing so as to get to the westward of *Bismarck* by dawn: at about 5 a.m. they crossed twenty miles ahead of the enemy's track, but in the poor visibility failed to see the destroyers' starshells. 'Throughout the night on the admiral's bridge', wrote Hugh Guernsey, 'we sat, stood or leant like a covey of disembodied spirits. It was dark, windy and rainy. None of us will ever know if it was cold. About two o'clock in the morning cocoa appeared. We drank it gratefully, but it might equally well have been pitch-tar; no one would have noticed.' Everyone's mind was on the coming battle. Now that it was as certain as anything could be, men asked themselves, as those in *Hood* and *Prince of Wales* had asked earlier, whether by this time next day they would be alive or dead, whether wounded and how, whether they would be able to do their duty as England and the ghost of Nelson expected. Other, duller, souls thought: I'm glad we've cornered the Hun at last, tomorrow we'll teach him a lesson.

Captains Dalrymple-Hamilton and Patterson stayed on their compass platforms all night, occasionally dozing in upright chairs. Tovey was up most of the time too, making frequent visits to the plot to see the enemy's latest position obtained by D/F bearings of Vian's destroyers (*Bismarck*'s wireless office was sending out similar signals to guide U-boats to her) and attending to incoming signals. From Somerville came news that twelve Swordfish would attack at dawn, from Vian that the enemy had made good eight miles between 2.40 and 3.40 and was still capable of heavy and accurate fire, while the Admiralty, desperately worried that having got this far Tovey might now have to break off and return for lack of fuel, gave approval for him to seek sanctuary in an Irish port, where an oiler would be sent.[5]

In the nerve-centres of Tovey's four ships (bridge, wireless office, engine and boiler rooms) there was activity all night, but elsewhere at their action stations, men not immediately needed, slept. George Whalley, a young officer in *Tartar*, found some of the after supply party asleep when he went to his cabin to fetch something. 'It was almost impossible to walk through them without treading on someone. They were all in duffel coats, sleeping as only a sailor can, in any attitude, wherever he happens to be. There was a complete silence, a sense of no soul about; only the sound of the ship in a sea-way, the creaking sounds, the wash, the drumming of the screws. There was no light except that coming through the slats of the pantry door. It fell across the still shapes in bars and moved across the duffel coats and outflung arms as the light swung to the ship's motion. It was strangely still and beautiful and ominous'.

Dawn broke at last, 'patchy rain squalls', wrote Guernsey, 'a tearing wind from the north-west and a rising sea'. Somerville thought the visibility too poor to risk the Swordfish attack, was afraid of a repetition of the *Sheffield* incident, signalled Tovey he was cancelling it. Tovey felt the same: with so many ships about and *Norfolk* and *Dorsetshire* approaching from north and south, he decided to stand off until full daylight, for he had no worries about the enemy escaping him now. He went to his sea-cabin as Nelson had done before Trafalgar, prayed, as he put it, 'for guidance and help'. He had no doubts that his ships would sink *Bismarck*, but was afraid they might get terribly damaged. The longer he prayed, the calmer he felt. It was, he said, 'as if all responsibility had been taken from me, and I knew everything would be all right', and he returned to the bridge refreshed and confident. About the same time his operations officer, Commander Robertson, went to his cabin to fetch his steel helmet. An astonishing sight met his eyes – four large rats running about in terror. Robertson remembered the adage about sinking ships, hoped it wasn't a bad omen.

During the night Tovey had been planning his battle tactics, now he revealed them to Captain Patterson and his staff. *King George V* and *Rodney* would approach the enemy head-on in line abreast, six cables (three-fifths of a mile) apart. 'I hoped', said Tovey, 'that the sight of two battleships steering straight for them would shake the nerves of the range-takers and control officers, who had already had four anxious days and nights'. The two ships would close as quickly as possible to a range of between seven and eight miles, then turn and fire broadsides: *Rodney* would have discretion to manoeuvre on her own. Dalrymple-Hamilton, receiving this message, was grateful to Tovey for giving him the freedom of action Holland had denied to *Prince of Wales*. He thought of his son North, at his action station in one of *King George V*'s anti-aircraft directors, hoped he would come safely through the battle. At 2.30 a.m. Tovey began to turn the fleet to port, in a long, slow arc to the eastwards, towards *Bismarck*, keeping informed of her position by D/F bearings on *Maori*. An hour later *Norfolk* came into sight dead ahead, having reached the scene of battle at the very last moment. She had mistaken *Bismarck* for *Rodney*, challenged her by lamp, only realised who it was when there was no reply, sheered away sharply to get out of range, as she had done in the Denmark Straits four days before. Then an alert *Bismarck* had fired on her within seconds, now, rolling sluggishly in the heavy seas, she made no attempt to. Nor did *Norfolk*. 'I felt it unwise to irritate her unnecessarily before she had someone else to distract her attention', wrote Wake-Walker, not realising her days of irritation were over. As *Norfolk* increased the range from the enemy, she sighted *King George V* and *Rodney* coming in from the west, became the first visual link between the three battleships. 'Enemy bears 130° 16 miles,' Wake-Walker signalled to Tovey, 'On tin hats!'

Tovey saw he was steering too far to the north, altered course to starboard to close. The ships came round, steadied on south. Tovey reached for his tin hat, hanging on a hook outside: when he put it on, a trickle of water ran down his face (during a rain squall some had collected in the bottom): he smiled, and those around him smiled to see their leader so relaxed. The minutes went by, Wake-Walker continuing to send reports of the enemy's position. On the bridge of *King George V* and *Rodney* officers and lookouts strained through binoculars to catch a first glimpse of the ship that for days now – it seemed like weeks – had been in the very marrow of their lives. Did she really exist? She had the same sort of grim reality as the giant in the boy's story-book. And what did she look like, this monster that had sunk their beloved *Hood*?

And then, suddenly, there she was; 'veiled in distant rain-fall,' wrote Guernsey, 'a thick, squat ghost of a ship, very broad in the beam, coming straight towards us'. 'Enemy in sight' came over the *Rodney*'s loudspeakers and telephones, and all over the ship men cheered. The time was 8.43 a.m., the range twelve and a half miles.

Four minutes later George Whalley in *Tartar*, walking aft along the upper deck, saw a cloud of brown smoke erupt from *Rodney*'s foremost guns, seconds later heard the rumble of her opening salvo. He ran down to the wardroom where some officers, having been at action stations all night, were sprawled asleep in every posture.

'They've found her!' he shouted. 'It's begun!'

CHAPTER

11

Before *Rodney*'s first salvo had landed, the fire-gong sounded in *King George V*. On the upper bridge Captain Patterson and his officers, on the lower the admiral and his officers, waited in tin hats and with cotton wool stuffed in their ears to deaden the sound, for the flagship's opening roar. Within seconds it came, like a small earthquake, the bitter cordite fumes catching at their throats, the explosion of the charges stunning them. The compass bounded out of its binnacle, Guernsey's tin hat was blown on to the deck, a pile of signals was sucked upwards like a tornado, scattered to the winds.

The salvoes fell as *Bismarck* was turning to starboard to bring all her guns to bear: great, white clumps rose all round her, higher than her foremast. Then it was her turn. In the British ships they saw a ripple of orange fire down the length of her, followed by a pall of cordite smoke, far blacker and thicker than their own. 'Time of flight 55 seconds,' announced a keen officer of the admiral's staff, and started counting off the time that was left. 'For heaven's sake,' said Tovey, not wanting to know the moment a shell might strike him, 'shut up!' Even so they waited anxiously on the bridges of the two battleships for the salvo to arrive, the men of each hoping it was aimed at the other. They felt an instinct to duck, then the thunderbolt fell off *Rodney*'s bow, short, in a pattern of huge splashes and Guernsey and others in *King George V* breathed a sigh of relief.

At ten miles range *Norfolk*, to the east of Tovey, joined battle with her 8-inch guns. *King George V* and *Rodney* continued firing with their foremost turrets and were soon claiming straddles and hits. But *Bismarck* was finding the range too, her third salvo straddled *Rodney*, a few splinters came aboard. One passed through the starboard side of the anti-aircraft director, smashed the cease-fire bell, passed thought a tin hat on a hook, severed the trainer's telescope, hit the fire gong and grazed the trainer's wrist, after which the director was evacuated and the crew took shelter below. Dalrymple-Hamilton turned to port to avoid the next salvo and bring the after turret into action. 'I watched *Rodney*,' said Guernsey, 'to see if she was being hit, but she just sat there like a great slab of rock blocking the northern horizon, and then suddenly belched a full salvo.' With his own eyes he saw some of the one ton shells come whizzing out of the barrels at 1,600 m.p.h., watched them 'like little diminishing foot-balls curving into the sky'.

At a minute before nine, when the range was down to eight miles, Tovey ordered *Rodney* and *King George V* to turn from south-east to south to bring the full weight of their guns to bear. Just before *Rodney* turned, Captain Coppinger, who was beside Captain Dalrymple-Hamilton on the bridge, taking notes of the battle, saw the burst of a heavy shell on *Bismarck*'s fo'c'sle, while another sent a sheet of flame up the superstructure. After the turn, *Bismarck* was seen to be altering to starboard too, to keep all her guns bearing, so that both forces were steaming on opposite courses, almost parallel.

Now a fourth British ship arrived to join the battle. It was the *Dorsetshire*, cutting things even finer than *Norfolk*. After 600 miles steaming at speeds that varied between 20 and 32 knots she had sighted *Cossack* forty minutes earlier, been directed by her to the scene, opened fire on the enemy from the south. She appeared at a useful moment, for the battleships were now steaming downwind, the funnel gases and cordite smoke hung about the bridge and round the gunnery control tower, making aiming at *Bismarck* difficult.

And now *Bismarck* shifted her fire from *Rodney* to *King George V*, spat out a salvo. Guernsey heard the whine of its approach, saw four tall fountains rise near the fo'c'sle, one short, three over. He wondered if the next would hit, found himself edging into the doorway at the back of the bridge, then remembering it was only splash-proof plating, stepped boldly forward. On the scan in the radar office they tracked some of *Bismarck's* shells coming toward them, held them from about three miles out to half a mile in. The radar officer said it was no more alarming than seeing enemy gun flashes, and the period of suspense was much less. They also tracked the flight of their own shells, lost them at five miles out.

Only a quarter of an hour after the two ships had turned south, Dalrymple-Hamilton found *Bismarck* beginning to draw past him: if he continued on this course he would be masking the fire of *King George V* on his other side, so interpreting in the widest sense Tovey's permission for him to manoeuvre independently, he did what no captain of a British warship had done since the Battle of Cape St Vincent 144 years earlier – took his ship out of the line, and while the enemy was engaging *King George V*, turned *Rodney* right round to a course of north. Tovey, following a few minutes later, called up to Patterson: 'Get closer, get closer, I can't see enough hits!'

In the big ships they were too occupied with fighting to take an objective view of the battle. It was different in the destroyers, in Vian's flotilla and in *Tartar* and *Mashona:* these last two Tovey had detached at the start of the action to return to Londonderry to fuel, but having come so far they weren't going to miss the battle for anything.

They were *aficionados* at the bull-fight, come to see how *torero* Tovey killed his first bull, spectators at a public execution. They saw things the combatants were unaware of, the sun for the first time in days shining from between white, racing clouds, and the wind, still strong, marbling and stippling the green water, whipping the tops from the short, high seas. One officer in *Tartar* was struck by the colour contrasts; bits of blue in the sky, a blue they hadn't seen for days, the blackness of *Bismarck* and the grey of the British ships, the brown pall of cordite smoke and the orange flashes of the guns, shell-splashes white as shrouds.

It was a lovely sight to begin with, a pageant, George Whalley called it, wild, majestic, almost too bright and clean for the matter in hand. It seemed strange to think that within those three Leviathans

were 5,000 men, it was irrelevant somehow, this was a contest between ships, not men. That was how it always was in a sea-fight, you
killed people whom you did not know and could not see, whom you
had little cause to think even existed.

Bismarck was a menace that had to be destroyed, they knew that, a
creature that would have cut the arteries that kept their country
alive. And yet to see her now, surrounded by enemies on all sides,
hopelessly outgunned and outnumbered, was not a pretty sight.
She was a ship after all, perhaps the finest they had seen, and ships
were their livelihood and life. As they watched the shells from the
battleships and cruisers tearing into her, they thought of her crew,
seamen like themselves. 'What that ship was like inside,' said George
Whalley, 'did not bear thinking of; her guns smashed, the ship full
of fire, her people hurt; and surely all men are much the same when
hurt.'

They stayed almost until the end, hopeful that Tovey might order
them to go in and fire torpedoes, dreadfully disappointed he didn't
(one officer in *Tartar* with perhaps the only movie camera in the
fleet had hopes of filming *Bismarck* at close quarters[1]). But their fuel
situation was acute, they had already stayed longer than they should.
The flags ran up *Tartar*'s yardarm, both ships turned, set course at 15
knots for Londonderry.

Now *Rodney* was only four miles from the enemy and closing, so
Bismarck shifted fire back to her. Deep down in *Rodney*'s bows, more
than 20 feet below the waterline, Chief Petty Officer Pollard and his
crew were reloading the ship's torpedo tubes. They had fired six
torpedoes during the run south, all without success, now were
getting ready to fire more. Like other parts of the ship they had
suffered much from the blast of their own guns, main lighting gone
and water pouring in from a cracked pipe, they were working on
three dim emergency lights and a couple of torches. Below the
waterline the explosion of *Bismarck*'s shells was magnified enor-
mously, and they knew that if the deck above them was hit and the
hatch buckled, they would be unlikely to get out. Now there was a
noise in their ears like a thunderclap, the compartment seemed to

rise and fall. A shell from *Bismarck* had landed just off the starboard bow, jammed the sluice-door of the starboard torpedo tube, rendered it useless.[2]

This was the nearest that *Bismarck* got to a direct hit, afterwards her fire began to fall off rapidly. Now untroubled by gases or cordite smoke, the British battleships closed the range, poured in salvo after salvo: *Norfolk* too was keeping up a steady fire from the east, while to the south-east *Dorsetshire*, which had previously checked fire because of the confusion of so many shell splashes, joined in again too. Looking at the enemy closely it was now possible to see something of the damage done. The hydraulic power that served A turret must have been destroyed, its two 15-inch guns were stuck at maximum depression, 'drooping' said one man, 'like dead flowers'. The back of B turret had been blown over the side, one of its guns like a giant finger pointed drunkenly towards the sky. In the after turret one barrel had burst, leaving a stub like a peeled banana. The main director control was smashed in and half the fore-mast had gone over the side. Inside the hull flames were flickering in half a dozen places, the fire from the few guns still in action was increasingly ragged and spasmodic.

She was now barely crawling through the water, so to avoid U-boats which the Admiralty had warned were gathering, Dalrymple-Hamilton found himself obliged to zigzag across her bows, firing broadsides alternately from port and starboard. The range was under four miles and still closing, so that Captain Teek in charge of X turret manned by the Royal Marines, found that the breech of his gun which had started the action down near the deck had risen almost to the roof of the turret. At one moment the foremost guns were pointing so far aft that the blast took Captain Coppinger's steel hat off his head and into a signalman, and sent his notebook flying (it was found later on the quarterdeck). At three and a half miles *Rodney* fired two more torpedoes through the undamaged port tube, neither of which hit. And still, because there was life in *Bismarck* and her flag flew, the huge shells went on being pumped into her. 'I can't say I enjoyed this part of the business much,' said Dalrymple-Hamilton, 'but didn't see what else I could do.'

207

King George V meanwhile was suffering from the same 'teething troubles' that in the Denmark Strait had so affected *Prince of Wales*. One after the other her main guns developed defects until at one moment their efficiency was down to 20%. At the time people were too busy repairing them to think about it, later they felt a chill of fear in reflecting what might have happened had they met *Bismarck* alone. Fortunately the secondary armament could now come into action and was soon straddling too. To Tovey it seemed incredible that any ship could stand such punishment and still float. He was worried too about his fuel situation and how much longer he could stay. 'Somebody get me my darts!' he said in exasperation, 'let's see if we can't sink her with those!'

By 10 a.m. the *Bismarck* was a battered burning wreck, her guns twisted and silent, full of huge holes in her sides and superstructure through which fires glowed and flickered, grey smoke issuing from a hundred cracks and crevices and drifting away on the wind, listing heavily to port, but at the foremast her admiral's flag and at the mainmast the German naval ensign still bravely flying. In the British ships they looked at her with awe and admiration, awe that such a magnificent ship should have to be reduced to this, admiration that her crew had fought so gallantly to the end. 'Pray God I may never know,' said Guernsey, echoing George Whalley, 'what those shells did as they exploded inside the hull.' It was a thought shared by many sailors that day, one rarely expressed by airmen who incinerate cities, nor by soldiers of those they kill in tanks.

As they watched, the lifeless ship took life – the enemy in person, a little trickle of figures running aft along *Bismarck*'s quarter-deck, climbing the guard-rails and jumping into the sea, unable to stand any more the inferno aboard, welcoming like lemmings death in the cool, kind sea. And presently in the British ships fire was checked, for the *Bismarck* no longer menaced anyone, her life was almost at an end.

Admiral Somerville, just over the southern horizon, with *Ark Royal*, *Sheffield* and *Renown* (whose crew were desolate to be deprived of a share in the battle) had been listening to the rumble of gunfire for the last hour. At 9.30 a.m. *Ark Royal* had flown off

34. *'After more than an hour's swimming, the first of them reached* **Dorsetshire's** *side.'* **Bismarck** *survivors waiting to be rescued*

35. 'It was an honour he was not to enjoy at liberty for long.'
*Lieutenant-Commander Herbert Wohlfarth receives the Knight's Cross from Admiral Dönitz on board **U.556** at Lorient*

twelve Swordfish to make a final torpedo attack on the enemy, but they arrived when the battle was in full spate, kept well clear. Now the gunfire had stopped. Somerville was desperate to have news, signalled Tovey as to whether he had finished the enemy off. The reply was surprising: *Bismarck* was still afloat, Tovey could not get her to sink by gunfire, he was discontinuing the action for lack of fuel and going home.

In fact there was nothing more for Tovey to do. Whether *Bismarck* sank now or later was immaterial: what was certain was she would never get back to port. He had already stayed ten hours longer than he had said his fuel would allow, and U-boats would soon be on the scene, if they had not reached it already. He signalled *Rodney* to form up astern, gave orders to Patterson to take the flagship home. And as he left he made a general signal to ships in company: 'Any ship with torpedoes to close *Bismarck* and torpedo her'.

Tartar and *Mashona* had already turned for home, Vian's ships had spent all their torpedoes, so had *Norfolk*, so had *Rodney* (firing her last two at the end of the action she claimed one hit which, if true, was the only instance in history of one battleship torpedoing another). Only one ship, *Dorsetshire*, still had torpedoes, and when Tovey's signal reached her, Captain Martin had already anticipated it. Closing in to a mile and a half on *Bismarck*'s starboard beam, she fired two torpedoes, both of which hit. She then went round the other side, at just over a mile fired another which also hit.

Far off now in *King George V*, half-way to the horizon, Tovey saw through his glasses the great ship slowly keel over to port until her funnel was level with the water, go on turning until she was completely upside down. He remembered Jutland and the sinking *Wiesbaden*, was already forming in his mind the words of his official despatch: 'She put up a most gallant fight against impossible odds, worthy of the old days of the Imperial German Navy'.[3] The stern dipped below the surface of the water, then the main keel: the great flared bows were last to go, and then all that was left to show where *Bismarck* had been were hundreds of men in life-belts, swimming in oil and water.

CHAPTER

12

Some died early in *Bismarck* and some late, and the luckiest were those who knew nothing of it.

When the battle started, despite tiredness, morale seems to have been good. Hans Riedel, loader in C turret, says that there was a certain amount of tension and restlessness beforehand, but once *Bismarck* opened fire, spirits were high. Able Seaman Heinz Staat, whose action station was at Commander Oels's control post, deep down below the armoured deck amidships, told of a Petty Officer there who kept taking off and putting on his tie – the same man, he said, who when the torpedo from *Victorious* had hit, had blown up his life-jacket and tried to leave the compartment without orders. Now Commander Oels said to him firmly, 'If you make other people nervous, I will find ways of keeping you quiet'. But the others hadn't been made nervous, said Staat, they seemed relaxed and confident, at any rate outwardly.

Müllenheim-Rechberg says the British ships took quite a time to find the range. When they had found it, and were hitting regularly, the fore part of the ship suffered more than aft. A and B turret were knocked out fairly early in the action, also the main gunnery control. Of those that survived the day none at all came from the fore part, not from A and B turrets, the bridge or bridge superstructure, the charthouse and gunnery control, the magazines and shell-rooms below. So we do not know how Lütjens and Lindemann, Schneider and Neuendorff, Netzbandt and Externbrink and all the other officers of the admiral's staff died. But there is much evidence of fires raging forward, both in the superstructure and below decks, and it would seem that the people who were not killed by shell bursts were burned to death by the fires or else trapped behind them, unable to get out, and drowned when the ship turned turtle.

After A and B turret had gone, and the fore plotting officer could get no more communication with Schneider in the main gunnery control, Müllenheim-Rechberg was ordered to fire C and D turrets with the after control. Schneider had been firing at *Rodney* but Müllenheim-Rechberg ranged on *King George V*. He remembers his first salvo as being one short and three over, which was the one that made Guernsey retreat to the after part of the bridge. His next three salvoes were less accurate, and then a British shell exploded near his position, which banged his head against an instrument and smashed the optics of the range-finder, so he had to order C and D turrets to fire in local control. D turret was the next to go when a shell burst in one barrel and there was a flashback into the turret that killed many of the crew: that left only C turret in action, and when one of its two barrels was hit, the lieutenant in charge ordered it to cease fire.

Like Müllenheim-Rechberg, others who survived knew little or nothing of what was going on elsewhere, for they stayed at their posts, behind armour plating, until the order came to abandon ship. In the engine-rooms they heard thuds and bangs distantly above them, couldn't tell the difference between their own guns firing and British hits. The lights continued to burn brightly and the engines to turn at slow speed: the only unusual thing was water slopping down from the air intakes, indicating near misses from enemy shells. Later smoke from shell bursts and fires came down the intakes, making breathing difficult, so in some compartments they put on gas masks.

Some people, like the flak crews and the merchant navy men for prizes, had nothing to do. Herzog and others of the after flak were ordered down to their mess on the after battery deck, near the barbette. It was uncomfortable sitting there, listening to the shells hitting the ship, not being able to strike back. After the forward turrets and superstructure had been hit, Chief Petty Officer Wienand, who had been talking to them of his home in Hamburg the night before, came to collect men to act as stretcher-bearers. When they had gone, Herzog opened his locker, took a couple of swigs from a bottle of *Rösenlikor* he kept there, stretched himself out. He felt exhausted after the exertions of the last few days, presently things began to get misty. He was aware of the loudspeaker saying the admiral and Lindemann had been killed, then that Lindemann hadn't been killed, and then there was a tremendous bang and the clatter and singing of iron and metal and afterwards sounds 'as though through cotton wool' of the cries of the wounded.

The duties of a few men like the medical orderlies and damage control parties took them about the ship. One damage control party was in the charge of Chief Mechanician Wilhelm Schmidt from Friedrichshafen. As they moved about, they were aware of British shells plunging down through the upper deck, sometimes the next deck too, bursting inside enclosed compartments, filling them with smoke and gases, putting out the main lights, showering splinters everywhere, twisting and buckling the ladders and doors and hatches. Some of the shells fell close to them, the splinters killed some men, wounded others. A messenger appeared to say that men were needed to fight the fire in the superstructure: those that went were all killed. Later, after the flashback in D turret, another messenger arrived with orders to flood D turret magazine, lest the ship blow up. So Wienand switched on the pump to flood the magazine, though whether the men in it got out or were drowned there or had already been killed by the flashback, no one knows.

Around 10 a.m., after C turret had packed up, but while the British ships were still firing, orders were given to prepare Measure 5, the order for placing scuttling charges, and to prepare to abandon ship. These orders came from the senior surviving officer, Commander Oels, the executive officer, from his post at the base of the superstructure. He had assumed command of the ship after the bridge had been knocked out.

There were several ways out of the command post, up a vertical ladder which ran through a narrow shaft to the superstructure, or through one of the doors in the bulkhead. Able Seaman Staat didn't fancy the ladder, went out of the port door, found the next compartment deep in water, hammocks floating about in it, the ship listing to port. He went up to the next deck, into a compartment full of yellowish-green smoke, full of wounded lying about and doctors and orderlies giving morphia injections, working so fast they were not even pausing to sterilise the needles.

He went through this compartment and up to the battery deck, into the main canteen alongside the funnel, and here he found Commander Oels and about three hundred men all struggling to get out. They couldn't go forward because of the fires raging there, and the midships hatch was jammed, so everyone was pushing and shoving to get through the narrow door aft: the canteen too was full of fumes, and those who hadn't got gas-masks were shaken by fits of coughing.

Another man in the canteen was Herbert Blum. A few minutes earlier he had been standing beside Commander Lehmann at the damage control command post when the order came by telephone to abandon ship. He remembered how Lehmann had replaced the telephone receiver 'as carefully as if it were the most fragile glass', and said to Blum and the others, as calm and friendly as ever: 'You may go now', and that was the last they saw of him.

Blum made his way to a workshop behind the funnel where he and his mates used to gather, was lying down there exhausted on the deck, when a shell burst in the next compartment. It blew the bulkhead door open and through the smoke Blum saw a wounded man being carried out and another without any arms.

So then he made his way up to the canteen and he hadn't been there long when there was a tremendous explosion. Blum saw a dazzling red ball of fire a few feet from his eyes, felt a terrible noise and agonising pressure in his ear drums, was flung to the ground. Staat saw it differently, as a flare, blue-green and yellow-white like phosphorus, and the after side of the funnel flaring a brilliant red.

Like Blum, Staat was thrown to the deck, momentarily concussed; after a few moments they picked themselves up, touched themselves all over, found they were unhurt. But all around was a scene of unspeakable carnage, at least a hundred dead, Oels among them, as many more wounded, some terribly: young men with bits of their faces blown away, limbs separated from bodies, splintered bones sticking through skin, blood gushing and flowing everywhere, men with stomach wounds watching their insides seep out and trying to shove them back, others vomiting with shock and disgust, the ghastly screams of the suffering.

These casualties made it easier for those untouched to get out. Staat picked his way over the dead and mutilated into the next compartment, found it almost as crowded as the one he'd left. Step by step he made his way aft, in the alleyway by the after canteen found a ladder leading to a hatch, with the help of five men opened it and came out on the upper deck. It was littered with dead and wounded: when the ship gave a lurch to port which was the windward side, many were washed overboard, then with the next wave washed back, smashed against the after superstructure. Staat and his companions ran up the sloping deck, found more dead and wounded, mostly flak crews lying behind C and D turrets. A flak Petty Officer with one leg blown off held up a hand with a big signet ring on it, implored Staat to throw him overboard, but Staat hardly had the strength to move himself. He lay exhausted by the starboard guard rails, saw a man taking off his trousers to jump overboard, thought it foolish as the man would get cold, then another shell exploded and when Staat looked again, the lower half of the man had vanished, his head and torso were falling into the sea.

Blum also managed to get to the upper deck, through a jammed hatchway, not more than two hands-breadths wide. Like Staat, Blum was horrified by what he saw, the wreckage everywhere, the huge shell-holes in the deck, grey smoke rising from below, the piles of dead and wounded. A man came up to him with one hand shattered, the other carrying a field dressing. While Blum was bandaging him up, he heard screams and yells coming from the after starboard 5.9-inch turret. He went over, found the hatch into it jammed, neither he nor the men inside could open it, he had to leave them there, trapped.

One of the crew of this turret, Ordinary Seaman Paul Hiller, was lucky. In the destroyer action during the night he'd injured himself loading, been ordered to change places with another man in the shellroom below. He didn't like this, felt trapped in such a small space so far below, but when the order came to abandon ship, he managed to get up the ammunition hoist, then through a small door on to the 'tween deck. He started to go forward but the fires drove him back: he managed to get to the battery deck, entered a compartment where the older merchant navy men for the prize crews were sitting patiently on their seachests. A shell plunged through the compartment, burst on the deck below. Many of the merchant navy men were wounded by splinters, Hiller called to them to follow him aft, but they just sat there silent and bleeding, waiting resignedly for the end.

In ones and twos other survivors reached the upper deck aft, some through hatches that were still free, others up ammunition hoists, a few like Adolf Eich up the wiring shaft from the switch room to Müllenheim-Rechberg's after control position. All had their tales of horror. One man, passing through the wireless office, until recently sending out beacon signals for U-boats, found the place a shambles, every man in it dead. Heinz Steeg reached the casualty station of the Adolf Hitler Platz (an open space on the main deck aft) just after a shell had burst there, killed all the medical staff and most of the wounded. Gerhard Schäpe passed a man who had gone out of his mind, was foaming at the mouth and yelling about German Stukas. Another saw an officer shoot himself. On the upper deck Eich found a Collani, a sailor's greatcoat named after the firm that made them, spreadeagled against the grating of an engine-room ventilator: behind it were the remains of its owner. A moment later Eich saw two men running aft, in the drifting smoke fail to see a gaping shell hole in the deck, plunge through it into the flames below. Gerhard Klotzschke arriving at D turret saw some of the survivors of the flashback sitting on the deck outside, badly burned, hair singed off, eyes half out of their sockets.

Some of the last men to come up were the people in the engine-room. Gerhard Junack was in the midships engine-room when Commander Lehmann on the telephone gave the order for Measure

5: at the time steam was coming from the boiler-rooms and all three engines were going slow speed ahead. Junack ordered his men to place explosive charges with time fuses in the cooling water intakes, and to open the seacocks. In the port engine-room Werner Lust and others weren't able to do this, because the deck was flooded with water from the ventilating shafts, but in the starboard engine-room the charges were laid by Klotzschke and others. When Junack's men had lit the fuses, which had nine minutes delay, he ordered them to evacuate the engine-room and go up top. The compartment was full of fumes but the lights were still burning brightly. They were burning too on the armoured deck, though no one was there. The firing had stopped, said Junack, and it was deathly still, quiet as a Sunday afternoon in harbour. In the silence he and his men heard the scuttling charges go off far below.

On the next deck they tried to get forward, were driven back by the fires, aft on the deck above they found a group of men in the smoke wearing gasmasks and lifebelts, wandering about, utterly confused. Junack ordered them to follow him, found a half-opened hatch, made the men take off gasmasks and lifebelts and they all just squeezed through, came out on the upper deck.

By this time a lot of men had gathered on the quarter-deck, two or three hundred, said Junack, and now they were joined by Müllen-heim-Rechberg and others from the after control, and by the crew of C turret, none of whom, said Hans Riedel, was even hurt. They were all horrified by what they saw; the tangled wreckage, smoke and flames, the piles of dead and mutilated, the moans of the wounded. Some helped to adjust the lifebelts of the less badly wounded, put them over the side: others found the screams got on their nerves, wanted to shut them up.

Before the British ships had ceased firing, many men had gone over the side on their own accord to escape the merciless shelling: they could be seen strung out like a row of beads in a long line astern, for the ship was still moving. Among them were Herzog and Manthey, both of the after flak, and a man called Höntzsch. They had been sheltering behind D turret and had loosened a rubber raft there when a huge shell splash landed alongside, swept them all and the raft

216

overboard. After fifteen minutes swimming they had managed to clamber aboard, saw the *Bismarck*, still being fired at, moving slowly away.

Junack gathered a group of men together, among them Blum, and said, 'We'll give three "Sieg Heils" and then we'll go overboard. Don't worry, comrades. I'll be taking a Hamburg girl in my arms again, and we'll all meet once more on the Reeperbahn'. The Reeperbahn is Hamburg's red light district, and Blum thought, my God, how on earth does he manage to think of that and taking girls in his arms in the middle of all this. So they gave three 'Sieg Heils' and Budich and a few others sang the national anthem, and then they went over the side. A few stupid ones went down the sloping deck over the port side, where the water was nearest, were soon thrown back against the ship, knocked unconscious. The others slid down the starboard side until they reached the bilge keel, jumped from there into the sea. Kenneth Pattisson in one of *Ark Royal*'s Swordfish flying overhead, saw hundreds of heads bobbing in the water, like turnips in a field of sheep, regretted he had no dinghy to drop to them, waved in a friendly useless gesture: as he turned away he observed smoke pouring out of *Bismarck*'s decks, smelt her burning, described her main gunnery control as a torch of fire.

When the survivors were clear of the ship, she slowly rolled over away from them until she was bottom up. Müllenheim-Rechberg and Junack looked for signs of torpedo damage, couldn't see any. Staat noticed two men sitting on the upturned keel, making no effort to save themselves. The stern went under and then the rest of her, taking all their personal belongings and hundreds of dead and wounded.

The *Dorsetshire* came round from the port side where she had fired her last torpedo, lay stopped in the sea a little way off; and survivors who had wondered if they were not escaping death by shellfire for death by drowning, felt a new surge of hope: even if it meant being taken prisoner, they were going to be rescued, they were going to live.

They struck out as well as they could towards the cruiser, though with the high seas and the oil from *Bismarck*'s tanks and the wounds of many, it wasn't easy. Müllenheim-Rechberg, swimming along, passed a man who said, 'I've no left leg any more.' Staat remembered being told that when you died of cold, you first felt it in the testicles, but it was his feet and fingers that were getting numb. After more than an hours' swimming the first of them reached the *Dorsetshire*'s side, where rafts, ropes, scrambling nets, fenders, lifelines of all kinds had been let down. Müllenheim-Rechberg noticed that many men, not seamen, didn't know how to grip a straight rope, urged them to get into ropes with bowlines. Staat's fingers were so frozen that he couldn't grip the rope at all, seized it with his teeth, was hauled on board that way. Müllenheim-Rechberg put his foot in a bowline rope, was pulled up by two sailors: when he reached deck level he tried to grab the guardrail, was too exhausted and fell back into the sea: he got into the same rope again, was hauled up by the same two sailors, this time took no risks, said in immaculate English, 'Please help me on board' which they did. Midshipman Joe Brooks of the *Dorsetshire* went down one of the lifelines, tried to get a bowline round a German who had lost both arms and was gripping the lifeline with his teeth: the ship rolled heavily, they both went under, Brooks never saw him again. Blum reached the *Dorsetshire*'s bow, was sucked under by a sea, felt himself under the keel, then came up the other side. The waves carried him away from *Dorsetshire*, but *Maori* was lying stopped a little way off, he managed to reach her and was hauled safely up.

The *Dorsetshire* had picked up some eighty men and the *Maori* some twenty, many more were in the process of being hauled up, and hundreds more were waiting in the water when an unexpected thing happened. *Dorsetshire*'s navigating officer, Lieutenant-Commander Durant, sighted on the starboard bow two miles away a smoky discharge in the water. He pointed it out to Captain Martin and others on the bridge. No one knew what it was but the most likely explanation was a U-boat: the Admiralty had sent a warning that U-boats were on the way, and they were lucky not to have encountered any already. And if it was a U-boat, *Dorsetshire*, laying stopped in the water, was a sitting target. In the circumstances Captain Martin had no choice but to ring down for full speed, and in *Maori* Commander Armstrong did the same. The water round *Dorsetshire*'s stern foamed and bubbled with the sudden exertion of the screws. Slowly, then faster, the ship moved ahead. *Bismarck* survivors who were almost on board were bundled over the guardrails on to the deck: those half-way up the ropes found themselves trailing astern, hung on as long as they could against the forward movement of the ship, dropped off one by one, others in the water clawed frantically at the paintwork as the side slipped by. In *Dorsetshire* they heard the thin cries of hundreds of Germans who had come within an inch of rescue, had believed that their long ordeal was at last over, cries that the British sailors, no less than survivors already on board, would always remember. From the water *Bismarck*'s men watched appalled as the cruiser's grey side swept past them, believed then that tales they'd heard about the British not caring much about survivors were true after all, presently found themselves alone in the sunshine on the empty, tossing sea. And during the day, as they floated about the Atlantic with only life-belts between them and eternity, the cold came to their testicles and hands and feet and heads, and one by one they lost consciousness, and one by one they died.

All except five. Ever since taking over from Wohlfarth early that morning, Kentrat in *U.74* had been cruising in the area. During the morning he had sighted a cruiser and two destroyers (possibly *Dorsetshire*, *Maori* and another of Vian's flotilla) later got a message from Dönitz to close *Bismarck* and take off her war diary (the same message went to Wohlfarth, but by this time he was homeward bound below the waves). Later still, when Kentrat learnt that *Bismarck* had sunk, he got a further message from U-boat headquarters to look for survivors. He searched in the area all day, and about 7 p.m. came across the raft carrying Manthey, Herzog and Höntzsch, took them on board, gave them warm food and drink and put them to bed. They had an adventurous voyage back to Lorient, for it was found that salt water had got into the batteries and the U-boat was unable to dive. Off the French coast, a British submarine, positioned in the area for *Bismarck*'s arrival, fired five torpedoes at *U.74* which, by Kentrat taking violent avoiding action, all missed. On arrival in France the three survivors were closely questioned about the time they had left *Bismarck*, for it seemed to some it might have been before the order to abandon ship. But their stories satisfied the authorities, and having told all they knew of the *Bismarck*'s last voyage, Manthey, Herzog and Höntzsch were sent on survivor's leave and then distributed to other units.

The German weather ship *Sachsenwald* commanded by Lieutenant Schütte, passing through the general area on return from a fifty-day meteorological patrol in the North Atlantic, was also ordered to search for survivors. They sighted nothing on the 27th or the night of the 27th, but at 1 p.m. on the 28th they came across a big oil slick, and beyond it many lifebelts, some with bodies in them, some without, and quantities of wreckage. *Sachsenwald* and two U-boats she met searched all day but found no survivors; but at 10.35 that night, she sighted two red lights to port. Through his glasses Schütte saw a raft with two men on it, steered towards them. One of the men shouted, 'Are you German?', and when Schütte said yes, they gave a faint cheer. They were taken on board, found to be totally exhausted, for they had been tossing in the raft for two days and a night without food or drink. They had the salt washed from their faces were given warm clothes and soup, and put in bunks. They gave, their names as Otto Maus and Walter Lorenzen, and said there was another raft with men on it nearby. Although *Sachsenwald* was by now very short of food, Schütte stayed in the area all night and searched again the following day; saw nothing but more wreckage and lifebelts.

At 12.45 a.m. on the morning of 30th May, he spoke the *Canarias* which had also been searching in the area and sighted only wreckage and bodies, five of which she had taken on board to check identity discs. At daylight both ships left the area to return to harbour, the *Canarias* to Ferrol and the *Sachsenwald* to Bordeaux.[1]

Of the other ships in the operation, Admiral Somerville with Force H set course for Gibraltar as soon as the twelve Swordfish, which had been unable to take part in the last battle, had jettisoned their torpedoes and landed on *Ark Royal*. While they were landing, two Heinkel bombers and a Focke-Wulf Condor were sighted: one Heinkel dropped a stick of bombs some distance from *Ark Royal* and that was the nearest that any of the numerous aircraft that had left France that morning to help the *Bismarck*, came to the British fleet. When *Ark Royal* reached Gibraltar two days later, every boat that was seaworthy came out to cheer her in.

On 28th May a big force of bombers set out from French bases in search of Tovey and his ships. They missed the main fleet, which was steering farther to the north-eastwards than they had supposed, found instead *Tartar* and *Mashona*, crawling along at twelve knots because of fuel shortage, 100 miles to the southward. They bombed them all day, at noon sank *Mashona* with the loss of one officer and forty-five men. Happily there was a lull in which Commander Skipwith in *Tartar* was able to pick up his friend Commander Selby and some 170 officers and men. Next day *Tartar* reached Londonderry with only 5 tons of fuel remaining.

At 12.30 p.m. on the same day Admiral Tovey with *King George V* and a reinforced destroyer screen entered Loch Ewe on Scotland's west coast and came to anchor: next day, after oiling, the flagship was back in its usual berth at Scapa. *Victorious* went briefly to the Clyde, then sailed on 31st May with her crated Hurricanes for the Mediterranean. On the way there Captain Bovell received the happy news that the crew of Swordfish 5H which had gone missing on the morning of 25th May – David Berrill, whom he had written about so glowingly, Pat Jackson and Leading Airman Sparkes, were safe in Reykjavik: with their last drop of petrol they had landed alongside an empty but provisioned life-boat – probably another casualty of H.X. 126 – and sailed about in it for nine days before being picked up by the Icelandic steamer *Lagarfoss*. *Maori* meanwhile with twenty-four *Bismarck* survivors had reached the Clyde, so had *Rodney* and *Norfolk*. *Dorsetshire*, due for a refit, was ordered to Newcastle-on-Tyne, on England's north-east coast. She had seventy-nine *Bismarck* survivors on board, including four cot cases: one died on passage and was buried at sea in the presence of his shipmates and a guard of honour from *Dorsetshire*, his body wrapped in an ensign of the old Imperial German Navy. The ship's bugler sounded the Last Post and as the body went over the side a former shipmate played '*Ich hatt einen Kamarade*' – 'I had a comrade' – on a mouth-organ borrowed from a British sailor.

In Britain the general reaction to the news of the sinking was one of relief rather than exhilaration. On the afternoon after the battle, in the House of Commons, Winston Churchill, not yet knowing the final outcome, told an enthralled House of events up to the beginning of the final action, then went on to other business. In the middle of the other business he was handed a note, read it, said to the Speaker: 'Mr Speaker, I crave your indulgence. I have just heard that the *Bismarck* has been sunk'. Members cheered wildly, waved their order papers, thankful that the cloud that had darkened their horizon for the last five days had at last been lifted. But one member, the writer Harold Nicolson, sat silent: more than some, he saw the thing in human terms, thought of the innumerable dead, sensed its high tragedy.

Now that *Bismarck* had been safely disposed of, it was time to think about *Prinz Eugen;* and next day Winston Churchill wrote a top secret memorandum, marked 'For First Lord and First Sea Lord alone. In a locked box':

> 'The bringing into action of the *Prinz Eugen* and the search for her raise questions of the highest importance. It is most desirable that the United States Navy should play a part in this. If would be far better, for instance, that she should be located by a United States ship, as this might tempt her to fire upon that ship, thus providing the incident for which the United States government would be so thankful.
>
> Pray let this matter be considered from this point of view, apart from the ordinary naval aspect. If we can only create a situation where the *Prinz Eugen* is being shadowed by an American vessel, we shall have gone a long way to solve the largest problem.'

But *Prinz Eugen* was unable to help Churchill and Roosevelt with their plans. After leaving *Bismarck* on 24th May she had steered for the southern group of supply ships, reached the tanker *Spichern* north-west of the Azores on the 26th with only 8 per cent of fuel remaining, next day got a report from an Italian submarine of sighting five battleships steaming south-west at high speed in the *Bismarck*'s area, (almost certainly Vian's flotilla) so broke off her journey to the convoy routes. On the 28th she oiled again from *Esso Hamburg*, then discovered she had serious defects in all three engines, as well as a chipped propeller blade caused by ice when going through the Denmark Straits. Captain Brinkmann therefore abandoned all further plans for commerce raiding and shaped course for Brest, which he reached safely on 1st June. Since leaving Gotenhafen *Prinz Eugen* had travelled 7,000 miles at an average speed of 24 knots.

U.556 meanwhile had also reached harbour on almost her last remaining drop of fuel: when Wohlfarth made fast alongside the submarine jetty at Lorient, he had only eighty litres left. Next day Admiral Dönitz came aboard, presented Wohlfarth with the Knight's Cross of the Iron Cross. It was an honour he was not to enjoy at liberty for long. On her next trip to the Atlantic *U.556* was sunk, and Wohlfarth and most of his officers and men taken prisoner.

In Germany, despite news of further successes by the Luftwaffe against the Royal Navy off Crete, people were as depressed by the news of *Bismarck*'s death as the British had been by the death of *Hood;* more so perhaps, for unlike the British, they had no hopes of a compensating victory. Hitler's intuitions, as often, were right: the ship symbolised the nation, reputation had become a little diminished, prestige a little dimmed. Meanwhile a special office was set up, in which thirty people were employed answering telegrams and letters from next of kin, informing them that no information could be given as to whether their son or husband had survived until returns had come in from the British Admiralty. One letter from a father said his son could not possibly have been on board, as he had been called up only a few days before *Bismarck* had sailed. Research revealed that he was a stoker in the Merchant Navy, had been drafted to *Bismarck* at the last moment as part of the prize crew. On 7th June the German Admiralty received the names of the 102 British-held survivors: with the three from *U.74* and two from *Sachsenwald*, that made a total of 107 out of a ship's company of over 2,000.

Yet if despondency was the dominant mood of the German people and relief that of the British, there were two small groups of people whose excitement knew no bounds. In Brest, when Philippon heard the news on B.B.C. radio, he ran down the Tourville steps four at a time, rushed to the French naval officers' mess – the big hall with its Louis XIV panelling – where some twenty officers were about to sit down to dinner. Slamming the door behind him, he cried, 'The *Bismarck*'s been sunk!' They all turned round. 'If I live to be a hundred', he wrote afterwards, 'I shall never forget the expressions on their faces'.[2]

He was not the only foreigner concerned with the operations to hear that B.B.C. broadcast. A thousand miles away in Southern Norway, Viggo Axelssen, Arne Usterud and others sat drinking in the Red Room of the Kristiansand club, listened with quiet concentration to the news of the battleship's sinking. Viggo and Arne remembered the evening only seven days before when walking on the Vesterveien they had sighted *Bismarck* and *Prinz Eugen* speeding northwards, how Arne Moen had carried the message about it in the engine of his bus to Helle; and how Odd Starheim and Gunvald Torstad had sent it out from there on their transmitter. They remembered too how quickly the German army's D/F unit had arrived at Helle, how narrowly Torstad and Starheim had escaped detection. Now Viggo raised his glass and said, 'Gentlemen!' They all stood up. Viggo said, 'Thirty-five thousand tons' (*Bismarck*'s 'official' tonnage). They repeated it, drained their glasses. Viggo opened the door to the dining-room where other members were at their evening meal, asked them to rise too, drink the same toast. They did, everyone knew what was meant.

And next day across the Norwegian border, in far off, spy-ridden Stockholm, no Englishman alive was more delighted than Captain Henry Denham when he received from the Admiralty this signal:

'Your 2058 of 20th May initiated the first of a series of operations which culminated yesterday in the sinking of the *Bismarck*. Well done.'

Epilogue

He that outlives this day and comes safe home,
Will stand a tip-toe when this day is nam'd
Shakespeare: Henry V

In a story of such nobility and high endeavour, it is sad to have to record what follows.

Sometime during the night of 26th May, Winston Churchill, not then knowing the enemy was crippled beyond repair, became obsessed with the idea that *Bismarck* must be sunk at whatever cost to our ships. He therefore drafted or had drafted for him the following signal to Tovey:

'We cannot visualise the situation from your signals. *Bismarck* must be sunk at all costs and if to do this it is necessary for *King George V* to remain on the scene, then she must do so, even if it subsequently means towing *King George V*.'

This was an extraordinary signal. To have suggested allowing the fleet flagship to run out of fuel in an area where U-boats were gathering and to which aircraft would soon be directed, was to invite her certain destruction – and the deaths of the admiral, his staff, and the ship's company. Furthermore, until *Prince of Wales* was repaired, *King George V* was the *only* British capital ship that had *both* the armour *and* the speed to match *Bismarck's*. If *King George V* had run out of fuel and been sunk, *Bismarck*, once repaired, would have had a more or less free hand in the Atlantic. Pound himself disagreed with the signal, and should not have approved it; but he was not always firm where Churchill was concerned, and it finally went out from the Admiralty at 11.37 next morning, by which time the battle was over and Tovey was on the way home.

Tovey and his staff thought the signal ridiculous: when it was read to them they laughed out loud. Later, when they had time to realise its import, they were angry. 'It was,' said Tovey, 'the stupidest and most ill-considered signal ever made',[1] and he told his staff that if the situation envisaged had arisen, he would have disobeyed the signal and risked court-martial. When the fleet reached harbour and the green telephone was connected to London, Pound apologised for the signal, agreed it should never have been sent. But Tovey never forgot it, it rankled with him for years.

An even more distasteful event occurred a few weeks later – one which proved that Wake-Walker was right in his suspicions on 24th May that the Admiralty were thinking him lacking in offensive spirit. Having read all the reports on the operation and studied the track-charts, Pound informed Tovey that he wanted Wake-Walker and Jack Leach of the *Prince of Wales* brought to trial by court-martial for failing to engage *Bismarck* during the run south after the action with the *Hood*. Tovey was appalled, replied that the conduct of Wake-Walker and Leach were exactly what he desired, the last thing he had wanted was a premature action that might force the enemy to the westward and away from *King George V*. Pound's answer to this was that he still wished the two officers to stand trial by court-martial and if Tovey would not order it, then the Admiralty would. To this Tovey replied that if they did, he would if necessary haul down his flag as Commander-in-Chief and appear at the trial as prisoners' friend. After that, said Tovey, 'I heard no more about it'.[2]

Pound's deputy, Vice-Admiral Tom Phillips, also allowed a sour note to cloud his comments on the operation. Both in his *critique* of the draft communiqué and later of the proposed Honours and Awards, he tried to belittle Dalrymple-Hamilton, said that *Rodney's* movements on the 25th had been 'ill-judged', she should have turned sooner for Brest. But Dalrymple-Hamilton had done what he was ordered to do, drawn a line between the D/F position of *Bismarck* (which unlike *King George V* he had plotted correctly) and Brest, and when he reached it, turned south-east and steered down it. In fact *Bismarck* had not gone direct for Brest but made a long loop to the south – a possibility the impetuous Phillips does not seem to have considered.

Winston Churchill preached magnanimity to one's enemies in victory: Admirals Pound and Phillips seemed unwilling to show it to their friends.

The pursuit and sinking of the *Bismarck* will remain one of the great sea-stories of all time, worthy to take its place with Salamis, Lepanto, the Armada, Trafalgar, Tsushima, Jutland, Midway, the Coral Sea. It covered an immense area of ocean, from the Baltic to the Arctic, the Arctic to the Atlantic, the Atlantic to the Bay of Biscay, and all in the space of only eight days. More than 4,000 sailors, British and German, were killed. People of other nationalities were caught up in it too: Poles, Swedes, Norwegians, Americans, French, Italians, Spanish.

The story itself, with fortunes veering from one side to the other with dramatic swiftness, embraced many of the elements of ancient mythology: pursuit, discovery, escape, re-discovery; fear, deeply felt, cowardice, and courage; hopes dashed and realised; tiredness to the point of exhaustion; joy and agony, death and the knowledge of death; victory, defeat, survival; a story which like a Greek tragedy was somehow inevitable, its end in its beginning, its beginning in its end.

Bismarck's mission came too late. Had she and her sister ship *Tirpitz* been completed a year earlier, sailed with *Scharnhorst* and *Gneisenau* for the Atlantic trade-routes in the early winter of 1940–1, it might have been a different story. Split into separate battle groups, there is no knowing what damage they might have done, what effect their actions might have had on Britain's war effort. Even now it had required a huge effort by the British Admiralty, the summoning of a multitude of forces to track down this one warship; eight battle-ships and battle-cruisers, two aircraft-carriers, eleven cruisers, twenty-one destroyers, six submarines, more than 300 air sorties; and of nearly sixty torpedoes (apart from *Dorsetshire*'s) fired at her, no more than three, or at the most four, hit.*

* One from *Victorious*'s Swordfish, two from *Ark Royal*'s Swordfish, possibly one from *Rodney*.

It was lack of oil that was the most direct cause of Lütjens's defeat (and very nearly of Tovey's withdrawal).[3] Had he sailed from Norway with full tanks, as he should have done, he might still, despite the hit from *Prince of Wales*, have considered turning west into the Atlantic to shake off his shadowers, then fuel from one of the waiting tankers before turning for home. Alternatively he could have steered direct for Brest at a much higher speed, one that would have outdistanced the approach of Force H. But undoubtedly luck was with the British. The hit on the rudders from *Ark Royal*'s Swordfish was, as the Germans said, one in a hundred thousand.

In theory Raeder could have sent *Prinz Eugen* to sea again together with one of the battle-cruisers as soon as their damage was repaired. But a number of things prevented it. First, the capture of the cipher machine from *U.110* as well as other captured intelligence meant the end of *Bismarck*'s supply ships. On 3rd June the *Belchen* was sunk by the cruisers *Aurora* and *Kenya* (her crew were picked up by *U.93*), on 4th June the *Esso Hamburg* by the cruiser *London*, and the *Gonzenheim* by the cruiser *Neptune*, on 5th June the *Egerland* by the *London*, on 12th June the *Friedrich Breme* by the *Sheffield*, and on 15th June the *Lothringen* was captured by aircraft from the carrier *Eagle* and the cruiser *Dunedin*.

Despite these losses German heavy warships could still have operated in the Atlantic for shorter periods, sailing from and returning to Brest. But by now other factors had entered into consideration. The hit on *Bismarck*'s rudders may have been a lucky one, but what had happened once could happen again. British air power was growing in strength daily. The combination of aircraft carriers, long-range flying-boats and radar meant that once a German warship was picked up in mid-Atlantic, she would be unlikely to get away: carrier planes by day and radar by night would maintain contact until superior forces could be brought up. Hitler was quick to see this, fearing further loss of prestige forbade Raeder to send any other German warships into the Atlantic. As a seaman Raeder could not be blind to it himself. 'The loss of the *Bismarck*', he wrote, 'had a decisive effect on the war at sea.'

That effect was the realisation (reinforced by Luftwaffe successes against the British Navy off Crete) that the aeroplane had now made the battleship obsolete. And if that were true, there was no point at all in keeping *Scharnhorst*, *Gneisenau* and *Prinz Eugen* bottled up in Brest, a nightly target for the bombers: they must be brought home to Germany, not via the Atlantic where they might be crippled by aircraft and sunk as *Bismarck* had been, but by the shortest route available, the one that gave them the maximum air cover, up the English Channel. It was a daring idea, Hitler's originally, but the more the naval staff looked at it, the more feasible it seemed. The three ships left Brest on the night of 11th February, and despite warnings of their imminent departure sent by Philippon to London, were unobserved until just before entering the Narrows.[4] Six Swordfish led by Eugene Esmonde attacked them with great courage, but the Germans had a huge air umbrella over the ships and all six were shot down: Esmonde was killed, got a Victoria Cross posthumously. Air power succeeded in the end when both *Scharnhorst* and *Gneisenau* hit mines laid by the R.A.F. off the Dutch coast: but all three ships reached German ports.[5]

Unfortunately the lesson that had been learnt by the Germans had to be learnt afresh by the British. When the situation in the Far East began to deteriorate towards the end of 1941, Winston Churchill decided to send the now repaired *Prince of Wales* and the *Repulse* to Singapore, hoping that such a show of strength might deter the Japanese from whatever devious plans they had in mind.[6] Pound appointed as commander of the force his deputy Vice-Admiral Sir Tom Phillips. The two ships and their escorting destroyers (*Electra* was one, with Cain still on board) reached Singapore on 2nd December. On the 7th the Japanese attacked Pearl Harbor, landed forces in Northern Malaya. On the afternoon of the 8th Phillips took the squadron northwards to attack the landing forces, but on the evening of the next day, having been spotted by Japanese reconnaissance planes, he turned back for Singapore. On the morning of the 10th, and without air protection of any kind, the squadron was attacked by waves of Japanese bombers and torpedo planes: they hit *Prince of Wales* and *Repulse* repeatedly, sank both ships: neither Admiral Phillips nor Captain Leach were among the two thousand saved.

And so it was brought home to the British, even more painfully than to the Germans, that battleships without massive air protection were sitting ducks, indeed that the day of the battleship was almost over. All four main protagonists continued to use them for the rest of the war, less to fight pitched battles than as support for ground forces and carriers, in which role many Japanese battleships were sunk.

The last battleship in service was the American *New Jersey* which went out of commission in 1972. Today the battleship and battle-cruiser are almost extinct; one or two still moulder in the world's dockyards as gaunt memorials to the past. Those of us who lived with, and in, those strange, lovely, vast, mysterious creatures, remember them with pride; are proud too to have been at sea in their company in the week that *Hood* and *Bismarck* sailed to glory and disaster.

Notes

CHAPTER 1 (pp. 17 to 36)
1. Not A.1. as stated in *Room 39*.
2. Commanded by the author's father, Captain E. C. Kennedy, R.N., who did not survive the action.
3. Flying Officer Campbell was awarded a posthumous V.C.

CHAPTER 2 (pp. 37 to 57)
1. Professor Arthur Marder, in *Winston is Back: Churchill at the Admiralty 1939–40* (*English Historical Review*, supplement 5, 1972) says of the wooden dummies: 'They served no useful purpose and were dissolved in May 1941'. Yet it would seem that on this last occasion at least they performed a priceless service.
2. Lieutenant Viscount Kelburn, now Rear-Admiral The Earl of Glasgow.

CHAPTER 3 (pp. 58 to 80)
1. 'In March 1939 the Board of Admiralty decided to take *Hood* in hand for major reconstruction, including the fitting of additional horizontal and vertical armour ... The war intervened and the work was never carried out'. (Director of Naval Construction to Director of Naval Ordnance, Feb. 9th, 1952, *Roskill Papers*.)
2. In *The War at Sea*, Vol. 1, page 400, Captain Roskill argues that Holland turned north to search for *Bismarck* after *Suffolk* and *Norfolk* had lost touch with her in a snowstorm. But *Suffolk*'s signal of 00.09 reporting this, said only: 'Enemy hidden in snowstorm', and Holland had no more reason to suppose that *Suffolk* had lost *radar* contact than when earlier that night (for nearly an hour) she was reporting *Bismarck* hidden in a fog.

Suffolk's log records the 00.09 signal as having been despatched at 00.20, *Norfolk*'s as having received it at 00.16. (All other ships' logs have been destroyed). Whichever of these two times was wrongly entered (for if *Suffolk* did despatch it at 00.20, *Norfolk* could hardly have received it at

00.16), neither could have influenced Holland's turn from 285° to 340° at 00.12. I have therefore followed the conclusions of Commander Pitcairn Jones that Holland altered to the north not to search for *Bismarck* but to bring on action.

3. The German Navy had developed a very sensitive listening device called GHG, which they imagined (wrongly) the British Navy had developed too. That is why U-boats crews under attack were always ordered to move about in stockinged feet and make the minimum of noise. Captain Giessler in *Der Marine-Nachtrichten-und-Ortungdienst* describes how *Prinz Eugen* was fitted with no less than sixty underwater 'listening posts', and says that the American Navy showed great interest in them when the ship was handed over to the United States at the end of the war.

CHAPTER 4 (pp. 81 to 93)

There were two Boards of Inquiry on the loss of the *Hood*. The first, a brief affair, reported on 2nd June, 1941. The second, much longer, took evidence from 89 witnesses from *Norfolk*, 71 from *Prince of Wales*, 14 from *Suffolk*, and 2 from *Hood* as well as a number of technical experts. It reported on 12th Sept., 1941. The conclusions of both Boards were almost identical, that the cause of *Hood*'s loss was not the cordite fire seen burning on the boat-deck ('and in which U.P. and/or 4″ ammunition was certainly involved' – Report of Second Board) but a 15″ shell from *Bismarck* penetrating *Hood*'s armour and exploding in or near her after magazines ('the probability is that the 4″ magazine exploded first' – Report of Second Board).

2. Mr A. J. Benson tells me that the notes on *Hood* in the 1935 edition of *Jane's Fighting Ships* contains the statement: 'Due for replacement in 1941'.

It should however be remembered that *Hood* and other battle-cruisers were never meant to take on battleships. They were built in order to engage and destroy marauding cruisers, for which purpose they did not need heavy armour but did need superior gunfire and high speed.

CHAPTER 5 (pp. 97 to 111)

1. This splinter was later analysed in Berlin as being part of a 14″ shell from *Prince of Wales*, not a 15″ shell from *Hood*. It was an 'over' from a salvo fired at *Bismarck* at a time when due to alterations of course *Bismarck*, *Prinz Eugen* and *Prince of Wales* were all momentarily on the same line of

bearing (*Prinz Eugen* on *Bismarck*'s disengaged side). (Letter from Commander Schmalenbach to the author, 23rd July, 1973.)

2. Historians who write of 'a hot and prolonged argument' (*Grenfell*, p. 85 *note*) between Lütjens and Lindemann on this matter seem to forget that the German Navy, like the British, was highly disciplined; and further that Lütjens was not living in isolation on board *Bismarck* but had his staff officers, Captain Netzbandt, Captain Melms, Commander Ascher and others with him.

3. Of course if *Bismarck* had gone on to sink the *Prince of Wales*, if she *had* succeeded in returning to Germany without further damage, if she *had* been repaired quickly and sent out again, there would have been two fewer ships left to oppose her in the Atlantic (indeed *King George V* would have been the *only* capital ship left of comparable speed and armour). But this is being very wise long after the event.

4. In *King George V*, as in other ships, it was assumed that Wake-Walker's signal '*Hood* has blown up' had been wrongly deciphered. Rear-Admiral Paffard writes that after it had been read out to Tovey, 'I went straight down to the cipher office in the bowels of the ship . . . the senior officer had already had the short message deciphered independently by three or four other cipher officers; there had certainly been no mistake in the deciphering. There could of course have been an error in ciphering or transmitting, and we tried every less devastating alternative to "blown up" that we could think of in the hope that something like "damaged" or "speed reduced" might be also the same four-figure group. But nothing was, and I had to report back to the admiral's bridge that there was no mistake.'

5. For two differing views on Pound, see Marder in *Winston is Back*, pp. 3–5, and Captain S. W. Roskill's reply in the *Journal of the Royal United Service Institution, Dec. 1972*.

CHAPTER 7 (pp. 129 to 150)

1. Captain Giessler, one of the German Navy's last war radar experts, has informed the author that *Bismarck* was not equipped with a FuMB, or radar search receiver, (an instrument designed to pick up enemy radar transmissions).

2. There has been much controversy as to how the D/F bearings came to be wrongly plotted in the flagship. It has been widely believed that it was because the flagship was not carrying gnomonic charts (special charts for plotting D/F bearings, which follow the great circle of the earth), and

that the bearings were plotted instead on an ordinary, navigational (Mercators) chart. 'Our own interpretation was inaccurate,' wrote Tovey to Roskill on 1st Jan. 1961, 'owing to lack of the requisite special charts.'

This evidence however is somewhat suspect, as in the same sentence Tovey also wrote, 'I only wish they (the *Admiralty*) had signalled their own interpretation of the wireless bearings much earlier', showing he had forgotten having asked the Admiralty *not* to send their own interpretation. There is also the strong evidence of Captain Frank Lloyd, Master of the Fleet (i.e. fleet navigating officer) on Tovey's staff. 'Of course we had gnomonic charts on board,' he has told the author, 'no one but a fool would have thought of plotting D/F bearings direct onto a Mercator chart. But the gnomonic charts didn't have compass roses printed at the position of most of the stations from which bearings were taken. One had to lay off the bearings with a protractor, set to true north at each station, but the graduations on the protractor didn't correspond with those of the missing roses.'

Captain Lloyd agrees that the Admiralty plotting team would also have experienced these difficulties, but points out that they were plotting D/F bearings every day, and therefore had far greater experience. He says that during the afternoon of that day he worked out the bearings 'by spherical trigonometry' and thus found the mistake.

3. Commander R. F. Jessel in the *Journal of the Royal United Service Institution*, Feb. 1953.

4. Suggestion of Lieutenant-Commander Peter Kemp.

5. Anquetil took great risks with his radio messages, and later that year was caught by a German detector unit, while almost in the act of transmission. Despite torture and, in the end, execution, he refused to reveal the names of his contacts. Philippon was at Puynormand when Rémy brought him the news. He returned to Brest to continue his work, not knowing whether Anquetil had talked or not.

6. In the end the note did not reach its final addressee until too late to influence events.

7. About an hour after Tovey had turned south-east, he received a signal from the Admiralty for all ships to assume that *Bismarck* was making for France. This signal was based on the first firm intelligence there had been – an intercepted message from a high-ranking German official in occupied Europe, whose son was in *Bismarck*, asking where the battleship was bound, and the reply from Berlin, 'Brest'.

CHAPTER 8 (pp. 151 to 161)

1. The relevant part of Smith's report to the Intelligence Division of the Department of Naval Operations, U.S. Navy, has not been published before, and runs as follows:

'We started leg EG of area at 1000, and at 1010 I sighted what was first believed to be *Bismarck* bearing 345° (*i.e. fine on the port bow, head assumed to be 000°*). Definite recognition was impossible at the time due to visibility. I immediately took control from "George" (automatic pilot), started a slow, climbing turn to starboard, keeping ship sighted to port, while the British officer went aft to prepare contact report. My plan was to take cover in the clouds, get close to the ship as possible; make definite recognition and then shadow the ship from best point of vantage. Upon reaching 2000 feet we broke out of a cloud formation and were met by a terrific anti-aircraft barrage from our starboard-quarter. Immediately jettisoned the depth charges, and started violent evasive action which consisted of full speed, climbing and S turns. The British officer went aft again to send the contact report. When making an S turn, I could see the ship was a battleship and was the *Bismarck*, which had made a 90° starboard turn from its original course (this was evident from wake made by his manoeuvring) and was firing broad-side on us.

The AA fire lasted until we were out of range and into the clouds. It was very intense and were it not for evasive action, we would have been shot down. The barrage was so close that it shook the aircraft consider-ably (one man was knocked from his bunk) and the noise of the bursts could be heard above the propellers and engine noise. Numerous bursts were observed at close quarters and small fragments of shrapnel could be heard hitting the hull ... '

2. See note 4 of Chapter 12.

CHAPTER 9 (pp. 162 to 180)

1. Later that week the British journalist Godfrey Winn went to Lough Erne to interview the crew of Z/209, and his article about them, '*Seek and Follow Men* Caught *Bismarck*' appeared in the *Sunday Express* of 1st June. There is not a word in it about Ensign Smith, nor could there have been, for Germany and America were still at peace, and his participation as an active crew member of Z/209 was a clear violation of American neutrality.

How disappointed Godfrey Winn was to find himself forbidden by the censor to make use of this scoop, it is hard to say. He may even have felt slightly relieved. In a major naval operation of this kind the British would have been loath to admit that they had needed 'outside' help.

2. This was optimistic. At present speed she could not be expected to reach Brest until 6 p.m. at earliest.

3. Of these three, only Friend survived the War.

4. Some journalists and historians have cited this signal (and the further one on page 238) as evidence that Lütjens was an ardent Nazi. But invoking the name of the Head of State on a nationally emotional occasion is not unusual. When in 1949 Commander Kerans brought the *Amethyst* to safety after being bottled up in the Yangtse by the Communists for two months, he signalled the Admiralty: 'Have rejoined the fleet south of Woosung. No damage or casualties. God Save the King.'

CHAPTER 10 (pp. 181 to 202)

1. I learnt of the participation of the American officers Smith, Johnson and Rinehart, entirely by chance. The only reference to them in the *Bismarck* papers in the Public Record Office is a memo dated 29th July, 1941 (signature illegible) to the Assistant Chief of the Naval Staff (Home) that it has 'unofficially' come to the author's notice that Ensign Smith was in the Catalina that sighted *Bismarck* and Ensign Carl Rheinhardt (*sic*) in one that later shadowed her (there is no mention of Lieutenant Johnson).

The memo is marvellously English. 'I am not quite clear,' the author says, 'why these American officers were in the Catalina', but goes on to say that if they did play a valuable part in the operation, 'I suggest it would be a good thing if the Admiralty were to recognise their services ... Perhaps "silver salvers" suitably inscribed would be a good way of doing this.'

My inquiries to Vice-Admiral Edwin Hooper, USN, Curator of the US Naval Archives, produced Smith's report to the Navy Department (and also that of Lieutenant-Commander Wellings). In the summer of 1973, when I was in Washington to cover the Senate Watergate Hearings for the BBC, I thought I would take a long shot and see if Smith was alive. I dialled the Navy Department and told the operator I was trying to trace an Ensign L. B. Smith, last heard of 32 years before, when flying with the RAF in England. The girl said 'One moment, please'. Within seconds another girl said, 'Officers' Locator'. I repeated my request, and she too said 'One moment please'. After about half a minute, she said 'Do you have a pencil, sir?' I said I had and she said, 'Captain L. B. Smith, 1709 West 39th Street, Kearney, Nebraska'. I thanked her, dialled Long

Distance, and within four minutes of my first call to the Navy Department, heard a voice in Kearney, Nebraska, saying, 'Smith speaking'.

As I had a spare day after Watergate, I flew out to Kearney and interviewed Smith. He told me of the part Johnson had played, and also how Rinehart spelled his name. Further inquiries at the Navy Department revealed that they too were alive, and we subsequently corresponded. The silver salver idea seems to have been dropped; at any rate none of the officers received one.

Captain Smith also told me that at the end of the war he was executive officer at a naval air station in California where a certain Lieutenant Richard Milhous Nixon was serving. Smith remembers him as a 'brown bagger', that is a man who brought his lunch with him in a brown bag and ate it at his desk rather than waste time and money eating in the mess. He describes Nixon as 'one of the most conscientious and hard-working officers I ever met'.

2. The *Bismarck*'s radar went out of action during her engagement with *Norfolk* in the Denmark Straits, and it is not known whether it was successfully repaired. Even if it was, further firing by *Bismarck* may have knocked it out again.

3. The nosecap of one of *Bismarck*'s 15'' shells was later found on *Zulu*'s fo'c'sle, squashed flat and looking like the head of a large fish. It was mounted and put in a glass case in the wardroom, and named 'The Bismarck Herring'.

4. When the British Admiralty heard from Madrid that the *Canarias* was to sail, they instructed their own naval attaché there to inform the Spanish Minister of Marine that in accordance with Article 13 of the 10th Hague Convention, 'any survivors taken on board a Spanish man-of-war must be so dealt with that they do not again take part in operations of war. They cannot thereafter be transferred to any other ship nor be returned to German controlled territory.' Later the naval attaché replied that this had been done, and the Spanish Minister of Marine 'seems to accept the point'.

5. Tovey received one other signal from the Admiralty that night. It was sent from Pound in 'admirals only' cipher, and said: 'Assume you are organising destroyer night attacks if possible. No answer required', which one historian has described as being as ludicrous as advising General Montgomery to use his artillery before Alamein. Tovey had complete faith in Vian and saw no reason to remind him of the blindingly obvious.

CHAPTER 11 (pp. 203 to 209)

1. This was the author.

2. The Germans have long believed that *Rodney* was severely damaged by *Bismarck* during the battle, and as late as the publication of *Profile Warship No. 18, KM Bismarck* in 1972 Commander Schmalenbach was writing: 'Contrary to British public announcements, American reports told of severe damage to the *Rodney* who subsequently had to go to the shipyard in Boston, Mass'.

The facts are that *Rodney* was already on her way to Boston, Mass., for a long overdue refit when she was diverted to take part in the *Bismarck* operation. She did suffer severe damage, not from *Bismarck* but from the blast of her own guns. Lieutenant-Commander Wellings, USN, wrote in his report to the American Navy Department:

'Considerable damage to *Rodney* was caused by firing over the fo'c'sle. The deck leaked very badly after the battle. It was necessary to remove the fo'c'sle wooden deck as far back as the end of B turret in order to repair these leaks. The stresses were transmitted to the decks below, causing some damage to bulkheads, stanchions and athwartships beams.'

Rodney's quarter-deck was also severely damaged by blast from X turret firing over the stern at maximum depression (Info F. J. Bell).

3. 'I should like to pay the highest tribute for the most gallant fight put up against impossible odds' – Tovey to Admiralty 1119/27, to which they replied at 1610/27: 'For political reasons it is essential that nothing of the nature of the sentiments expressed in your 1119 should be given publicity, however much we admire a gallant fight'.

CHAPTER 12 (pp 210 to 224)

1. Much of the information contained in this chapter comes from *Schlachtschiff Bismarck* by Jochen Brennecke, to whom I am indebted.

2. In 1947 Jean Philippon was received by the British Ambassador in Paris, Sir Duff Cooper, and presented with a citation from the British Government for his work in Brest. Part of this citation reads:

'On another occasion his information that arrangements were being made to receive a large battleship contributed to the success of the British Navy in intercepting the ship before it reached France.'

Philippon rose to be Commander-in-Chief of the French Mediterranean Fleet and today lives in retirement in Paris.

1. At the time Pound did not tell Tovey that it was Churchill who had originated the signal and not himself. Years later Tovey wrote that if he had known it was Churchill, he would have certainly referred to the fact in his despatch. (Tovey to Rear-Admiral Bellairs, 2nd Oct. 1950 – Copy in *Roskill Papers*). As it was, Tovey was most generous to the Admiralty in his despatch: 'The accuracy of the enemy information supplied by the Admiralty and the speed with which it was passed were remarkable, and the balance struck between information and instructions passed to the forces out of visual touch with me, was ideal' (*Despatch* paras 92/93).

2. Pound's most disastrous piece of interference came the following year when Convoy P.Q. 17 to Russia was threatened by the move to northern Norway of *Bismarck*'s sister ship *Tirpitz*. Against the advice of all his colleagues but one, and of Commander Denning, the intelligence officer, who assured him he would know from wireless traffic and agents' reports the instant *Tirpitz* sailed, Pound ordered it to scatter. Tovey had previously told him on the telephone from Scapa that if it did scatter, the result would be 'sheer, bloody murder', and he was right. Two thirds of the convoy was sunk by U-boats and aircraft.

In fairness to Pound, it should be said that in later life Tovey's memory let him down, and he was apt to exaggerate. The occasion of his having forgotten that he had asked the Admiralty *not* to send their own interpretation of D/F bearings has already been related in note 2 of Ch. 7 (pp. 233-4). Again in 1954 he was under the impression he had received the signal about the *King George V* being towed home *before Ark Royal*'s last attack and decided that 'if *Ark Royal* failed to damage the *Bismarck* . . . to disobey the signal and turn back while we still had enough oil to get back to an English port.' In another letter in the same year he imagined that the signal had ordered him to continue the chase 'up to the shores of France'. (Tovey to Roskill, Nov 11, 1954 and Nov 20, 1954).

His secretary of the time, now Rear Admiral R. W. Paffard, writes of these events as follows:

'. . . I think his memory only began to play tricks after he had suddenly retired from all public life and virtually became a hermit. With no current interests and nobody to talk to other than his wife, it was understandable that he brooded more and more on the past, and particularly on the controversial aspects of his command of the Home Fleet; and Lady Tovey, in constant pain from arthritis, and always by nature inclined to put the worst construction on everything, undoubtedly nurtured his resentment and encouraged him to magnify the disagreements he had had with Churchill and Pound. (Letter to the author, 5th May, 1973.)

3. In a personal minute to the First Lord and First Sea Lord dated 21st March, 1941, and referring to Lütjens's successful cruise with *Scharnhorst* and *Gneisenau*, then about to enter Brest, Churchill wrote:

'When I was at the Admiralty, I repeatedly asked that more attention should be paid to the development of fuelling at sea. Now we find the German battle-cruisers are able to remain out for many weeks at a time without going into any base or harbour to replenish. If they can refuel at sea, it is a scandal that we cannot do so. Again and again our ships have to be called off promising hunts in order to go back to fuel, six or seven hundred miles away . . . Arrangements should be made to have a few tankers in suitable positions off the usual routes so that if our ships are operating as they are now, they could call one of these up and make a rendezvous . . . ' (*First Lord's Papers.*)

The possession of an Empire and world-wide fuelling bases had blinded the British Navy to the importance of being self-sufficient in war-time. The American Navy had already adopted the idea of a fleet train, and today all the major navies of the world take tankers and supply ships with them. Churchill's thoughts, as in other matters, were ahead of his time.

4. The author has been informed by Vice-Admiral Sir Norman Denning that, because of some incredible oversight, some of Philippon's most important messages never reached the Operational Intelligence Centre, and were thus never acted on by the operational staff.

5. *Scharnhorst* was sunk when returning to Norway from an unsuccessful attack on a North Russian convoy on 26th Dec. 1943. *Gneisenau* was paid off in Gotenhafen in 1943 as a result of severe damage suffered in an R.A.F. attack on Kiel soon after the successful Channel dash. *Prinz Eugen* survived the war, only to meet her end as a victim of American atom bomb tests at Bikini in 1948.

6. The aircraft carrier *Indomitable* was scheduled to accompany the force, but had been damaged by grounding off Jamaica.

NOTES ON ILLUSTRATIONS
1. Plate No. 2
This photograph has often been captioned, '*Bismarck* putting to sea for the last time.' There is no indication when or where it was taken, but probably during exercises in the Baltic in the spring of 1941.

2. Plate No. 13

This photograph came into my hands in an unusual way. In a letter to the *Daily Telegraph* in July 1973, I asked if anyone could help me find a photograph I was sure I had somewhere seen of a *King George V* class battleship firing shells which were clearly visible in the top right hand corner.

No one had (it seemed I was confusing the *Duke of York* with the USS *Missouri*) but Commander W. A. E. Hall wrote saying he had a photograph of *Bismarck* leaving Grimstad Fjord, and would I like it?

He had obtained this photograph in peculiar circumstances. In 1964 he was sent to Bergen to help the Norwegian Navy in certain exercises. As part of the exercises, and being the only non-Norwegian naval officer taking part, Hall was 'arrested' by a local police officer, Jørgen Garmann. During Hall's 'detention', Garmann mentioned he had a photograph taken by his brother Christoffer of *Bismarck* leaving Grimstad fjord. When Hall said he had witnessed the end of the *Bismarck* as a midshipman in the *Dorsetshire*, Garmann gave him the photograph.

Sources

1. BOOKS:

ANON. *Coastal Command* (H.M.S.O. 1942)

APPS, Lieutenant-Commander Michael: *Send Her Victorious* (William Kimber, 1971)

BEKKER, C. D.: *Swastika at Sea* (William Kimber 1953)

BERTHOLD, Will: *Sink the Bismarck* (Longmans 1958)

BRADFORD, Ernle: *The Mighty Hood* (Hodder and Stoughton 1959)

BRENNECKE, Jochen: *Schlachtschiff Bismarck* (Koehlers Verlagsgesellschaft, Herford and U.S. Naval Institute, Annapolis, Maryland U.S.A., 1960)

BREYER, Siegfried: *Schlachtschiffe und Schlachtkreuzer 1905–1970* (J. F. Lehmanns Verlag München 1970)

BROOME, Captain Jack: *Make a Signal* (Putnam 1955)

BUSCH, Fritz-Otto: *The Story of the Prinz Eugen* (Hale 1960)

CAIN, Lieutenant-Commander T. J., as told to A. V. Sellwood: *H.M.S. Electra* (Frederick Muller 1959)

CHURCHILL, Winston S.; *The Second World War, Vol 3, the Grand Alliance* (Cassells 1950)

COOKRIDGE, E. K.: *Inside S.O.E.* (Arthur Barker 1966)

DÖNITZ, Grand Admiral Karl: *Memoirs: Ten Years and Twenty Days* (Weidenfeld and Nicolson 1958)

FRANK, Wolfgang: *The Sea Wolves* (Weidenfeld and Nicolson 1955)

FRANKLIN, Alan: *One Year of Life* (Blackwoods 1944)

GIESSLER, Helmuth: *Der Marine-Nachrichten-und-Ortungsdienst* (J. F. Lehmanns Verlag München 1971)

GRENFELL, Captain Russell: *The Bismarck Episode* (Faber and Faber 1948)

HANSSON, Per: *Det Største Spillet* (Oslo, Gyldendal, 1965)

HAUGE, E. O.: *Mannen som stjal Galtesund* (Oslo, Cappelen, 1955)

HILARION (Capitaine de Vaisseau Philippon): *S & G* (Editions France-Empire, Paris, 1957)

JAMES, W. D. (Ed): *Hamptonians at War* (Privately printed for Hampton Grammar School)

JAMESON, Rear-Admiral William: *Ark Royal* (Rupert Hart-Davies 1957)

KEMP, Lieutenant-Commander P. K.; *The Fleet Air Arm* (Herbert Jenkins 1954)

KEMP, Lieutenant-Commander P. K.: *Victory at Sea 1939–1945* (Frederick Muller 1957)

KENNEDY, Ludovic: *Sub-Lieutenant: A Personal Record of the War at Sea* (Batsford, 1942)

LOHMANN, Walter, and HILDEBRAND, Hans H.: *Die Deutsche Kriegsmarine 1939–1945* (Verlag Hans-Henning Podzun, Bad Nauheim, 1956)

MACINTYRE, Donald: *Fighting Admiral: The Life and Battles of Admiral of the Fleet Sir James Somerville* (Evans Bros, 1961)

MCLACHLAN, Donald: *Room 39* (Weidenfeld and Nicolson 1968)

MCMURTRIE, Francis: *The Cruise of the Bismarck* (Hutchinson 1942)

MARTIENSSEN, Anthony: *Hitler and his Admirals* (Secker and Warburg 1948)

MOORE, John: *The Fleet Air Arm* (Chapman and Hall 1943)

NICOLSON, Nigel (Ed): *Diaries and Letters of Harold Nicolson* (Collins 1966–68)

POOLMAN, Kenneth: *Ark Royal* (William Kimber 1956)

RAEDER, Grand Admiral Erich: *Struggle for the Sea* (William Kimber 1959)

RICHARDS, Denis: *The Royal Air Force, Vol. 1, The Fight at Odds* (H.M.S.O. 1953)

ROHWER, J. and HUMMELCHEN, G.: *Chronik des Seekrieges 1939–1945* (Gerhard Stalling Verlag, Oldenburg 1968)

ROSKILL, Captain S. W.: *The War at Sea, Vol 1, The Defensive* (H.M.S.O. 1954)

ROSKILL, Captain S. W.: *The Navy at War, 1939–1945* (Collins 1960)

ROSKILL, Captain S. W.: *Naval Policy Between the Wars* (Collins 1968)

ROSKILL, Captain S. W.: *The Secret Capture* (Collins 1959)

RUGE, Vice-Admiral Friedrich: *Sea Warfare 1939–1945* (Cassells 1957)

SALEWSKI, Michael: *Die Deutsche Seekriegsleitung 1939–1945, Band 1: 1935–1941* (Bernard und Graefe Verlag für Wehrwesen, Frankfurt-am-Main 1970)

SCHOFIELD, Vice-Admiral B. B.: *Loss of the Bismarck* (Ian Allen 1972)

SHIRER, W. L.: *All about the sinking of the Bismarck* (W. H. Allen 1963)

THOMPSON, Kenneth: *H.M.S. Rodney at War* (Hollis and Carter 1946)

TULEJA, Thaddeus V.: *Eclipse of the German Navy* (J. M. Dent 1958)

VIAN, Admiral of the Fleet Sir Philip: *Action This Day* (Frederick Muller 1960)

VULLIEZ, Albert, and MORDAL, George, (Trans. George Malcolm): *Battleship Scharnhorst* (Hutchinson 1958)

WILLOUGHBY, Malcolm F.: *The U.S. Coastguard in World War II* (United States Naval Institute, Annapolis, Maryland, 1957)

WINTON, John (Ed): *Freedom's Battle, Vol 1, War at Sea* (Hutchinson 1967)

2. DOCUMENTS, MAGAZINES, PAMPHLETS, NEWS-PAPERS, etc.

British and German official naval papers. (Ministry of Defence.)

PUBLIC RECORD OFFICE.

Admiralty: War of 1939–1945: War History, Cases and Papers.

ADM 199/1187–1941   Pursuit and Destruction of German Battleship *Bismarck.*

ADM 199/1188–1941   Pursuit and Destruction of German Battleship *Bismarck.*

ADM 199/1933–1941   April–June. First Lord's Papers.

ADM 205/10–1941   April–Dec. First Sea Lord's Papers. Correspondence with Prime Minister and accompanying papers.

Admiralty and Secretariat Cases.

ADM 116/4351–1941   Loss of *HMS Hood* in action with German Battleship – Boards of Inquiry.

ADM 116/4352–1941   Loss of *HMS Hood* in action with German Battleship – Boards of Inquiry.

Air Ministry: Coastal Command.

AIR 15/204–1941   July–1946 Aug. Sinking of the German Battleship *Bismarck.*

AIR 15/415–1941   May–Nov. Sinking of the *Bismarck.* Report.

Air Ministry: Operations Record Books: Groups.

AIR 25/254–1939   Mar–1943 Dec. No. 15 (General Reconnaissance) Group Operations Record Book.

Air Ministry: Operations Record Book: Squadrons.

AIR 27/1294–1941   Jan–1943 Dec. No. 209 Squadron Operations Record Book.

AIR 27/1299–1941   Jan–1943 Dec. No. 210 Squadron Operations Record Book.

AIR 27/1459–1941   Jan–1943 Dec. No. 240 Squadron Operations Record Book.

Atlantic Monthly, The, No. 206, 1960 ('The Sinking of the Bismarck – an Eye-Witness Account' by George Whalley).

Blackwood's Magazine, No. 1515, January 1942 ('Enemy in Sight' by Esmond Knight).

Coast Guard at War, The, Greenland Patrol II (Public Information Division, U.S. Coast Guard Headquarters 1945).

English Historical Review, Supplement 5, Longmans 1972 ('Winston is Back: Churchill at the Admiralty 1939–1940' by Arthur Marder).

Faedrelandsvennen, 4th March, 26th May, 28th May, 1971. (Articles on Norwegian underground.)

Führer Naval Conferences: Report on Rheinübung, 6th June, 1941.

Hewel, Walter, Diary of (Courtesy of David Irving).

Journal of the Royal United Service Institution, February 1953 ('The Bismarck Operation – The German Aspect' by Commander R. F. Jessel).

Journal of the Royal United Service Institution, August 1959 ('Hitler's Admirals' by Commander M. G. Saunders).

Journal of the Royal United Service Institution, December, 1972 ('Marder, Churchill and the Admiralty. 1939–42' by S. W. Roskill).

Log of U.S. Coast Guard Cutter Modoc 24th–25th May, 1941 (National Archives and Records Service, Washington D.C.).

Operations and Battle of German Battleship Bismarck, Intelligence Division, Chief of Naval Operations, U.S. Navy Department: Enclosure (A) Narrative of Operations by Lieutenant-Commander Wellings and (H) Report by Special Observer (Ensign L. B. Smith) in Catalina Z/209. (Archives of the U.S. Navy Department, Washington D.C.).

Profile Warship No. 6, K.M. Prinz Eugen, by Commander Paul Schmalenbach (Profile Publications 1971).

Profile Warship No. 18, K.M. Bismarck, by Commander Paul Schmalenbach (Profile Publications 1972).

Profile Warship No. 19, H.M.S. Hood, by R. G. Robertson, CA (Profile Publications 1972).

Purnell's History of the Second World War, Vol. 2, No. 5, 1967 (Articles by Lieutenant-Commander P. K. Kemp and Captain Gerhard Junack).

Roskill Papers.

Sunday Express, 1st June, 1941 (Article on crew of Catalina Aircraft Z/209 by Godfrey Winn).

Times, The (Launching of the *Bismarck*, 15th Feb. 1939, Obituary notices of

Vice-Admiral L. E. Holland, 31st May, 1941, Admiral of the Fleet Sir Dudley Pound, 22nd Oct. 1943, Admiral Sir Frederick Wake-Walker, 26th Sept. 1945, Air Chief Marshall Sir Frederick Bowhill, 14th March, 1960, Admiral of the Fleet Sir Philip Vian, 29th May, 1968, Admiral of the Fleet Lord Tovey, 13th January, 1971).

Tovey, *Admiral of the Fleet Lord:* 'God and the War' (World's Evangelical Alliance 1944, British Museum No. 3458 aa 25) and 'Why do I believe in God?' (World's Evangelical Alliance 1949, British Museum No. 04430 df 41).

U.S.C.G.C. Modoc (Public Information Division, U.S. Coast Guard Headquarters, Washington D.C. 1959).

United States Naval Institute Proceedings, Vol. 84, No. 7, July 1958 (Exploits and End of the Battleship *Bismarck* by Commander Gerhard Bidlingmaier).

United States Naval Institute Proceedings, Vol. 85, No. 6, June 1959 (Correspondence between J. P. Thornton and Commander Gerhard Bidlingmaier on the scuttling of *Bismarck*).

3. RADIO AND TELEVISION
Extracts from BBC broadcasts made in May and June 1941 by:
Flying Officer Dennis Briggs, Signalman A. E. Briggs, Captain Frederick Dalrymple-Hamilton, Lieutenant-Commander Hugh Guernsey, Rear-Admiral Frederick Wake-Walker, and in March 1960 by Commander Kenneth Pattisson.

Extracts from interviews conducted by the author in 1970–71 for the BBC television documentary *Battleship Bismarck* with:
Captain E. S. Carver, Commander G. R. Carver, Commander H. G. Dangerfield, Rear-Admiral Percy Gick, Captain Gerhard Junack, Esmond Knight, Captain Frank Lloyd, Werner Lust, Baron von Müllenheim-Rechberg, Captain Ludovic Porter, Captain Pitulko, Commander Paul Schmalenbach, R. E. Tilburn, Herbert Wohlfarth.

4. *Correspondence and/or interviews with:*
Viggo Axelssen, F. J. Bell, A. J. Benson, David Berrill, Admiral Sir Alexander Bingley, Captain C. M. Blackman, Commander Joe Brooks, George Clark, Admiral Sir Frederick Dalrymple-Hamilton, Captain North Dalrymple-Hamilton, Admiral Sir Charles Daniel, Captain Henry Denham, Vice-Admiral Sir Norman Denning, Grand Admiral Karl

Dönitz, Captain Robert Ellis, Hon. James Galbraith, Jørgen Garmann, Rear-Admiral Percy Gick, Captain Helmuth Giessler, Rear-Admiral the Earl of Glasgow, Vice-Admiral Sir Peter Gretton, Commander W. A. E. Hall, Commander R. F. Jessel, Captain James Johnson, Captain Gerhard Junack, Lieutenant-Commander Peter Kemp, H. G. Knight, Captain Frank Lloyd, Beatrice Lockhart, Werner Lust, Captain Donald Macintyre, Captain Colin McMullen, Otto Maus, Captain Charles Meynell, Baron von Müllenheim-Rechberg, Commander the Rev. A. G. Oliver, Rear-Admiral R. W. Paffard, Vice-Admiral Jean Philippon, Captain Ludovic Porter, Captain Carl Rinehart, Captain S. W. Roskill, Commander Paul Schmalenbach, Vice-Admiral B. B. Schofield, Captain H. W. Sims-Williams, H. G. Sitford, Captain A. G. Skipwith, Captain L. P. Skipwith, Eric Smith, Captain Leonard B. Smith, Margot Williams, Herbert Wohlfarth, Hans Zimmermann.

Index

Cardinal, Sub-Lieutenant, 31
Carls, Rear-Admiral, 32, 100, 156, 189
Carver, Edmond, 173
Churchill, Winston S., 20, 38, 48, 107, 132, 222, 225
Clayton, Rear-Admiral Jock, 106, 130
Coode, Lieut.-Commander Tim, 168, 169-70, 173-4
Coppinger, Captain, 128, 204, 207
Cossack, 141, 142, 183-4, 186, 187, 204
Cunningham, Admiral, 155
Curteis, Rear-Admiral Alban, 104, 121, 126

Dalrymple-Hamilton, Captain F. H. G., 128, 163, 172, 199, 200, 204, 205, 207, 226
Dalrymple-Hamilton, North, 200
Daniel, Captain Charles, 106, 131
Darlington Court, 136
de la Perière, Lothar von Arnauld, 133
Denham, Captain Henry, 18, 224
Denning, Commander N., 106
Deutschland, 20, 21, 156
Dixon-Child, Sub-Lieutenant, 173
Doelker, Lieutenant, 122
Dönitz, Grand Admiral Karl, 21, 28, 101, 136, 141, 167, 223
Dorsetshire, 155, 182, 200, 204, 207, 209, 217, 218-19, 221
Dundas, Midshipman, 86, 92-3
Durant, Lieut.-Commander, 218

Earl, Lofty, 91
Echo, 43
Edinburgh, 102, 127, 131, 182
Edwards, Captain Ralph, 106, 131, 132
Egerland, 32, 228
Eich, Leading Seaman A., 87, 178, 197, 215
Electra, 43, 68, 92, 229
Ellis, Captain Robert, 53-4, 65, 70, 112, 124, 125
Emden, 29
Ermland, 167, 190
Eskimo, 128

Esmonde, Eugene, 42, 115, 119, 120, 229
Esso Hamburg, 32, 223, 228
Externbrink, Dr, 30, 49, 50, 137, 191, 197, 210

Fancourt, Captain Henry St J., 46-7
Force H, 57, 66-7, 123, 124, 156-8, 181, 220
Friedrich Breme, 32, 228
Friedrich Eckholdt, 34
Friend, Sub-Lieutenant, 174
Furious, 157

Galatea, 48, 104, 156
Galbraith, Sub-Lieutenant James, 185
Gensoul, Admiral, 61
Gick, Percy, 115, 119, 120
Giese, Lieutenant, 179
Gneisenau, 20, 21, 22, 23, 27, 28, 50, 134, 157, 198, 229
Goddard, Lieutenant Noel E., 47
Godfrey-Faussett, Lieutenant ('Feather'), 174, 175
Gomez, Señor, 91
Gonzenheim, 32, 228
Göring, Hermann, 32, 167, 195
Gotland, 19, 34
Graf Zeppelin, 32
Graham, Commander H. R., 185
Graser, Commander, 79
Guernsey, Lieut.-Commander Hugh, 199, 201, 204, 208

Hane, Lieutenant, 78-9
Hansen, Leading Seaman, 119, 120, 137
Hans Lody, 34
Hartley, Sub-Lieutenant, 159
Hatfield, Flight-Lieutenant, 183
Havers, Lieut.-Commander, 86
Heide, 32
Hermione, 48
Hertel, Petty Officer, 78
Herzog, Leading Seaman, 177-8, 180, 211, 216, 219-20
Hewel, Walter, 31, 32